THINKING THE
CONTEMPORARY LANDSCAPE

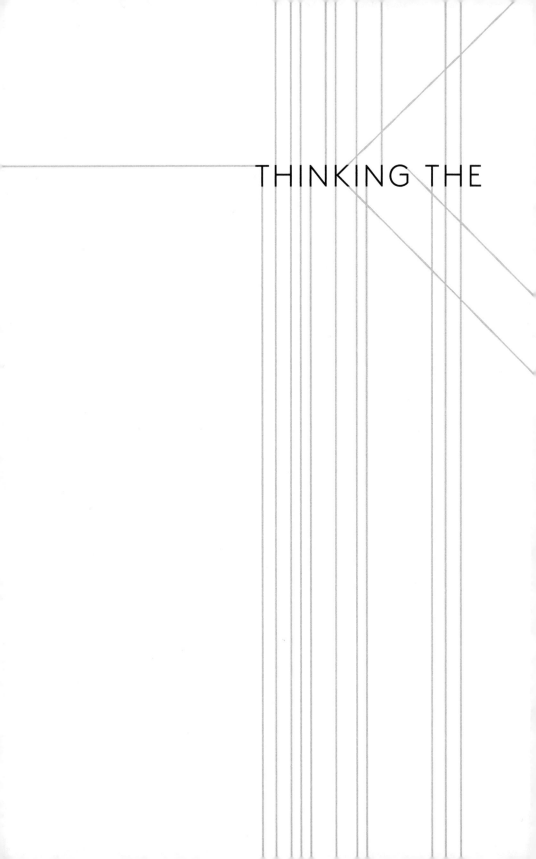

THINKING THE

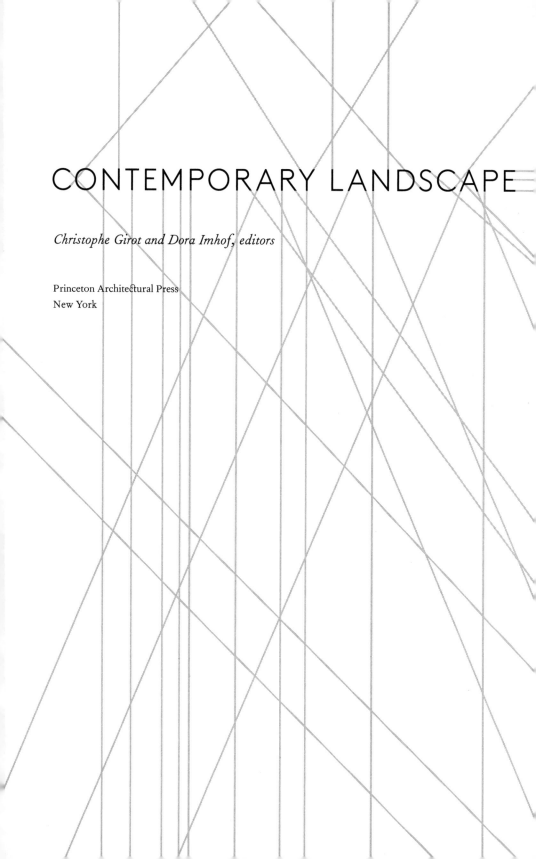

CONTEMPORARY LANDSCAPE

Christophe Girot and Dora Imhof, editors

Princeton Architectural Press
New York

CONTENTS

INTRODUCTION

Thinking the Contemporary Landscape is a compilation of essays that look at the profession of landscape architecture as it reacts to new challenges posed by both societal and environmental change and considers new fields of action. Landscape architecture suffers from broad intellectual dispersion and tremendous cultural disparity, precisely at a moment when direction and cohesion are indispensable to our civilization. Our editorial line seeks to identify aesthetic concerns that, recently, have all too often been overshadowed by a positivistic scientific discourse about nature. This seventeen-essay collection aims to contrast the current discourse with a more philosophical and poetic stance. It pinpoints a contemporary form of intelligence about landscape by relating positions from outstanding academic thinkers and practitioners. Most of the authors took part in a symposium that was organized in 2013, with generous support from the Volkswagen Foundation, at Herrenhausen Palace in Hanover, Germany. Additional authors were solicited thereafter, to complement certain facets of a contemporary debate on representation and politics that we found to be lacking at the symposium. This book reflects on current thinking in landscape architecture and is meant to open the discussion and nurture further inquiry into design methods and aesthetics.

Landscape is a cultural artifact—a construct resulting from the belabored shaping of terrain and the making of place; it has, in fact, very little to do with the ideal of an untouched wilderness. This plain definition of the word as the product of successive stages of human culture enables us to frame a discussion about symbolic expression and form giving within the realm of the politics of space. What actually constitutes the proper immanence of a landscape in our age? What role does memory play in this reading of place? How does one identify concretely the contemporary aesthetic and intelligence of a given landscape, particularly through the virtual realm? At a moment of relentless conceptual oscillation and environmental uncertainty, the timeless quality of a landscape is strikingly frail, idealistic, almost idiosyncratic—it has neither the solidity nor the proper physical resilience to resist the centrifugal thrust of our age.

The juxtaposition of science and memory, of exponential development and history, points to one of the major contradictions in contemporary landscape thinking, which mirrors a multitude of heterogeneous and often conflicting ideologies that attempt to define a world that is constantly being reshaped and reinterpreted by newer forces. As a result, there exists a schism between the way a landscape is understood scientifically and the way it exists cognitively, mnemonically, and emotionally for people. This mix of rational scientific discourse and poetic interpretation about landscape has never been so murky and inextricable as it is today. The authors were asked to take issue on a variety of subjects in which the topic was either reframed, recomposed, or rethought, to see whether a dialogue could even occur between the individual experience of secular myths of landscape on the one hand, and scientific positivism on the other. Some authors were asked to reflect on the relevance of science and memory in relation to aesthetics; others were asked to comment rather on the expression of power on the terrain. A discussion about heuristic and empirical methods was intended to shed light on differing, yet sometimes complementary, approaches to landscape design. Is it actually possible to reconcile science and memory in our present culture? Paying critical attention to the way we conceive our environment, both symbolically and scientifically, may indeed help restitute a stronger vision and direction in landscape architecture.

This book is organized into three parts. However, these sections should not be seen as completely autonomous from one another; there are indeed many thematic correspondences between them.

Part one addresses the societal and epistemological shifts that have occurred in our conception of nature and perception of place. Effects of climate change, combined with a rapid increase in population growth and neoliberal globalization, provide an incentive to rethink nature and landscape in many disciplines. The popularization of the concept of the Anthropocene by the atmospheric chemist Paul J. Crutzen and the biologist Eugene F. Stoermer in 2000 has brought us to question not only domains pertaining to nature, such as landscape architecture, geology, and geography, but also art production and art history, philosophy, and sociology. While the ecological debate has been ongoing for several decades now, a broader theoretical interest in landscape theory has been rekindled by a wider discourse on nature and its recent history.[1]

The first part of the book, with essays by Vittoria Di Palma, Saskia Sassen, Emily Scott, Sonja Dümpelmann, and Charles Waldheim, focuses on the concept of wastelands, which is central to the transformation of urban areas. It is not so much with some idyllic landscapes, but rather through the mirror of contested,

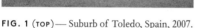

FIG. 1 (TOP) — Suburb of Toledo, Spain, 2007.

FIG. 2 (BOTTOM) — Imperial Wharf, Chelsea, London, 2008.

FIG. 3 — Central Business District, Montreal, Canada, 2009.

All photos by Christophe Girot.

contaminated, and capitalized areas that contemporary issues about landscape thinking become most acute and visible. This is also where questioning idiosyncratic solutions has become of vital importance. (**FIGS. 1-3**) Conflicting ideas about what is actually possible and desirable in a landscape and how the field of action narrows down for given interventions become all the more apparent in the essays of Susann Ahn, Regine Keller, and Jörg Rekittke.

Part two explores different methods of design with an international perspective, focusing on Europe, China, and the United States. Over the past century there has been a tendency to reduce the field of action of landscape design both pragmatically and scientifically. Large-scale landscape analysis has in part taken over the realm of design, through engineering and with the help of elaborate mapping overlay techniques that selectively arrange layers of information pertaining to a site with no particular regard to a landscape's given physical, historic, and aesthetic qualities. This empirical fragmentation, in which landscape is treated repeatedly in separate divisions, has created a highly abstract, scientific vision of terrain that is quite removed from any reality of place. In turn, such a highly reductive and deductive approach to design, combined with strong eidetic evocations, has enabled the global transfer of an idealized brand of landscape mapping, as a substitute for design without any specific consideration for cultural appropriateness and specificity.

Authors were asked to dispute the "mapping" approach and to discuss whether landscape architecture could integrate other heterogeneous realities, taking into account the importance of cultural tropes within a more physical, heuristic, and poetic understanding of design. Authors were challenged to define new methods in the field while remaining open to other disciplines and cultural fields, paying particular attention to the deeper significance of place. The goal of this discussion was to enhance a fuller sense of a landscape, in its actual making, that is as much about its inherent novelty as it is about the complexity of context and tradition embedded within it. Differing approaches ranging from mapping to topology are developed in the essays of James Corner and Christophe Girot, while questions of scales of design become central in differing ways within the texts of Kathryn Gustafson and Kongjian Yu. In addition, Kristina Hill's contribution shows how closely landscape theory and practice, as well as science and memory, can be connected to a greater environmental cause.

In part three, the concepts of terrain, territory, visualization, and perception become central to the essays of David Leatherbarrow, Alessandra Ponte, Anette Freytag, Stanislaus Fung, and Adriaan Geuze. Great spatial disparity and territorial dispersion tend to prevail in today's modern landscapes. This phenomenon is attributed to a multitude of actors and factors that currently shape the land. Landscape has often been associated with the direct expression of power, but in an age of pluralism and urban sprawl, mass transit, and spatial relativity, what is the place of landscape and how does it relate back to terrain?[2] What is sometimes perceived as a general lack of congruence in our landscapes is often due to the emergence of a new layer of infrastructure that calls for an entirely different kind of territorial reading, as well as a new kind of engagement toward nature, which is itself becoming an expression of power. Landscape has shifted its focus away from the notion of *terroir*, founded on the intrinsic understanding of local topologies and lore, toward a more general and disconnected discourse on global environmental trends and economic functionalism. Authors were asked to take a position and trace back the intellectual uprooting of landscape back to unresolved issues of power on the terrain, as local custom regresses everywhere. By reflecting on the relevance of power and terrain in contemporary society, they weaved meaning back into their approach, entrusting the common landscape good with a deeper sense of purpose.

This book will certainly raise more questions than it will bring answers. Thinking the contemporary landscape requires at present as much attention toward the future as it does summoning selective memories and schemes from the past. The fact is that time—and the experience with botanical time—is of the essence in any sort of landscape architecture that wants its roots to leave marks within a culture. This is precisely what is lacking in our world, which values the short term in such a way that thinking about a specific territory over a century seems plainly intangible. Landscape architecture must be one of the few disciplines capable of merging a deeply symbolic and cultural understanding of nature with the massive environmental transformations to come. We should take the opportunity of these challenges that await us as an open invitation to reconsider landscape's pivotal role in society.

Christophe Girot and Dora Imhof, 2016

Notes

1
See, for instance, James Corner, ed., *Recovering Landscape: Essays in Contemporary Landscape Theory* (New York: Princeton Architectural Press, 1999); Mark Dorrian and Gillian Rose, eds., *Deterritorialisations: Revisioning Landscape and Politics* (London: Black Dog Publishing, 2003); Charles Waldheim, ed., *The Landscape Urbanism Reader* (New York: Princeton Architectural Press, 2006); Rachael Ziady DeLue and James Elkins, eds., *Landscape Theory* (New York: Routledge, 2008); Lucy R. Lippard, *Undermining: A Wild Ride Through Land Use, Politics, and Art in the Changing West* (New York: The New Press, 2014); and Emily Eliza Scott and Kirsten Swenson, eds., *Critical Landscapes: Art, Space, Politics* (Oakland: University of California Press, 2015).

2
See, for instance, Martin Warnke, *Political Landscape: The Art History of Nature* (London: Reaktion Books, 1994); Denis E. Cosgrove, *Social Formation and Symbolic Landscape* (London: Croom Helm, 1984); and W. J. T. Mitchell, ed., *Landscape and Power* (Chicago: University of Chicago Press, 1994).

PART 1

—LANDSCAPE REFRAMED

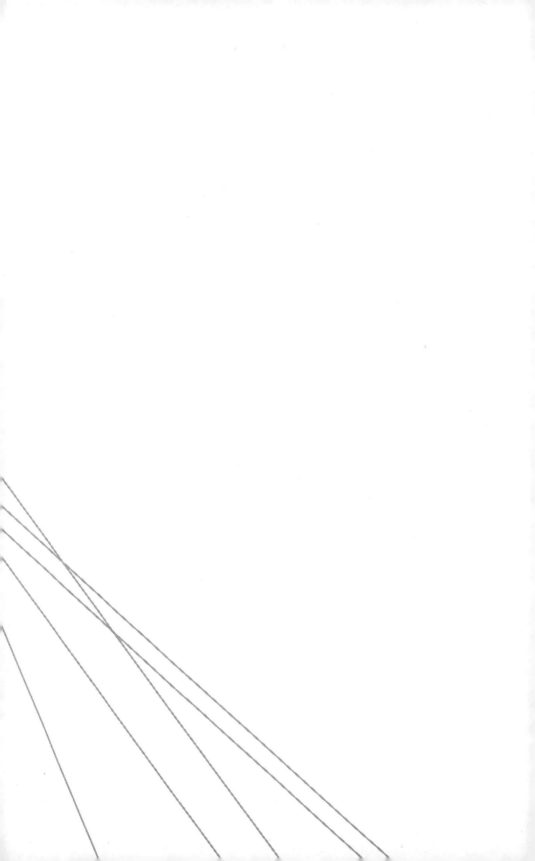

IN THE MOOD FOR LANDSCAPE
—*Vittoria Di Palma*

What might it mean to be "in the mood for landscape"? Or to pose the question another way: What might it *do* for landscape to understand it as a mood? Considering it as such privileges interpretations that focus on mental states, types of response, varieties of emotion, and patterns of interaction, rather than on objective descriptions, disinterested evaluations, or big data. To be (or not to be) in the mood for landscape suggests an impassioned engagement, perhaps a polemical stance, or even a flag-waving call to action. This essay aims to explore the history and consequences of understanding landscape as a mood, rather than as a picture, an object, a territory, or a system. Although these other frames of reference can also offer fruitful insights, I will examine the conditions and possibilities generated by viewing landscape through the lens of emotion.

An emotional perspective offers an apt vantage point from which to address issues central to contemporary landscape. Moreover, it is particularly suited to the challenges associated with postindustrial sites. Whether we operate as critics, designers, historians, or global citizens, the kinds of landscapes we are increasingly called upon to respond to—garbage dumps and landfills; disused mines and quarries; outmoded urban infrastructure; derelict factories, power plants, and military installations; and tracts littered with abandoned buildings or polluted by the toxic residues of industrial processes—are neither garden nor wilderness but instead fall into the category of wasteland. (FIG. 1) These kinds of sites (no matter whether we use the term *wasteland* or one of a number of alternatives including Ignasi de Solà-Morales Rubió's "terrains vagues," Antoine Picon's "anxious landscapes," Niall Kirkwood's "manufactured landscapes," Mira Engler's "waste landscapes," or Alan Berger's "drosscapes") have one important thing in common: they are united not by physical properties (such as geographical location, ecological characteristics, or degree and type of contamination), but rather by the types of reactions they elicit.[1] In other words, what makes these kinds of sites comparable—what brings them together under the category of wasteland—has less to do with *what they are* than with *how they make us feel*. Indeed, the history of the concept of wasteland indicates that the term was created to encompass all those (often very different) landscapes that evoked feelings located on the aversive end of the emotional spectrum—feelings like fear, horror, contempt, and disgust.[2]

In this context, disgust is particularly suggestive. Disgust is unique among the six "basic emotions" (the other five are happiness, sadness, fear, anger, and surprise) in that it occurs as both a seemingly instinctual, reactive response, and a highly developed, culturally and socially inflected tool of discrimination and moral judgment.[3] Disgust is visceral, powerful, and immediate; but it is also a feeling, according to William Ian Miller, "connected to ideas, perceptions, and cognitions, and to the social and cultural contexts in which it makes sense to have those feelings and ideas."[4] For Norbert Elias, disgust was a key motor of the civilizing process; for Mary Douglas, it was the foundation of a society's notions of pollution and taboo.[5] Disgust is an emotion that operates powerfully in the formulation of a culture's ordering systems: it establishes and maintains hierarchies; it is fundamental to the construction of a moral code.[6] Disgust can therefore help to shed light on the systems through which different kinds of landscapes are valued, and the reasons why ethical or moral arguments so often appear in the context of discussions regarding derelict or polluted sites. Furthermore, because of this dual nature, which is at once biological (and therefore universal) and culturally and socially inflected (and therefore relative), disgust may allow us to complicate established distinctions between the biological and the cultural, offering strategies for uniting ecological or quantifiable factors with the various cognitive, poetic, and affective qualities of a landscape.

THE AESTHETICS OF DISGUST

The English word *disgust* derives from the French *dégoût* and thus is specifically associated with the sense of taste on an etymological level. The term begins to appear sporadically in English during the first quarter of the seventeenth century, and then with increasing frequency after about 1650, in concert with a growing interest in the notion of taste and discussions regarding its role in aesthetic judgment.[7] (FIG. 2) *Aesthetics* was a term coined by Alexander Gottlieb Baumgarten in the eighteenth century to mean "received by the senses"; it defined an emerging discipline that focused on human reactions to objects rather than on the inherent qualities of objects, thus reformulating canons of beauty as questions of taste.

For the philosopher Aurel Kolnai, disgust's nonexistential and perceptual emphasis made it "an eminently *aesthetic* emotion."[8] Kolnai differentiated between the *ugly* object (in which the ugliness derives from the object's properties or characteristics) and the *disgusting* object (in which the definition arises from our reaction to the object). Disgust has a particularly close connection to

previous:

FIG. 1 — The High Line, New York City, November 2007.
Photo by Caleb Smith.

FIG. 2 — James Parsons, "Human Physiognomy Explain'd," *Philosophical Transactions* (London: Printed for C. Davis, 1747).
Henry E. Huntington Library and Art Gallery.

aesthetics because it focuses exclusively on how the repellent object *appears to us* rather than on what it *is*. This interpretation was corroborated by the experimental psychologist Paul Rozin through studies he conducted in the 1980s, in which volunteers were presented with what appeared to be feces, and were asked to eat them. The reaction of disgust was both immediate and universal—even when the volunteers were informed that the feces were actually made out of fudge. Once the disgusting object presents itself to our senses, it overpowers our reason, triggering an emotion of startling immediacy and power.

Furthermore, as both Kolnai and Carolyn Korsmeyer have argued, the disgusting object is unique in that it "rivets our attention, even at the same time that it repels."[9] This may be the root of the attraction of disgust, for, as Kolnai observed, "there is contained already in its inner logic a possibility of a positive laying hold of the object, whether by touching, consuming, or embracing it."[10] Disgust is thus an emotion that harbors a contradictory duality, a mixture of repulsion and allure. When in the grip of its effects, we are both repelled and transfixed, overcome by an impulse to remove ourselves as quickly as possible from the disgusting object's presence, yet also often strangely impelled to draw near. In this way, disgust, when considered in terms of its aesthetic dimension, may help to explain the paradoxical fascination of a garbage dump or derelict industrial site.

Before we turn to the possibilities disgust offers for understanding and engaging with landscapes such as these, however, it is imperative that we look back to the moment when increased attention began to be paid to the relationship between emotion and aesthetics. For the proliferation of *disgust* as a term and the invention of aesthetics also coincides with the emergence of new attitudes toward landscape. The concept of mood was a central feature of this development.

MOOD AND MODE

The figure primarily responsible for connecting landscape with the concept of mood was the painter Nicolas Poussin. On November 24, 1647, Poussin wrote a letter to his patron Paul Fréart de Chantelou, to whom he had recently sent *The Sacrament of Ordination*. (**FIG. 3**) Chantelou had been dissatisfied with the painting, and had written a letter to Poussin (now lost) expressing his disappointment. Comparing *The Sacrament of Ordination* unfavorably with another painting, *The Finding of Moses*, which Poussin had sent to the collector Jean Pointel, Chantelou expressed his preference for Pointel's painting, and wondered whether Poussin's choice meant that the painter did not love him. (**FIG. 4**) In his reply, Poussin expostulated with Chantelou, and asked, "Cannot you see that it is the nature of the subject which has produced this result and your state of mind, and that the subjects I am depicting for you require a different treatment?"[11] It was not that one painting was better than another, but that their different subjects necessitated the adoption of different modes, leading the two paintings to produce different effects on the spectator.

The modes derived from Greek music theory; according to Poussin, they produced "marvelous effects." However, their application to visual art was novel, and Poussin felt the need to begin with a definition. The modes, he explained, were a creation of "[t]hose fine old Greeks, who invented everything that is beautiful." The ancients had observed that particular kinds of musical compositions "had the power to arouse the soul of the spectator to divers [*sic*] emotions," and had "attributed to each [mode] a special character." These included the Dorian mode, which was "firm, grave, and severe"; the Phrygian mode, used for "pleasant and joyous things" because "its modulations were more subtle than those of any other Mode and because its effect was sharper"; the Lydian mode, "for mournful subjects"; the Hypolydian mode, which "lends itself to divine matters" because it "contains within itself a certain suavity and sweetness which fills the soul of the beholders with joy"; and the Ionic mode, used for "dances, bacchanals, and feasts because of its cheerful character."[12] Poussin did not reveal to Chantelou which mode he associated with either *The Finding of Moses* or *The Sacrament of Ordination*, but his discussion established a direct link between the general aspect of a painting and the emotional effect it was capable of producing. Even more importantly, as argued by Anthony Blunt, Poussin's extension of the concept of the modes to visual art differed from earlier theoretical treatments, because whereas other writers had argued that a mood or emotion could be conveyed by the gestures of the depicted figures,

FIG. 3 (TOP)— Nicolas Poussin, *The Sacrament of Ordination*, 1647. Oil on canvas, 46 x 70 in. (117 x 178 cm).
Edinburgh, National Gallery of Scotland (Bridgewater Loan, 1945).

FIG. 4 (BOTTOM)— Nicolas Poussin, *The Finding of Moses*, 1647. Oil on canvas, 46.5 x 78 in. (118 x 199 cm).
Louvre, Paris, France/Bridgeman Images.

Poussin's theory of the modes instead posited that an emotional response could be elicited by the general style of a painting.[13] Furthermore, it suggested that the means by which a painting became capable of eliciting particular emotional responses could be systematized. Mood and mode were joined together through the art of painting.

LANDSCAPE AND EFFECT

Although Poussin was renowned for his representation of landscape, and *The Finding of Moses* devotes as much attention to its landscape setting as it does to the figures grouped around the salvaged infant, it was not Poussin but his younger contemporary Roger de Piles who extended the concept of emotional effect to landscape painting in a truly comprehensive manner. In 1708, near the end of his life, de Piles published a treatise entitled *Cours de peinture par principes* (translated into English as *The Principles of Painting*).[14] Structured like a course of lectures, and intended for de Piles's fellow academicians, the book set out principles that de Piles had been developing for much of his career. De Piles's overarching aim, in keeping with the goals of the Académie royale de peinture et de sculpture was to determine the grounds by which high art could be differentiated from technically accomplished craft, and thus to establish the definition of "la véritable peinture" or "true painting." Along with extended discussions of painterly techniques like line, color, shading, and composition, the book also included a long section on landscape.

Works by the great masters of landscape painting, Nicolas Poussin and Claude Lorrain in particular, were associated with different styles. Poussin, whose cerebral landscapes and noble themes evoked the geometrical perfection of a vanished classical world, was the exemplar of the heroic style. Lorrain, whose classical landscapes were characterized by limpid skies, clear light, harmonious forms, and soft colors, excelled at the pastoral style. Each of these styles was associated with a particular effect: whereas Poussin elevated the mind through the contemplation of glorious thoughts and actions, Lorrain soothed the spectator with placid visions of classical Arcadia.[15]

The principal means of communicating these effects was through what de Piles termed the *tout ensemble*. The tout ensemble (translated as "the whole together") was an aspect of composition according to which all the parts of a painting were so mutually interdependent that none would dominate over any other.[16] (FIG. 5) A successful tout ensemble ensured that a painting, rather than being perceived by the eye as a collection of disparate objects, was instead seen

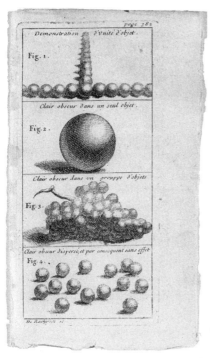

FIG. 5 — Roger de Piles, *Cours de peinture par principes* (Paris: Jacques Estienne, 1708). *Avery Architectural and Fine Arts Library, Columbia University.*

all at once (compare the scattered spheres in the fourth register of the plate, which have no effect, to the bunch of grapes in the third register, which produces a strong effect). The tout ensemble was the facet of a painting's composition that guaranteed a unified impact.

But the tout ensemble was also much more than a successful engagement with the laws of human vision, for it was this quality that raised painting from an artisanal craft to a high art. The tout ensemble was analogous to "the spiritual part" of painting; it was what differentiated "true painting" from more mundane productions. In de Piles's memorable formulation, a true painting calls out to its spectators; it compels us to approach and engages us in conversation.[17] For painters to succeed in producing this kind of intense communication with their viewers, de Piles contends, they must be transported out of themselves, seized by the enthusiastic raptures of the sublime. Then, and only then, will they be able to kindle a similar rapturous state in their audience, making the viewing of their work akin to a divine revelation. The true work of art transcends its objecthood to address its beholders, transfixing them, calling out to them, and overcoming their reason in order to infuse them with a kind of sublime ecstasy.[18] Thus, in de Piles's treatise, the articulation of an aesthetics of effect was closely bound up with the genre of landscape.

Although de Piles was primarily interested in painting, it is in his treatise that we find an important indication of a wider transformation that was to have fundamental implications for landscape theory and design. The relative quality of a work of art was gauged less by criteria related to its production than by the circumstances of its reception—in other words, by its ability to have an emotional effect on its spectators. This transformation had two important consequences: First, the shift in emphasis from production to reception introduced problems of individual preference, reformulating discussions of beauty into debates about taste. Second, the growing interest in effect meant that objects were valued with respect to the degree of their emotional impact. Thus, objects capable of generating strong responses became those that were most highly esteemed. Pastoral landscapes composed of verdant meadows, meandering brooks, and flowering shrubs were displaced in the cultural imagination by sublime landscapes featuring jagged rocks, desolate plains, towering cliffs, thundering cataracts, and exploding volcanoes. In this way, understanding landscape through the lens of emotion gave a new prominence to those aversive landscapes that fell into the category of wasteland.

WASTELAND AND DISGUST

These developments and their consequences can be illustrated by considering three types of wasteland that achieved particular prominence in early modern Britain: swamps, mountains, and forests. Each can be associated with a distinct modality of disgust.

A notorious example of a swamp wasteland was the vast stretch of mud, mire, and mere located in eastern England that was known as the Fens. Early descriptions of the region characterize its earth as mud, its waters as putrid, its fauna as vermin, its inhabitants as disease ridden, and its odors as stenches. Description after description expresses reactions of a visceral disgust, an indication that the fears provoked by swamp wastelands went far beyond mere concerns for safety, instead touching upon deeply held notions of contamination, corruption, and impurity.

Drainage was the only solution. Two of William Dugdale's maps, "A Mapp of the Great Levell, Representing it as it lay Drowned" and "A Map of the Great Levell Drayned," show the effects of an ambitious scheme that was pursued over the course of the seventeenth century. (FIGS. 6-7) In the first image, a vast extent of fen, moor, and common marsh oozes over the landscape, blanketing and obliterating its distinguishing features. In the second, a host of new drains have been carved into the landscape, gathering and channeling the irregular waters between parallel banks and revealing, in their wake, thousands of acres of fertile plough land now divided and arranged into neat orthogonal plots. By separating the elements and relegating them to distinct categories—dividing earth from water

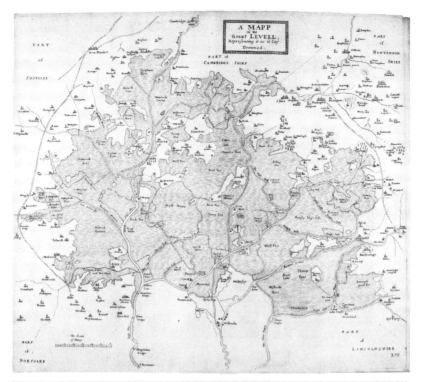

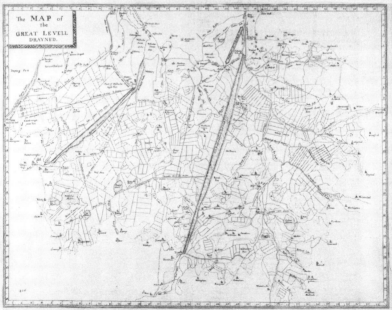

FIG. 6 (TOP) — William Dugdale, "A Mapp of the Great Levell, Representing it as it lay Drowned," *The History of Imbanking and Drayning of Divers Fenns and Marshes* (London: Printed by Alice Warren, 1662).
William Andrews Clark Memorial Library.

FIG. 7 (BOTTOM) — William Dugdale, "A Map of the Great Levell Drayned," *The History of Imbanking and Drayning of Divers Fenns and Marshes.*

with ditches and dikes—this comprehensive scheme aimed to impose rational control over a wayward landscape, mitigating its power to defile by subjecting it to the discipline of private property. What this case study of swamps reveals is an innate disgust that inspires actions, involving the application of technology, designed to transform the landscape entirely to make it conform to protocapitalistic notions of use and productivity.

Mountains, on the other hand, furnish insights into the relationship between disgust and aesthetics. Derbyshire's Peak District, one of the earliest sites of domestic tourism in England, provides a good case in point. Drawn by descriptions of the region's seven "wonders," which included two caves, a chasm, two unusual springs, a "shivering mountain," and the Duke of Devonshire's house at Chatsworth, visitors came to experience these assorted aberrations of nature, and described their experiences in terms that suggested a grand tour of hell. One of the earliest visual representations of this area, an engraving published in Charles Leigh's *The Natural History of Lancashire, Cheshire and the Peak in Derbyshire* of 1700, is a view of the cave known as "Poole's Hole." (FIG. 8) The plate indicates that the cave is understood according to conventions of the monstrous—the inclusion of other images such as a fossil, a boy born with a birthmark, and a woman with horns growing out of her head makes this point clear. Yet early descriptions of the region express not simply fear and revulsion, but that precise mixture of repulsion and fascination that tends to characterize disgust in its aesthetic dimension. Mountains thus provide the template for a powerful emotional reaction that mingles repulsion and fear with attraction, a reaction that later in the century is identified as the sublime. The products of this modality of disgust are artistic ones: literary descriptions of mountainous landscapes, and works of visual art like paintings, sketches, and watercolors. The distance inherent in the act of representation is what allows for the play of a horrified fascination, that simultaneous tug of attraction and repulsion, which is the hallmark of the sublime. Thus, what the case study of mountains reveals is an aesthetic disgust that uses the techniques of art to generate representations: words and images that distance the object sufficiently for it to become an object of pleasurable (and perhaps even frisson generating) contemplation.

Turning to forests, however, the questions change. Unlike swamps and mountains, which were understood as wastelands given by God or nature, the forests of England were instead seen as wastelands created by culture. By the second half of the seventeenth century, they had been decimated by unscrupulous tree felling, the growth of the iron and glass industries, and the upheavals

FIG. 8 — Poole's Hole, from Charles Leigh, *The Natural History of Lancashire, Cheshire, and the Peak in Derbyshire* (Oxford: Printed for the author, 1700).
William Andrews Clark Memorial Library.

FIG. 9 — Charcoal making in a forest. John Evelyn, *Sylva, Or A Discourse of Forest-Trees*, 2nd ed. (London: J. Martyn and J. Allestry, 1670).
William Andrews Clark Memorial Library.

of the English Civil War. (FIG. 9) Contemporary literature on forests reveals that disgust was not directed toward the landscape, but rather at the people who were judged as misusing it. Furthermore, the censure of particular activities within the space of the forest went hand in hand with social distinctions. Hunting (an elite activity associated with the Crown) was celebrated, while foraging, poaching, wood gathering, agriculture in forest clearings, and building construction (all practiced for the most part by commoners) were condemned.

Looking at forests furnishes an early example of human industry being identified as harmful rather than as beneficial, and reveals the articulation of a moral disgust, directed at the works and actions of humans rather than at the precultural landscape itself. The solution to the waste of England's primeval forests was a campaign of tree planting spearheaded by the Royal Society fellow and horticultural enthusiast John Evelyn. Evelyn's magisterial *Sylva* of 1664 was written to encourage wealthy landowners to plant trees on their estates for economic, strategic, and aesthetic reasons. Thus, in the case of forests, we find a moral disgust directed at human actions that inspires the deployment of a form of gardening understood in redemptive terms. Planting trees would atone for the sins of an unscrupulous culture and produce an "Elysium Britannicum," a new Eden, proof positive that the nation (or at least its wealthy landowners) had been saved.

FIG. 10 — Lachenaie Landfill, Québec, Canada, June 2008.
Photo by Vittoria Di Palma.

THE WASTELAND TODAY

Today we do not understand landscape as early modern British people did. Yet even though their fens have become our wetlands and their dangers have become our risks, and even though climate change has permanently confounded the constructs of "nature" and "culture" and united what we used to call nation-states into one common global ecosystem, we continue to react toward landscapes we designate as "wasteland" in strikingly similar ways. We continue to look to science and technology for solutions to the threats posed by toxic, polluted (and, by extension, polluting) landscapes, just as they did with their swamps. We continue to use art to generate pleasure when we contemplate oil spills, strip mines, slag heaps, and garbage dumps, just as they did with their mountains. And we still use gardening (or landscape design, as we now call it) to redeem landscapes that inspire our guilt because we have laid them to waste, just as they did with their forests. But when faced with toxic and derelict sites, it is not enough to turn away, assume that someone else will clean them up, take photos that will only be shown in a museum or art gallery, or cover them over with such stand-ins for "nature" as grass and trees. We must do more.

The aversive landscape mounts a challenge of a particular kind. (**FIG. 10**) Wasteland arouses our strongest feelings: it attracts at the same time as it repels. This emotional appeal, which is fundamental to the definition of wasteland, engages us both on a biological, universal level and on one that is culturally specific, uniting us through our common humanity while allowing for individual difference. Furthermore, the powerful emotions wasteland elicits can be channeled into action, used to construct a passionate, ethically and politically motivated stance that has the force to challenge the status quo. Finally, the equivocal nature of these emotions helps us to recognize that our desires may not always conform to what is socially sanctioned, and in this way aids in formulating an agenda that does not fall prey to the more simplistic forms of moral self-righteousness. Of all our contemporary environments, it is wasteland that most fully engages with the challenges and possibilities confronting landscape today. Wasteland not only shows us what an emotional response to landscape has meant in the past, but also suggests how being in the mood for landscape could lead to a more environmentally and socially equitable future.

Notes

1

Ignasi de Solà-Morales Rubió, "Terrain Vague," in *Anyplace* (Cambridge, MA: MIT Press, 1995), 118–23; Antoine Picon, "Anxious Landscapes: From the Ruin to Rust," trans. Karen Bates, *Grey Room* 1 (Fall 2000), 64–83; Niall Kirkwood, *Manufactured Landscapes: Rethinking the Post-Industrial Landscape* (London: Taylor and Francis, 2001); Mira Engler, *Designing America's Waste Landscapes* (Baltimore: Johns Hopkins University Press, 2004); Alan Berger, *Drosscape: Wasting Land in Urban America* (New York: Princeton Architectural Press, 2007).

2

Vittoria Di Palma, *Wasteland: A History* (New Haven, CT: Yale University Press, 2014).

3

See Andrew Ortony and Terence J. Turner, "What's Basic About Basic Emotions?" *Psychological Review* 97, no. 3 (1990): 315–31; Paul Ekman, "An Argument for Basic Emotions," *Cognition and Emotion* 6 (1992): 169–200; and Lisa Feldman Barrett, "Are Emotions Natural Kinds?" *Perspectives on Psychological Science* 1, no. 1 (March 2006): 28–58.

4

William Ian Miller, *The Anatomy of Disgust* (Cambridge, MA: Harvard University Press, 1997), 8.

5

Norbert Elias, *The Civilizing Process*, trans. Edmund Jephcott (Oxford: Blackwell Publishing, 1994); Mary Douglas, *Purity and Danger: An Analysis of Concepts of Pollution and Taboo* (London: Routledge, 1966).

6

For recent assessments of the evolutionary role of disgust, see Valerie Curtis, "Why Disgust Matters," in "Disease Avoidance: From Animals to Culture," ed. R. J. Stevenson, T. I. Case, and M. J. Oaten, special issue, *Philosophical Transactions of the Royal Society B* 366, no. 1538 (December 2011), 3478–90.

7

Miller, *Anatomy of Disgust*, 1.

8

Aurel Kolnai, "The Standard Modes of Aversion: Fear, Disgust, and Hatred," in *On Disgust*, ed. Barry Smith and Carolyn Korsmeyer (Chicago: Open Court, 2004), 100.

9

Carolyn Korsmeyer, *Savoring Disgust: The Foul and the Fair in Aesthetics* (Oxford: Oxford University Press, 2011), 37.

10

Kolnai, "Disgust," in *On Disgust*, 43.

11

Anthony Blunt, *Nicolas Poussin*, 2nd ed. (Washington, DC: National Gallery of Art, 1967; London: Pallas Athene, 1995), 368.

12

Blunt, *Poussin*, 369–70.

13

Ibid., 226.

14

Roger de Piles, *Cours de peinture par principes* (Paris: Jacques Estienne, 1708), translated as *The Principles of Painting* (London: J. Osborn, 1743).

15

De Piles, *Cours*, 200–259.

16

Ibid., 104–14.

17

Ibid., 3, 6.

18

Ibid., 114–21.

LAND AS INFRASTRUCTURE FOR
LIVING—*Saskia Sassen*

The biosphere's capacity to renew land, water, and air is remarkable, but pred-
icated on specific temporalities and life cycles that have been outpaced by our
technical, chemical, and organizational innovations over the last few decades.
We now have vast stretches of land and water that are dead—land dead from the
overwhelming, relentless use of chemicals, and water dead from lack of oxygen
due to pollution of all sorts. Here I examine extreme conditions of land. This is
a partial view that rests on the assumption that extreme conditions make sharply
visible what is more difficult to apprehend in milder circumstances. Thus, while
most of the land on our planet is still alive, more and more of it is dying.

LOSING AND ACQUIRING LAND

Just as there are many types of land, there are multiple forms of land degradation.
Erosion, desertification, and overuse through monocultures, as in plantations,
are critical causes of agricultural destruction. Climate change has brought heat
waves of a kind rarely seen before, affecting agricultural areas across the world
and increasingly including places that have been successful food producers for a
very long time. These heat waves and their consequences are probably the key
source of land degradation in agricultural regions. Mining and industrial waste
degrade land in a very different way. Scattered evidence in news media signals
that the extent of the fragility of land on our planet may not be widely understood or recognized. For instance, polls suggest that few in the United States
seem to know that more than a third of the country's land, including much of the
cherished, fertile Midwest, is actually stressed according to scientific measures.
Nor is it widely known in much of the West that we have at least four hundred
clinically dead coastal ocean zones worldwide, which can add to the fragility of
coastal land. We created this fragility and these deaths.

The eviction of fauna and flora in order to develop plantations and mines
has repositioned vast stretches of land as nothing more than sites for extraction.
The destruction of land is such that over twenty countries today have acquired
extensive stretches of land in foreign countries to grow the food they need for
their people. Some countries, notably Japan and Saudi Arabia, have been doing
this for decades, but the last decade has seen a vast escalation in such acquisitions
and in the number of countries and firms doing so.

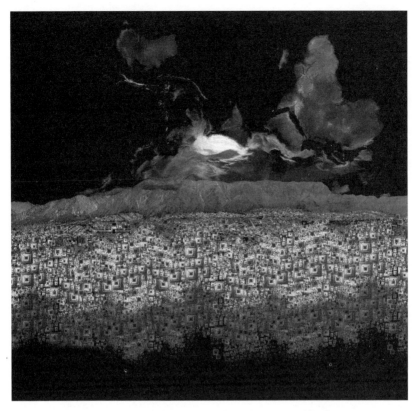

FIG. 1 — Hilary Koob-Sassen, "Polis Extension," from the series Models of aggregate endeavour, 2005–2015. Presented by the Errorists as *The Ascendant Accumulation of Error*, Institute of Contemporary Arts, London, 2015.
Courtesy of the artist.

A major shift began in 2006, marked by a rapid increase in the volume and geographical spread of foreign acquisitions, as well as the diversity of the buyers. Foreign governments and firms are estimated to have acquired more than 200 million hectares of land from 2006 to 2011. Much of the purchased land is in Africa, but a growing share is now in Latin America and, a first since the post–World War II era, in several countries in Europe and Asia, notably Russia, Ukraine, Laos, and Vietnam. Finally, the buyers are increasingly diverse, and include purchasers established everywhere from China to Sweden, and firms from sectors as different as biotechnology and finance. Two significant factors contribute to this sharp increase in acquisitions: The first is the growing demand for industrial crops—notably, palm for biofuels and food crops, the latter still coming largely from the states of the Persian Gulf and China. The second is that the growing demand for land and the sharp rise in global food prices in the 2000s made land a desirable investment, even for speculative reasons.

This global demand has repositioned land on a diversity of global circuits, from governmental to corporate and, particularly, financial. Financial institutions have also bought land, not to become farmers, but to commodify land and

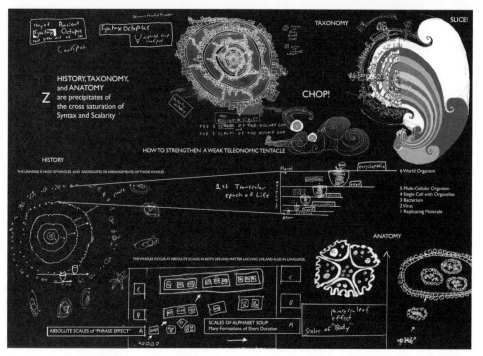

FIG. 2 — Hilary Koob-Sassen, "Syntax and Scalarity," from the series Models of aggregate endeavour, 2005–2015. Presented by the Errorists as *The Ascendant Accumulation of Error*, Institute of Contemporary Arts, London, 2015.
Courtesy of the artist.

speculate on its value. The sharp growth in foreign ownership is also significantly altering the character of local economies, particularly land ownership, and diminishing the sovereign authority of the state over its territory. The process of acquisition may be less violent and disruptive than the imperial conquests of the past. But that does not mean that they should be confused with more benign examples of foreign ownership—the placement of job-generating Ford motor plants in Europe or a Volkswagen plant in Brazil. The scale of land acquisitions leaves a large global footprint, marked by a vast number of microexpulsions of small farmers and villages, and by rising toxicity in the land and water surrounding the plantations constructed on the acquired land. There are growing numbers of displaced people, rural migrants moving to slums in cities, destroyed villages and smallholder economies, and, in the long run, much dead land.

At its most general, *land degradation* can be defined as "a long-term loss of ecosystem function and productivity…from which land cannot recover unaided."[1] It is difficult to measure accurately on a large scale. The few studies that have attempted to map the global process estimate that about 40 percent of the world's agricultural land is seriously degraded. The worst-affected regions are Central America, where 75 percent of agricultural land is infertile; Africa, where a fifth of the soil is degraded; and Asia, where 11 percent has become unsuitable for farming. Today our world is 0.8 degrees Celsius above preindustrial levels of the eighteenth century. A recent global examination of land by the World Bank mentions the findings of several scientists who state that "if the world warms by 2 degrees Celsius—warming which may be reached in 20 to 30 years—it will cause widespread food shortages, unprecedented heat waves, and more intense cyclones. We could see a 2-degree-Celsius world in the space of one generation."

The area of land affected by drought has increased over the past fifty years, and has done so somewhat faster than projected by climate models. For instance, the 2012 drought in the United States affected about 80 percent of agricultural land, making it the most severe drought since the 1950s. In sub-Saharan Africa, with "warming of less than 2 degrees Celsius by the 2050s, total crop production could be reduced by 10 percent. For higher levels of warming, there are indications that yields may decrease by around 15 to 20 percent across all crops and regions." A warming of 3 degrees Celsius is estimated to reduce savannas from "a quarter at present to approximately one-seventh of total current land area."

There are a few detailed studies on the evolution of land degradation worldwide starting in the late 1980s and early 1990s. Overall, researchers estimate (with diverse adjustments for particular variables) that 24 percent of global land area suffered degradation between 1981 and 2003. This is, for example, shown by Zhanguo Bai, David Dent, Lennart Olsson, and Michael E. Schaepman, who used twenty-three years' worth of data from the remotely sensed Normalized Difference Vegetation Index, generated mostly by satellite observation of green vegetation.[2] The index measures the amount of light spectrum absorbed by photosynthesis, adjusted for rain-use efficiency, to create a proxy for net primary productivity that can be tracked over time. In addition to the overall findings, these results have been validated empirically in several very diverse places—northern China, Kenya, and Bangladesh.

Over the past few years, heat waves have become the main source of agricultural land degradation, with all this entails for the global food supply, particularly for the poor. Based on studies of specific heat waves around the world, the World Bank's 2013 report illustrates that the past decade has seen extreme heat waves with major societal impacts. "These events were highly unusual, with monthly and seasonal temperatures typically more than 3 standard deviations (sigma) warmer than the local mean temperature—so-called 3-sigma events. Without climate change, such 3-sigma events would be expected to occur only once in several hundreds of years."

Heat waves can lead to a variety of problems. A decline in precipitation, for instance, is the major issue in some areas. Extreme cases include southern

Africa, where annual precipitation "is projected to decrease by up to 30 percent under 4-degree-Celsius warming…and parts of southern and west Africa [will see] decreases in ground-water recharge rates of 50 to 70 percent." A worldwide warming of 1.2 to 1.9 degrees Celsius by 2050 would increase the proportion of the global population that is undernourished by 25 to 90 percent. In South Asia, such an increase would require a doubling of food imports to meet per-capita calorie demand. "Decreasing food availability is related to significant health problems for affected populations, including childhood stunting, which is projected to increase by 35 percent compared to a scenario without climate change by 2050."

The facts about these increased temperatures and their causes have been convincingly established. The Fourth Assessment Report of the Intergovernmental Panel on Climate Change (IPCC) found that the rise in global mean temperature and warming of the climate system were "unequivocal." Furthermore, "most of the observed increase in global average temperature since the mid-twentieth century is very likely due to the observed increase in anthropogenic greenhouse-gas concentrations." Recent work reinforces this conclusion. Global mean warming is now approximately 0.8 degrees Celsius above preindustrial levels. Further, in the absence of human activity during the past fifty years "the sum of solar and volcanic forces would likely have produced cooling, not warming," as stated by James Hansen, Makiko Sato, and Reto Ruedy in 2012.[3]

Extreme summer temperatures can largely be attributed to climatic warming. Grant Foster and Stefan Rahmstorf, among others, show that if one removes known factors that affect short-term temperature variations (solar variability, volcanic aerosols, El Niño, and others), natural factors cannot explain warming.[4] Hence it can be largely attributed to anthropogenic factors—man-made factors. In the 1960s, summertime heat extremes (more than three standard deviations warmer than the mean of the climate) were practically absent, affecting less than 1 percent of the earth's surface. The affected area increased to 4 to 5 percent between 2006 and 2008, and by 2009–11 such extremes occurred on 6 to 13 percent of the land surface. Now such extremely hot outliers typically cover about 10 percent of the land area.

Beyond the gradual degradation of agricultural land, there are processes that cause extreme destruction to land of all sorts. Mining and manufacturing are the most obvious culprits in much of the world. Their capacity to kill land is enormous; it is particularly hard for land to recover from the type of degradation they create. Consider, for instance, that much of the estimated one billion tons of industrial waste produced by Organisation for Economic Co-operation and

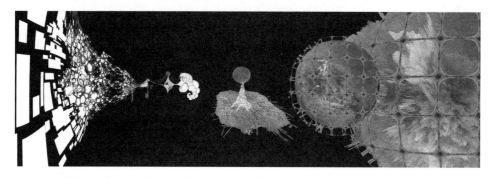

FIG. 3 — Hilary Koob-Sassen, "Transcalar Investment" from the series Models of aggregate endeavour, 2005–2015. Presented by the Errorists as *The Ascendant Accumulation of Error*, Institute of Contemporary Arts, London, 2015.
Courtesy of the artist.

Development (OECD) countries in 2001 still lives with us more than ten years later. And industry generates more waste than agriculture, forestry, and power production *combined*.

In sufficient concentrations, industrial waste, including heavy metals and greenhouse gases, can render an environment so toxic that plants cease to grow and even people become sterile. Some heavy metals (a misnomer, as this category includes some elements that are neither heavy nor metals), such as iron and zinc, are vital to human health in controlled amounts. Others, such as mercury and lead, are toxic at any level. However, the output of waste generated by modern industry is so massive it can render even a benign substance such as carbon dioxide toxic.

A MULTISITED SPACE OF DEVASTATION

We can think of such devastated and dead land as holes in the tissue of the biosphere. In the book *Expulsions*, on which this essay is based, I conceive of these holes as sites marked by the expulsion of biospheric elements from their life space.[5] Further, I conceive of the facts on the ground as the surface expression of deeper subterranean trends that are cutting across the world, regardless of the local politico-economic organization or mode of environmental destruction. In each place there is a specific alignment of issues that explains the outcome. But from a conceptual distance, all these differences become visible as a sort of generic condition: a global, multisited array of dead patches of land and water in the tissue of the biosphere.

There is a profound disjuncture between this planetary condition and its sources, on one hand, and the dominant logics shaping governmental responses and much policy, on the other. Destroyed air, land, and water become a generic condition, a facticity disembedded from the geopolitical landscape of countries and mainstream politics. States mostly focus on benefitting from today's basic consensus policy approach to climate change, which is carbon trading. The effort is not to reduce destruction but to maximize a state's advantage in the right to destroy: governments push to increase their "lawful" quota either to augment the right to pollute or augment what they can sell to governments that want to pollute more. Leaderships of all sorts appear to find it impossible to address the fact of planetary destruction and prefer to scale down their efforts to the lowest common denominators, which makes them seemingly more manageable.

Do the cases discussed suggest that some forms of political and economic organization prevent some of this destruction? Yes, but to a surprising extent the differences are minor compared to the scale of destruction. Those organizational differences fall mostly beneath the consequential levels for reducing destruction at the global scale; they matter more for the place than for the overall planetary condition. Do newer technologies prevent more destruction than older ones? Some of the newest, most complex technologies being deployed are not much better than the older, far more elementary modes of producing. They are only different—fracking or removing an entire mountaintop versus digging a coal mine. It all points to the limits of our current dominant approach, with its emphasis on the differences among countries, and the common proposition that more advanced modes of producing will allow us to reduce environmental destruction.

The multisited space of devastation tells a story about biospheric destruction that is much more than a tale of the individual, specific ways in which countries and sectors are destructive. In *Expulsions*, I examine dozens of instances worldwide as constituting a space of destruction that cuts across the familiar divisions of our geopolitical system. In much of the discussion about the environment, there is often an overemphasizing of these familiar differentiations, and a blaming of specific practices and policies in countries (coal-mining pollution in China, the chemical industry in Russia, land strip mining in the United States, and on and on).

But, in fact, at ground level what matters is the capacity to destroy the environment. From this angle, all these cases are generic—they are all negatives, regardless of the politics or United Nations votes of the countries involved. I use cases from countries with different forms of political and economic organization to signal that while environmental destruction may take on specific shapes and contents in each country, and may be worse in some than in others, it is their destructive capacities that really matter in my analysis. A mine that pollutes in Russia looks different from a mine that pollutes in the United States, but both are polluting above the threshold of the sustainable. In this sense, then, mine is a call for a return to ground level, in order to go beyond the divisions emphasized by the interstate system and its international treaties.

We thank Harvard University Press for allowing use of material from Expulsions: Brutality and Complexity in the Global Economy *(2014), especially chapter 4, "Dead Land, Dead Water."*

Notes

1
Zhanguo Bai, David Dent, Lennart Olsson, and Michael E. Schaepman, "Proxy Global Assessment of Land Degradation," *Soil Use and Management* 24, no. 3 (July 24, 2008): 223. In this paragraph all other quotes are from World Bank, *Turn Down the Heat: Climate Extremes, Regional Impacts, and the Case for Resilience, A report for the World Bank by the Potsdam Institute for Climate Impact Research and Climate Analytics* (Washington, DC: World Bank, 2013). Additional sources are World Bank, *Turn Down the Heat: Why a 4° Warmer World Must Be Avoided* (Washington, DC: World Bank, 2012); and R. T. A. Hakkeling, L. R. Oldeman, and W. G. Sombroek, *World Map of the Status of Human-Induced Soil Degradation: An Explanatory Note* (Wageningen, Neth.: International Soil Reference and Information Center, 1991).

2
Bai et al., "Proxy Global Assessment," 223–34.

3
James Hansen, Makiko Sato, and Reto Ruedy, "Perception of Climate Change," *Proceedings of the National Academy of Sciences of the United States*, 109 (2012): 14726–27.

4
Grant Foster and Stefan Rahmstorf, "Global Temperature Evolution 1979–2010," *Environmental Research Letters* 6, no. 4 (2011).

5
Saskia Sassen, *Expulsions: Brutality and Complexity in the Global Economy* (Cambridge, MA: Harvard University Press, 2014).

DENATURALIZING THE AMERICAN
LANDSCAPE—*Emily Eliza Scott*

> Landscape outlives history; it surpasses it. Over time—and almost as a function
> of its earth, its soil—landscape absorbs the events played out on its surface; it
> inters the marks of past practices as much as it also bears their traces…. [L]and-
> scape is ideological insofar as it allows history to decompose.
> —Jessica Dubow

In the past two decades, landscape has taken center stage within art and architecture—if for somewhat different reasons and to different ends. In both fields, there
seems to be a driving sense that material-environmental conditions are intensi-
fying and becoming less stable, and, moreover, that attention to entanglements
between the human and nonhuman might offer one way beyond postmodernism's hermetic fixation with representation. This essay focuses on contemporary
art that reveals the often hidden and often violent social, political, economic, and
historical facets of seemingly natural sites in the American landscape. Here land
is understood to be neither pregiven—static, neutral, or *natural*—nor something
to which we have unmediated access. Rather, it is approached as an outcome and
index of complex procedures. The artworks I will examine open onto questions
of power, and, furthermore, the role of visual representation (or a lack thereof)
in struggles over space. More precisely, they probe the ways that landscape, when
taken as an embodiment or extension of "nature," has served to sanitize, obscure,
and/or *naturalize* various conflicts, as in cases where differing environmental
values collide with regard to the same plot of ground.[1]

Around Crab Orchard (2012), the first feature-length film by the interdisciplinary artist and writer Sarah Kanouse, explores a specific wildlife refuge in southern
Illinois in terms of the way nature imagery has masked highly unsettling activities
taking place within its borders. Early on in Kanouse's sixty-nine-minute piece,
archival clips from an official United States Fish and Wildlife Service (USFWS)
promotional video showcase familiar-looking footage of waterfowl and other
wildlife in their presumably native habitat, set to twangy bluegrass and a voice-
over that beckons, "Ahhh, peace at last, away from the hustle and bustle of urban
life. […] Welcome to Crab Orchard National Wildlife Refuge, a unique place to
experience nature."[2] Shortly thereafter, we learn that Crab Orchard is simultaneously home to General Dynamics, a multibillion-dollar defense company that

produces munitions within the refuge and, in the process, leaves behind danger-
ous contaminants such as polychlorinated biphenyls (PCBs), depleted uranium,
and various leads. This wildlife refuge is unique in that it is the only USFWS site
where weapons production is still actively ongoing. It is quite typical, however,
in having undergone the "military-to-wildlife conversion" process, whereby
former federal military areas are refashioned into habitat for wildlife and outdoor recreation enthusiasts.[3] Also included in Kanouse's counterofficial portrait
of this place is the nearby Marion Prison, where inmates, along with local area
residents, have long been exposed to toxins leaking beyond the boundaries of
the refuge. Porosity is a key theme of Kanouse's story: the very notion of a
refuge—a place that is cordoned off, protected in a baseline state, outside of time
and politics, and managed in a one-dimensional way—is a fiction to be troubled.

Her own endeavor began, as she puts it, "with an impasse"—a blockade
to visual and informational access. Upon attempting to photograph a cluster
of anonymous-looking buildings owned by General Dynamics on the refuge
grounds, she and her companions were stopped by a private security guard, who
questioned them about why they'd want to take pictures of anything other than
scenery, flora, and fauna—these being the proper subjects of "real photography," he implied. (FIG. 1) This encounter was soon followed by an unannounced
visit from two Federal Bureau of Investigation (FBI) agents on Kanouse's front
porch, and then an explicit prohibition from any future filming within the park.
The impetus for *Around Crab Orchard*, then, was the artist's confrontation with
an at-once literal and conceptual problem: What other ways can we picture a
place like this?

Kanouse's "answer" involves an assemblage of diverse sources. Perhaps
uneven, or unlike, is a better way to describe the amalgam comprising this film,
which is furthermore punctuated by the artist's eloquent reflections about her
own research process—a "metanarrative" that provides a kind of horizon line
throughout the piece. A number of firsthand interviews with local residents,
environmental and social justice activists, and cultural geographers are interspersed with licensed press material from the USFWS and the US Army—
together forming a bricolage of voices. (The USFWS denied Kanouse's repeated
attempts to speak with them, and eventually stopped replying to her letters and
phone calls altogether.) While the interview is, of course, a staple format within
the documentary genre, *Around Crab Orchard* gives equal weight to less straightforward elements. At several, repeated points, Kanouse's camera dwells upon
the details of a "natural history" display: at one point, we face the fragment of

FIGS. 1–3 — Still from Sarah Kanouse, *Around Crab Orchard* (2012), HD video, 69 min. *Courtesy of the artist.*

a diorama mannequin fashioned as an American Indian tribesman in traditional local garb; elsewhere, we linger within the dripping, green humidity of a botanical garden presenting indigenous, regional plants; further on, we hover along the clinical corridors of a laboratory—all of these are spaces where authorized knowledge about Crab Orchard is forged. (FIG. 2) The artist's own body appears during many intervals, as well: we see her standing at each of the refuge's four directional boundaries, holding a sign to mark it, and, later, observe her finger tracing these same geographical contours on a road atlas. We watch as she hastily draws, cuts, and pastes foamcore into miniature architectural mock-ups of the elusive white buildings that have prompted her inquiry. (FIG. 3) She steps into and zips up a hazmat suit in one scene; in another, she scans through reels of microfiche to uncover a long-forgotten news story from the nineteenth-century addressing local race relations. Taken together, this constellation of performative gestures and varied source materials poses larger epistemological questions about what, exactly, counts as valid information, or evidence—one of the key subtexts of the film.

As becomes ever more clear, Kanouse's aim is not to build a coherent truth, a tidy image, or a tale with clear edges. Rather, *Around Crab Orchard* reminds us of the limits of embodied observation—of how much is *impossible* to know by standing on a piece of land and looking. Speaking to the conundrums entailed in representing any particular place with attunement to the inevitable intricacies, paradoxes, and contingencies at play, Kanouse asks within her narrative script:

> Where do we start a story like this? The story of a place, what it contains, what it does? It doesn't have a plot, some kind of beginning, middle, and end. Instead, it unfolds in space. It has contiguities and adjacencies. [...] The appearance of isolation is a function of scale, where we choose to focus and from what distance. Or maybe it's a parallax, a perceived shift in an object's location caused by the position of the observer. The closer we are, the more we distort. Parallax is often called an error, but accounting for it allows explorers to navigate without the aid of a map. At some scales of vision, if we back up far enough, every place seems to touch every place else.[4]

I am interested here in considering the strategies employed by contemporary artists who take familiar sights/sites and make them strange or legible in new ways—who attempt to undo what seems "natural," to highlight the ideological workings of landscape.[5] Critical documentary films like *Around Crab Orchard*, which often incorporate extensive and multipronged research, are one breed (other examples that come to mind include the Otolith Group's 2012 *The Radiant* and Lucy Raven's *China Town* from 2009); tours and other kinds of on-site "interventions," another.[6] The question of whether or not painting and photography—as media that collapse the worldly into the two-dimensional and the motionless—are capable of relaying the frictions, layers, and interrelations of place is one that hovers in the background, for me. Are there inherent limits to using a medium that, in essence, translates its subject into a scene?

I have begun with Kanouse's artwork, because I think it is emblematic of a shift in recent years from artists engaging with *landscape* (as tied to composition, view, or frame) to *land use*. The term *landscape* has a longstanding association with the pictorial, with formal composition, and with the aesthetic, in modern art history. The anthropologist Tim Ingold attributes this entire disciplinary orientation—a profound misorientation, in his opinion—to a simple etymological error, albeit one that has had far-reaching consequences:

> Of early medieval provenance, [landscape] referred originally to an area of land bound into the everyday practices and customary usages of an agrarian community. However, its subsequent incorporation into the language of painterly depiction—above all through the tradition of Dutch art that developed in the seventeenth century (Alpers, 1983)—has led generations of scholars to mistake the connotations of the suffix *-scape* for a particular "scopic regime" of detailed

FIG. 4 — Pieter Bruegel the Elder, *The Harvesters*, 1565. Oil on wood, 46 x 63 in. (116.5 x 159.5 cm).
Courtesy of the Metropolitan Museum of Art (Rogers Fund, 1919).

and disinterested observation (Jay, 1988). They have, it seems, been fooled by a superficial resemblance between *scape* and *scope* that is, in fact, entirely fortuitous and has no foundation in etymology. "Scope" comes from the classical Greek *skopos*—literally "the target of the bowman, the mark towards which he gazes as he aims" (Carruthers, 1998: 79)—from which is derived the verb *skopein*, "to look." "Scape," quite to the contrary, comes from Old English *sceppan* or *skyppan*, meaning "to shape" (Olwig, 2008). Medieval shapers of the land were not painters but farmers, whose purpose was not to render the material world in appearance rather than substance, but to wrest a living from the earth. [...] Nevertheless, the equation of the shape of the land with its look—of the *scaped* with the *scopic*—has become firmly lodged in the vocabulary of modernist art history. Landscape has thus come to be identified with scenery and with an art of description that would see the world spread out on a canvas, much as in the subsequent development of both cartography and photography, it would come to be projected onto a plate or screen, or the pages of an atlas.[7] **(FIG. 4)**

The trend in contemporary art I wish to identify, in line with Ingold's corrective, reflects a move beyond, or sometimes even against, "the art of description," and a renewed emphasis on the material rather than the primarily visual aspects of land, often with special attention to issues of labor. The cultural theorist Raymond Williams, in his 1980 essay "Ideas of Nature," in fact cites a fundamental divide between those who approach landscape as a product of nature versus human shaping: "A considerable part of what we call the natural landscape [...] is the product of human design and human labour, and in admiring it as natural it matters very much whether we suppress that fact of labour or acknowledge it."[8]

The landscape photography of Ansel Adams, at least within the past half-century of American art, may best demonstrate the impulse to *suppress*, or evacuate, the "fact of labour" that goes into landscape's making. His exquisitely composed, black-and-white pictures feature sweeping landscapes of the American West, typically devoid of any hint of human presence. The scenes are monumental, conjuring a seemingly original moment—and one that is specifically American, yoking the birth of American national identity to the vision of an unpeopled, wild Western frontier. (Williams's reminder of the etymological link between *nature*, *native*, and *nation*—all derived from the Latin *natus*, meaning "to be born"—is particularly apt here.[9]) Formally, Adams's images hark back to

FIG. 5 — Robert Adams, *Mobile Homes,
Jefferson County, Colorado*, 1973.
© *Robert Adams, courtesy Fraenkel Gallery, San
Francisco.*

the sublime depictions of the nineteenth-century Hudson River School painters, while simultaneously harnessing the deep tonal contrasts of twentieth-century modernist "straight" photography to extreme dramatic effect.

In the 1960s and 1970s, certain artists were already seeking to counter Adams's representational schema and the romantic notions of landscape it embodied, some of them taking up industrial and otherwise visibly impacted landscapes to do so.[10] Those photographers who participated in the highly influential 1975 exhibition New Topographics: Photographs of a Man-Altered Landscape, at the George Eastman House in Rochester, New York, adjusted their frame of view (in some cases, we can imagine, only ever so slightly) to capture those marks erased by Adams. Instead, they portrayed the mundane, unglamorous processes of suburbanization, industry, and everyday habitation in the American West—underscoring the human-land dialectic of landscapes in formation.[11] (FIG. 5)

In 1973, the American artist Robert Smithson wrote about the "dialectical landscape" in what would be the last published essay in his life. From the mid-1960s onward, he engaged explicitly "disrupted" or "pulverized" sites (e.g., rock quarries, slag heaps, partially constructed highways) in favor to those that evoked a sense of either careful finish or untouched beauty.[12] He was deeply critical of the ecology movement quickly gaining steam at the time and derided a budding "wilderness cult" (his term) for its reductive division between the human and nonhuman worlds, arguing that "[s]piritualism widens the split between man and nature."[13] (Ansel Adams's widely circulated images were both an illustration and a driver of such a wilderness ethic during this period.) Smithson insisted upon the importance of confronting contemporary environments in all their messy complexity: "The artist cannot turn his back on the contradictions that inhabit our landscapes."[14]

Many artists today similarly turn to the American West, although—differently from their predecessors—they approach it as a locus for dramatic displacements and erasures, highlighting links between longstanding myths of a national frontier and the systematic colonization and militarization of space there. (FIG. 6) Their works foreground the politics of land use, reminding us furthermore that the constitutive forces of landscape are for the most part *not* visible. Artists are perhaps uniquely inclined to sense the less evident dimensions of landscape, to look sideways at how processes become forms, to excavate and *recompose*

FIG. 6 — Emmet Gowin, *Subsidence Craters, Northern End of Yucca Flat, Nevada Test Site*, 1996. Toned gelatin silver photograph, 14 x 14 in. (35.5 x 35.5 cm).
© Emmet Gowin; courtesy Pace/Mac Gill Gallery, New York.

FIG. 7 — Trevor Paglen, *Detachment 3, Air Force Flight Test Center, Groom Lake, Nevada, Distance ~ 26 miles*, 2008. Chromogenic print, 40 x 50 in. (102 x 127 cm).
Courtesy of the artist, Metro Pictures, Altman Siegel, and Galerie Thomas Zander.

FIG. 8 — Nicholas Brown, from *Vanishing Indian Repeat Photography Project*, 2011–.
Courtesy of the artist.

the marks of submerged and/or suppressed events—whether historical or current—that have played out on a particular surface. (I leave it to other authors in this volume to explore the ways that landscape architecture might also interpret and amplify the behind-the-scenes of landscape.)

Trevor Paglen, an artist and "experimental geographer," appropriates amateur technologies such as limit telephotography in order to probe the "black world" of the US military-industrial complex: covert testing grounds and other spaces of wartime production that are actively "produced as nowhere," smudged off of the map, and kept under the public's radar.[15] His grainy photographs of military bunkers in Nevada or streaks left by top-secret flights in the "other night sky" depict not only the existence of such sites and activities, but also the limits of visuality itself. (FIG. 7)

The cultural landscape historian and indigenous rights activist Nicholas Brown is meanwhile building a "re-photographic" archive of Glacier National Park in northern Montana. His *Vanishing Indian Repeat Photography Project* (*VIRPP*), begun in 2011, is part of a larger inquiry into what he calls the "vanishing logic" that underpins and binds narratives about the disappearance of indigenous peoples in the late nineteenth century—generated by the US National Park Service, among other institutions—with those about melting glaciers today. Brown explains,

> [...] the *VIRPP* interprets colonization as an ongoing process rather than an historical event, which, in turn, sheds light on the structural dimensions of settler colonialism. [...] By exploring the conjunction of vanishing glaciers and Indians at Glacier National Park, the *VIRPP* [...] ruptures a temporal boundary that has kept the story of yesterday's vanishing Indian separate from that of today's vanishing glacier, insisting, instead, that we consider them as parts of the same story.[16]

His practice of re-photography is significant not only because it has been employed by certain photographers associated with "new topographics" to document historical developments in the American West, but also because it is a central tool for scientists studying environmental change, such as glacial retreat, over time. (FIG. 8)

In one final example, the Boston-based collective the Institute for Infinitely Small Things reproduced for their 2011 piece *The Border Crossed Us* a segment of the US-Mexican border fence from southern Arizona—an infrastructural element that is largely invisible to most Americans, yet literally marks and organizes the space of the nation-state—on the campus of the University of Massachusetts,

FIG. 9 —The Institute for Infinitely Small
Things, *The Border Crossed Us*, 2011.
Courtesy of the artists.

Amherst. (FIG. 9) The artists specify that "[t]his particular section of the fence
divides the Tohono O'odham indigenous community along seventy-five miles
of their reservation, disrupts ceremonial paths, desecrates sacred burial grounds
and prevents members from receiving critical health services."[17] Their own intervention, which orchestrated a direct physical confrontation between the university public and this highly charged, temporary transplant, was coupled with an
impressive roster of events led by representatives of the Tohono O'odham tribal
community, among others, and involving a strong dialogic component. With its
multiple participatory dimensions, *The Border Crossed Us* posed thorny questions about the political and social dynamics of borders as well as the relations
between seemingly distant places.[18]

Today the forces that produce landscape are arguably more decentralized, dema-
terialized, and delinked from the actual ground than ever before. More accurately,
the distances have widened between the places where decisions regarding land use
are *made* and where they are *enacted*. Whereas Ingold's medieval worker-shapers,
who "with foot, axe and plough, [...] trod, hacked and scratched their lines into
the earth," performing labor that was "close-up, in an immediate, muscular and
visceral engagement with wood, grass and soil," in our own day and age, a whole
series of geographically dispersed factors and agents—some virtual and others
"analog" (e.g., international trade and patenting laws, migrant worker streams,
stock market figures, transportation systems)—prefigure any moment before foot
or plough pierce ground.[19] Critical geographers have been especially helpful in the-
orizing the "uneven development" that characterizes our contemporary condition
of globalized deferrals and displacements, whereby violence (to land, humans, and
nonhumans) is often shifted from one place to another, and in the process further
from common view.[20] The literary and postcolonial theorist Rob Nixon further
elaborates upon the "slow violence" entailed in many environmental operations
(e.g., long-term contamination owing to extractive industries, the severing of ties
between indigenous communities and their homelands and ways of life) that unfold
across vast scales and in forms and temporalities that are often hard to perceive,
compounding their intensity. This, he describes, is "a violence that occurs gradually and out of sight, a violence of delayed destruction that is dispersed across time
and space, an attritional violence that is typically not viewed as violence at all."[21]

Although globalization is not a new phenomenon, since the 1980s and 1990s, various neoliberal economic policies such as the deregulation of financial markets, together with the expansion of transnational corporations and advancements in telecommunication technologies, have ushered in an era in which the global economy operates with unprecedented power and swiftness. The present moment, we might say, is distinguished by the degree to which finance orders space. The sociologist Saskia Sassen has described "finance [as] the steam engine of our time," a vast force that is "flattening everything around us" as it "grabs more and more terrain" amid an ongoing shift from a world organized largely by national territories to one of global connectivity and jurisdiction.[22] As faraway places become ever more entangled via flows of labor and capital, it is increasingly impossible to tease apart one place from another—a more *territorial* optic of analysis is demanded.

I want to close with a case taken not from art, but from contemporary land use practices. Hydraulic fracturing, or *fracking*—the process of injecting water and chemicals at extremely high pressure into geologic strata below ground in order to "free" gas and oil encased within rock—is creating a new topography across the American landscape. Its residual landforms—less monumental and *consolidated* than those produced by open-pit mining or mountaintop removal—superficially resemble both the pockmarks left by repeated atomic tests in the desert hinterlands, and those apertures quickly enveloping the surface of glaciers and polar ice caps melting due to anthropogenic climate change (itself the result of carbon released into the atmosphere via the burning of fossil fuels). (FIG. 10) Although not exclusive to the United States, the rampant application of this method of resource extraction there is attributable to a combination of specific historical developments, from early white settlers' perceptions of "open land" being free for the taking under the rubric of "Manifest Destiny," to the allocation of land into gridded parcels for individual ownership. A distinction between surface and subsurface property rights is furthermore now coming into unprecedented play, as private landowners are increasingly approached by energy companies who want to buy or lease rights to terrain underground—leading to the widespread phenomenon of backyard (and even front yard) drilling, including within densely populated residential neighborhoods. (FIG. 11) This emergent frackscape is arguably the neoliberal landscape par excellence. (And, as is always the case, its repercussions are distributed unequally, exacting disproportionate impact upon those with less power.) It has moreover begun to produce unexpected seismic

FIG. 10 — Hydraulic fracturing ("fracking") pads, Jonah Field, Wyoming, 2012. *Courtesy of EcoFlight.*

FIG. 11 — A deep, horizontal hydraulic fracturing well in a residential backyard in Ogemaw County, Michigan, 2012. *Courtesy of the photographer LuAnne Kozma and Ban Michigan Fracking.*

happenings, such as frequent earthquakes in Midwestern states like Oklahoma, that signal not only the retreat of any supposed baseline state of nature, but also landscape itself pushing back in unruly, lively fashion. If, as the artists I have discussed insist, the American landscape is not, and never has been, solid, self-evident, or neutral ground, today, it would seem we are entering a phase of previously unknown instability that penetrates the earth's deep layers, catalyzing new, postnatural fissures and tremblings underfoot.

Notes

Epigraph:
Jessica Dubow in "The Art Seminar" roundtable
discussion reproduced in Rachael Ziady DeLue
and James Elkins, eds., *Landscape Theory*
(London: Routledge, 2007), 100.

1

An earlier version of this essay was presented
at the College Art Association annual meeting
in Chicago, Illinois, on February 14, 2014,
within the context of a panel titled "Still on
Terra Firma? The American Landscape in
Contemporary Art." I pursue similar ideas in the
introduction to *Critical Landscapes: Art, Space,
Politics*, a book I coedited with Kirsten Swenson
(Berkeley: University of California Press, 2015),
1–15.

2

The US Fish and Wildlife Service is a federal
government agency within the US Department
of the Interior that manages the National
Wildlife Refuge System, in its own words: "a
national network of lands and waters set aside
to conserve America's fish, wildlife, and plants."
Official agency page: http://www.fws.gov
(accessed July 20, 2015).

3

Many such "military-to-wildlife conversion" (or
"M2W") sites furthermore carry "superfund"
status, determined by the government to be
the most acutely polluted places in the country.
The geographer Shiloh Krupar, who appears at
several points in Kanouse's film, describes them
as "green brownfields," elaborating that cleanup
at superfund sites is often minimal, following
"a different standard for allowable levels of
contamination to remain" than elsewhere.
Her own research has focused on the Rocky
Mountain Arsenal and Rocky Flats National
Wildlife Refuges, both near Denver, Colorado,
the former of which has been repopulated
with various megafauna including bald eagles
and American bison. She surmises that these
creatures, "as signs of purity and the native,"
play a crucial role in the fabrication of creation
stories for such places. She elaborates: "a
stockpile of genetically pure bison would return
the land to a mythic origin, drawing on imperial
nostalgia for the frontier and reversing the
historic decimation of the animal and the forced
removal of Plains-area American Indians who
relied on the bison." Countering this familiar
and moralistic conservationist paradigm, she
calls for an environmental ethics that "responds
to the M2W division of nature/human with a
commitment to more uncertain materialities—to
stewardship of the wastes and material remains
of militarization" and that acknowledges the
ways in which violences are still enacted at these
sites. Shiloh Krupar, "Where Eagles Dare," in
Critical Landscapes: Art, Space, Politics, ed. Emily
Eliza Scott and Kirsten Swenson (Berkeley:
University of California Press, 2015), 132–33.
In 2011 Kanouse and Krupar established a
collaborative research project on the toxic legacy
of the military-industrial complex in the United
States, in the form of a fake government agency.
The National Toxic Land/Labor Conservation
Service, according to its mission statement,
attends to "the ongoing environmental, eco-
nomic, and health effects of the Cold War and
the American nuclear state." Project website:
http://www.nationaltlcservice.us/ (accessed
July 20, 2015).

4

Sarah Kanouse, *Around Crab Orchard* (2012), HD
video, 69 min.

5

Among the many significant texts on landscape
and ideology, see in particular: Leo Marx,
*The Machine in the Garden: Technology and the
Pastoral Ideal in America* (New York: Oxford
University Press, 1964); W. J. T. Mitchell, ed.,
Landscape and Power (Chicago: University of
Chicago Press, 1994); and Bruce Braun and Noel
Castree, eds., *Remaking Reality: Nature at the
Millennium* (New York: Routledge, 1998).

6

The London-based artist Kodwo Eshun,
cofounder of the Otolith Group, has written
about the essay film—an apt descriptor of

Kanouse's piece—as a genre of moving image that is both self-reflexive and adequate to the intricacy and contingency of its subjects. "We can think of the essay film as a space-time in which to realize the adventure of thinking. Mainstream film is in too much of a rush. Plots demand that things happen in the right place and the right time." In addition to reflecting a different temporality than typical films, he states, the essay film understands events themselves in radically other terms: "To return to the event through the image and thereby to use images to provoke new events: it is through double logics such as this that the film essay proceeds." Kodwo Eshun, "The Art of the Essay Film," *DOT DOT DOT* 8 (October 2004): 58. More than disrupting familiar modes of image production and consumption (e.g., in which the viewer remains a passive spectator), the essay film—and what I am calling critical documentary practices, more generally—imagine alternative, and highly fluid, scenarios of past, present, and future.

7

Tim Ingold, "Landscape or Weather-world?" in *Being Alive: Essays on Movement, Knowledge, and Description* (London: Routledge, 2011), 126.

8

Raymond Williams, "Ideas of Nature," in *Problems in Materialism and Culture* (London: Verso, 1980), 78.

9

Raymond Williams, "Nature," in *Keywords: A Vocabulary of Culture and Society* (New York: Oxford University Press, 1976), 219.

10

Emily Eliza Scott, "Wasteland: American Landscapes in/and 1960s Art" (PhD diss., UCLA, 2010).

11

This important exhibition has been reprised multiple times since 1975, most recently in 2010 by the Center for Creative Photography in Tucson, Arizona, in an exhibition entitled "New Topographics" that subsequently traveled to several national and international venues. See Britt Salvesen, ed., *New Topographics* (Göttingen,

Ger.: Steidl, 2010); and Greg Foster-Rice and John Rohrbach, eds., *Reframing the New Topographics* (Chicago: Center for American Places, distributed by University of Chicago Press, 2011).

12

Liza Bear, ed., "Discussions with Heizer, Oppenheim, Smithson," *Avalanche* (Fall 1970): 53–54.

13

Robert Smithson, "Frederick Law Olmsted and the Dialectical Landscape," *Artforum* (February 1973). Reprinted in *Robert Smithson: The Collected Writings*, ed. Jack Flam (Berkeley: University of California Press, 1996), 163.

14

Ibid., 164.

15

Trevor Paglen, "Groom Lake and the Imperial Production of Nowhere," in *Violent Geographies: Fear, Terror, and Political Violence*, ed. Derek Gregory and Allan Pred (New York: Routledge, 2007), 246–47.

16

Nicholas Brown, "The Vanishing Indian Repeat Photography Project," in *Critical Landscapes: Art, Space, Politics*, ed. Emily Eliza Scott and Kirsten Swenson (Berkeley: University of California Press, 2015), 136–37.

17

The Institute for Infinitely Small Things, "The Border Crossed Us," accessed July 20, 2015, http://www.ikatun.org/thebordercrossedus/.

18

Within architecture, Teddy Cruz has done likewise compelling work on borders, for instance, in his series of conferences and field excursions on the "political equator" between San Diego, California and Tijuana, Mexico: http://politicalequator.blogspot.ch (accessed July 20, 2015).

19

Ingold, "Landscape," 126.

20

The geographers Neil Smith and David Harvey are credited with first articulating a theory of uneven development in texts including Smith's

Uneven Development: Nature, Capital and the Production of Space (Oxford: Blackwell, 1984). In 2010, the contemporary art historian T. J. Demos and Alex Farquharson curated an exhibition on the theme, "Uneven Geographies," at Nottingham Contemporary: http://www. nottinghamcontemporary.org/art/uneven -geographies (accessed July 20, 2015).
21
Rob Nixon, *Slow Violence and the Environmentalism of the Poor* (Cambridge, MA: Harvard University Press, 2013), 2.

22
Saskia Sassen, "The Global Street: Where the Powerless Get to Make History," (keynote lecture, "Thinking the Contemporary Landscape: Positions and Oppositions" conference, Herrenhausen Gardens, Hanover, Germany, June 21, 2013. Also see T. J. Demos on the "naturalization of finance" and "financialization of nature" in "Art After Nature: The Post-Natural Condition," *Artforum* (April 2012): 191–97.

FALSE NATURE?

Susann Ahn and Regine Keller

HARDY'S FLIES

It takes great skill, experience, and, above all, a steady hand to master the art of making a deceptively real-looking fly. It's not only about capturing a re-creation of the external anatomy of the insect, but also about perfectly producing a body capable of flying in just the same way as the original. William Hardy developed that art over decades of devoted attention to detail, achieving a level of crafts-manship over time that had no equal. He was convinced that his flies were far better than Mother Nature's originals; apart from anything else, the latter could be used only once. As far as Mr. Hardy was concerned, if real flies had any con-structive reason to exist at all, it was merely to provide a model for the perfected replicas used to catch salmon. In 1872, Mr. Hardy and his craftsmanship founded a company in Alnwick, Northumberland, that would ship handmade copies all over the world. Fly fishermen soon developed a veritable obsession with "gen-uine" Hardy flies, and his originals were traded for top prices worldwide. The most important thing was the "authenticity" of the flies, and a myth grew that word had spread among the salmon that they should only bite if the line boasted a real *Hardy* fly. Soon, nobody was interested in using nature-made flies to fish anymore, which downgraded the insect's existence to sheer meaninglessness, at least as far as Hardy was concerned.[1]

Nature is probably the oldest teacher of creative people, and Hardy's flies are a lovely example of our aptitude for copying nature to develop self-serving technologies. But a closer look at imitations of nature provides illumination in more than just the technical sense; our entire concept of nature depends upon it. The way we classify objects, and our surroundings, as natural or unnatural is completely formed by the image of nature that we carry within us. These days, it appears that what might be considered natural in our urbanized world is no longer particularly important. It seems to be sufficient that something suggest a semblance of the natural. (FIG.1)

But what do we mean by "nature" or "the natural"? The English philosopher John Stuart Mill (1806–1873) addressed the problem long ago, pointing out that many of the connotations attached to the two terms led to terminological confu-sion, because they were based on a commingling of moral concepts, legitimiza-tion, and normative aspects.[2] This article, however, is not primarily concerned

FIG. 1 — Hardy's Salmon Flies.
Photos by Regine Keller.

with the Millsian definition of nature, which characterized it as, among other things, "a name for the mode, partly known to us and partly unknown, in which all things take place."[3] This article deals much more with the concept of "nature as ideology," which the German landscape designer Joachim Wolschke-Bulmahn described as, "Nature, understood in this way, is a (more-or-less) systematic scheme of ideas, held by particular social, political, cultural, and other groups."[4] In that assessment, nature represents an intellectual construct. And according to Wolschke-Bulmahn, it is only human reflection on nature that produces an emotional bond and the assignment of values to nature.[5]

The terms *nature* and *naturalness* are associated with positive or negative values depending on the cultural context. In the European context, "natural" is assigned a predominantly positive value and often functions as a kind of seal of approval, with which products, but also landscapes, are stamped. Urban dwellers in particular often express a yearning for "the natural." But the German philosopher Thomas Schramme argues that when people think of "the natural" they mean only a specific part of "nature"—to wit, exclusively the beneficial part of nature. Everything else, such as the dangers or unpleasantness associated with nature, is ignored.[6] The historian Rolf Peter Sieferle characterized nature as "that which is elementary, self-contained, spontaneous, sprouted, unavailable, unproduced, while on the other side is that which is artificial, technical, regulated by arrangements and agreements, made and compelled, designed and cultivated."[7] And even things that have the positive connotations of "natural" are subject to differing levels of meaning: "the natural as biological, as self-evident, as non-artificial, as non-cultural, and as non-technical." When we talk about the "naturalness" of a landscape in a landscape architecture project, the emphasis is often on the "non-artificial" aspect. However, landscape architecture has in fact a long, historical-cultural tradition of dealing with artificial representations of nature, with the imitation of putatively untouched landscapes. Landscape architects have always been busy creating images that suggest "nature" and "natural," but are thought through down to the tiniest technical detail and "artificially" effectuated by humans.

Representing landscape as a facsimile of nature is a gardening tradition that has its roots in the Chinese gardens, in which the emphasis was not on the construction of a paradise, but rather on a devotion to honoring nature, by creating as perfect a copy of real landscapes as possible. Chinese garden designers adhered to geomantic principles and focused on designing an effigy of an ideal microcosm that was closely allied to traditional, allegorical Chinese landscape painting.[8] No trouble was spared, and they constructed artificial seas as well as artful replicas of entire mountainous massifs. In Asia, the "natural landscape garden," which had spread out over Japan, was replaced over time by sublimely excessive citations of landscapes. Landscapes were reproduced on a smaller scale, or individual aspects, such as water, were symbolized by materials like gravel, turning them into artifacts. An artificial refinement of "raw nature," in place of purely replicating it, became the expression of the gardening art.

RENATURALIZATION AS AN IMITATION OF NATURE

In the past—but also in the present—many of those artifacts led to the belief that in the eye of the beholder, the imitation was better than the original. That phenomenon of "counterfeit nature" or the "perfect imitation of the natural" acquired a new meaning in efforts of renaturalization, which was based on the assumption that nature could be restored (as many times as desired).[9] The starting points for numerous renaturalization projects are designed and controlled river environments such as can be found in many cities around the world. Often linked to the myth of a city's founding, many of these rivers were once important to settlement activities and in addition to the benefits they provided to humans, that meaning almost always included the threatening nature of a river. Regulating a river's flow meant power, and safeguarded the sovereignty of the site. The once vitally necessary benefits of rivers as infrastructure elements have become obsolete in many places today. Regulation has come under fire and the desire for a natural reconfiguration of those spaces corresponds to society's current concept of a *new urban nature*—highly secure yet as if part of the wilderness; urban and yet scenic or even pastoral.

Taking this into consideration, interdisciplinary teams of landscape architects and planners develop concepts for green spaces that, in the best-case scenario, put their function within the ecological system on a par with their aesthetic and societal ones. The mediation of these objectives and the citizen's desire for *new urban nature* is challenging and often a source of controversy as the example of the renaturalization of the Isar River in Munich shows.

THE ISAR IN MUNICH

Upon close examination, the renaturalization of the inner-city section of the Isar raises the question of what actual concepts were used to effect an imitation of an untamed river. Expectations for renaturalization are high. Therefore, we must first understand the connotations inherent in the nature of rivers in a historical context.

THE FLOWING

The name Isar most likely stems from the Indo-Germanic word *es*, or "is," originally meaning "flowing water" and later taking on the meaning of "ice" (as the river flows into Italy's South Tyrol, it is called the Eisack—in Italian, Isarco). An earlier interpretation that it came from the Celtic words *ys* (torrential) and *ura* (water) has since been discredited. The Isar is an Alpine river starting in Austria, whose lower lengths in Germany have decisively shaped the cities of, above all, Bad Tölz, Munich, Freising, and Landshut. In the Middle Ages, the river was the impetus for settlements, and the bridges built across it were, in the final analysis, the reason for founding the cities of Munich and Freising. A society that controlled the river had power and, since only a few bridge construction techniques were capable of subjugating the savage stream, the centers of power in the region in the Middle Ages were restricted to those sites. Initially used as a trade route, the Isar would become important for delivering hydraulic power for skilled trades and provisioning. For many centuries, the townspeople considered the river a necessary evil rather than a romantic, glorious natural space. Regular flooding brought catastrophe, so the savage river spread feelings of horror rather than pleasant associations.

THE TAMED

Following the great bridge-building spate in the Middle Ages, during the Renaissance era numerous measures were undertaken to regulate the flow of many of Europe's rivers with the construction of artistic canals and weirs. In Munich, water use was optimized primarily by regulating the flow of the city streams that fed the Isar. It was not until the end of the eighteenth century that the Isar in Munich was properly "tamed." In order to reduce the amount of flooding and ensure that the river could be used to supply energy, the river was directed into a fixed canal, where it carved out an ever-deeper channel. Enormous dams, constructed by the topographer and engineer Adrian von Riedl in the late eighteenth century, eventually made the city completely safe from flooding, however they also created an increasingly severe physical and visual separation between city and river. The Isar, once a resource for millers, tanneries, laundries, and incipient small industry degenerated into nothing more than a gutter for effluent. After an 1854 cholera epidemic hit the city, the theories of the local chemist and hygienist Dr. Max von Pettenkofer were put into effect, and Munich undertook the ending of the city's catastrophic hygienic conditions by installing a sewer system. The improved quality of the water, as well as a changed concept of nature in the romantic era, eventually resulted in an entirely new way of looking at the river. As riverside industry with its unequivocally harsh working conditions disappeared, it became possible to appreciate the river as a romantic piece of scenery. Between 1856 and 1861, Carl von Effner, court gardener and later director of royal gardens for the Bavarian court, was charged with landscaping the banks of the Isar, creating what would be called the Maximiliansanlagen, or Maximilian Gardens, in the style of English landscape gardens. In 1857, construction began on the Maximilianeum, a palatial building housing a student foundation and pages' school, to complement the new river scene. The building stood high in splendor above the parks along the Isar's edge, but had no direct contact with the river. At the same time, the river's character was still heavily shaped by the rafting trade, which used the river to

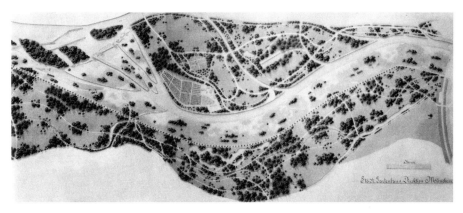

FIG. 2 — Municipal Recreation Area along the Isar in Munich (Partial Plan), Jakob Heiler, ca. 1900. *Stadtarchiv München, Plansammlung, Gartenbau.*

deliver timber and coal from the mountains down to the city and its industries. The best evidence of that was what was called "Coal Island" in the center of the city, which was the repository for vast quantities of the fuel until 1870, when it was turned into a recreational and exhibition area. It was a sign of the first step in the conversion of the river from an industrial location into a place of recreation and culture, with exhibitions beginning in 1898 transforming it. Further antiflooding measures made the island even better suited to its new use and with the start of construction of the Deutsches Museum for science and technology in 1906, the site underwent further changes.[10] (FIG. 2)

In the nineteenth century, the flow of the entire length of the Isar within the city's borders was regulated and the now flood-free banks were lined with numerous green spaces in the style of landscaped gardens. Inspired by the gardeners and landscape architects Friedrich Ludwig von Sckell and Peter Joseph Lenné, the royal and city parks departments in and around Munich comprised the idea that beautifying existing landscapes not only created lovely scenery, but also had a beneficial effect on a city's hygiene standards. A beautiful landscape was believed to have an intact nature. Natural beauty often served as the model. That belief took root in the consciousness of the beholders.

THE RENATURALIZED

In the late Middle Ages, intensive underground and surface mining in Europe had turned large swathes of land into moonscapes, decimating forests and completely destroying some sites. The depletion of nature was slowed as early as the sixteenth and seventeenth centuries by Germany's first forestry management laws.[11] The reforesting measures were the first consequence of the idea of restoring the natural state, of renaturalization; this was the birth of the concept of sustainability. Mining landscapes are the drastic protagonists in our unbridled search for raw materials, and the basis of industrialization in every country in the world. The "discharge" of mining management laws and the efforts that follow to recreate something of nature that is "valuable" in the ecological sense is common practice these days, and often well regulated by law.

By contrast, the endeavor of renaturalizing rivers began to gain favor in Germany in the mid-twentieth century with the rise of renaturalization ecology as a scientific discipline. Efforts at renaturalization developed primarily from the environmental movement and are coupled with the American concept of "restoration ecology."[12] Since the end of the 1980s, renaturalization projects for rivers, streams, meadows, and marshes have been implemented with the aim of restoring ecosystem functions that have been severely compromised or curtailed by anthropogenic activity.[13] This is based on the thesis that intact ecosystems contribute to human well-being, whether directly or indirectly and, from an anthropocentric perspective, provide economic, material, health, or psychological benefits.[14] A renaturalization ecology tries to combine precepts of basic ecological research with theoretical concepts from landscape architecture and planning, and with nature conservation, in order to influence societal and political decision-making processes using specialized technical doctrine.[15] The "renaturalization" trend became very popular in light of arguments for sustainability, despite the fact that the basic idea of "ecologically planning" was not at all new, as historical examples prove. As a result, the flow of rivers was deregulated, fish passes were built to ensure intact migration patterns in acknowledgment of findings in biology, buffer zones along waterway banks were instituted to create aquatic and limnological systems conducive to the health of flora near or under the water. Thus, from the standpoint of biology and engineering, it was possible to get the issue under control. And the ecological idea of renaturalization could be popularized by creating picturesque country scenes. The renaturalization of the Isar in Munich is closely bound to the desire and longing of the city's residents for "intact nature."[16] While conservationists may still put forth arguments based on the environmental aspects, the majority of the population also wants to see the picture of a romantic riverscape. This became abundantly clear in a 2003 competition for the third planning section of the "Isar-Plan" seeking submissions

opposite:
FIGS. 3 + 4 — First- and second-prize "Isar-Plan" competition plans, 2003. TOP: Irene Burkhardt Landscape Architects with SKI + Partner, Reichenbach and Schranner Architects, and Mahl-Gebhard Landscape Architects.

BOTTOM: Winfrid Jerney Landscape Architects with the Institute for Hydrotechnology, Prof. Dr.-Ing. Wilhelm Bechteler, Engineers, Dr.-Ing. Joachim Dressler, Prof. Dr.-Ing. Victor Lopez Cotelo, Dipl.-Ing. Stephan Zehl Architects. both: *Baureferat der Landeshauptstadt München, Wasserwirtschaftsamt München.*

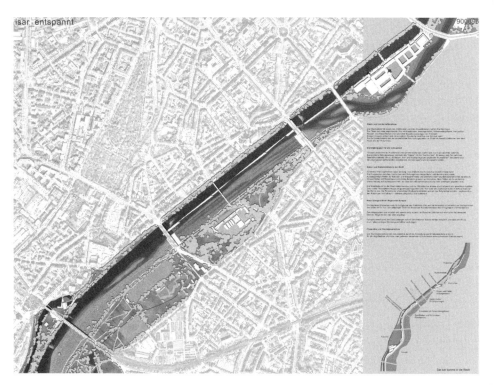

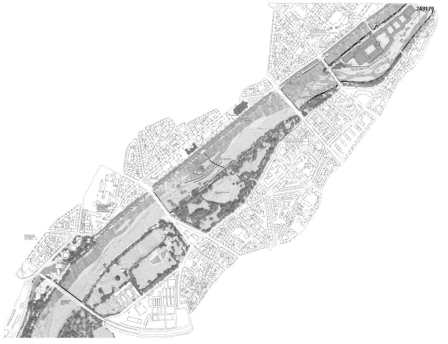

for the remodeling of an inner-city section of the Isar. Interdisciplinary teams of urban planners, landscape architects, and hydraulic engineers were asked to tender plans to transform the stretch between the Braunau rail bridge and the Deutsches Museum, which sported retaining weirs and buildings along the banks. The objective was to combine flood protection with attractive recreation areas for the public, and create a nature-oriented character of the riverbed. The winning design of the interdisciplinary working group comprising SKI+Partner, Reichenbach and Schranner Architects, and Mahl-Gebhard Landscape Architects that formed around Irene Burkhardt Landscape Architects suggested gravel islands and large, concrete river plates that structure the riverbanks and allow easy access to the water as well as spots for sunbathing. Existing groundsills were transformed and included in an ecological concept strengthening the biodiversity. However, the design openly displayed all the technical mechanisms and necessary building materials, such as concrete, to create the weirs and riverbanks. Clearly constructed, straight borders made the delineation between the edge of the river and the city both visible and usable.

The award committee was majoritarian in agreement about the winner, but the plan brought the citizenry to the barricades, as residents saw the "clean and modern engineering" of the construction as something akin to the downfall of Western civilization. Two months after the jury selected the winning team, the citizens of the adjacent neighborhoods started to show their resentment in an open council followed by several petitions, open letters, and newspaper articles creating public awareness. The main critique was about the lack of "naturalistic" design, which was put on par with poor recreation quality and decreased ecological function.[17] In the end, the people fought to have the commission awarded a hybrid between the first- and the second-place design, which included curving riverbanks and edging in natural-looking stone. (FIGS. 3–4)

The end product evokes the former savage river, with its shingled banks and presumably dynamic flooding scenarios. "So in a way, it's an attempt to reconstruct the river that ran through Munich 150 years ago. Despite the addendum that the natural character of an untamed river is irretrievably lost, that bygone image is projected onto the future, albeit with different safety requirements."[18] The naturalness is in essence artificial: during construction, stones that had apparently washed loose from the river had to be "glued" in place with great effort and a lot of concrete to resist the actual force of the water. So the remodeling of the renaturalization took place "between the poles of an illusory space of free and unbridled nature and a compensatory space that […] offers security and refuge."[19] The renaturalization has been deemed successful among experts, but particularly among Munich's citizenry.[20] After all, it provides a picture that borrows from nature, has positive connotations and is widely accepted. But should we really accept artificial nature as a method of repair to be sold under the label of naturalness and added value to the ecology?

TOWARD NEW URBAN NATURE

Is landscape architecture in this case simply camouflage for the urban nature the public really wants to see? Do we want nothing more from landscape architectural design than an imitation of natural scenes while promoting ecological values? One could get the impression that this is what would satisfy the residents and politicians best—the more deceptively "natural," the better. New urban nature is this: providing ecosystem services wrapped in packaging that is identical to nature. "These days, protection of nature and the environment is increasingly justified with 'providing ecosystem services.' Those 'services' are also generally called 'cultural.' But there is no such thing as cultural ecosystem services," says Ludwig Trepl.[21] In his writing, Trepl clearly distinguishes between the natural sciences' understanding and the scientific idea of an ecosystem. He differentiates between scientific fact and cultural expectation, namely that an ecosystem must be useful. There is an apparent contradiction in this, as well as in the explanation of a currently very popular way of building political consensus. Because many representatives of the nature conservation movement, in their discussions about value, tend to equate artificially created nature scenes with the capacity to provide ecosystem services, the impression arises that only such systems are ecologically valuable. And because such debates are held among a broad public, the emphasis is not on the scientifically verifiable impact, but rather the social-cultural aspect of the phenomenon, which is fortified with the creation of nostalgic scenery. So for a landscape architect, designing something that services that nostalgic desire for nature—the idea of a new urban nature, as we call it here—ensures a high level of acceptance for a project. That new urban nature is evident in Munich in the image of a surrogate that is wild, natural, and even functional, and that promises to have a healing effect on the ravaged urban soul. But doesn't an artifact, the illusion of a natural landscape, such as the renaturalized Isar, cheat the beholder? Nietzsche describes those complex observational levels as the "consciousness of appearance."[22] This conflicts with the fact that an "honest" approach to engineering demands, i.e., putting the technical mechanism on clear display in the design, currently finds no favor with the wider public. It remains to be clarified exactly what duties a landscape architect is expected to fulfill. What kind of camouflage must he or she design? Do projects that counterfeit nature correspond to the idea of so-called ecological aesthetics that Peter Finke called for in his 1986 article "Landschaftserfahrung und Landschaftserhaltung" (Landscape experiences and landscape preservation) and which, in turn, find their origins as early as 1969 in Ian McHarg's *Design with Nature*.[23] Or do they serve only to feed what James Corner critically described thusly: "The landscape idea throughout much of this century has come mostly in the form of picturesque, rural scenery, whether for nostalgic, consumerist purposes or in the service of environmentalist agendas"?[24] That conflict within the brotherhood seems to continue unabated. But society appears to have long since decided what it wants. In his dissertation "Landschaft und Lüge" (Landscape and Lie), Thomas Hauck writes, "McHarg and Corner's positions illuminate the dialectic discourse in landscape design. Using rational methods, McHarg strives for the picturesque superorganism, while Corner wants to use intuition to design places and open spaces that are serviceable and can be appropriated, for communities in the urban landscape of the twenty-first century."[25] The beholder simply likes counterfeit nature far better than the original, just like with Mr. Hardy's flies. The question remains whether, and when, just like with Hardy's flies, the imitation will render the original meaningless.

Notes

1
Andy Heathcote and Heike Bachelier, *The Lost World of Mr. Hardy* (London: Trufflepig Films, 2008), 93 min.

2
John Stuart Mill, "On Nature" (1874), in John Stuart Mill, *Nature; The Utility of Religion; Theism* (London: Watts, 1904), 9.

3
Ibid., 8.

4
Joachim Wolschke-Bulmahn, "The Nationalization of Nature and the Naturalization of the German Nation: 'Teutonic' Trends in Early Twentieth-Century Landscape Design," in *Nature and Ideology: Natural Garden Design in the Twentieth Century*, Dumbarton Oaks Colloquium on the History of Landscape Architecture, vol 18, ed. Joachim Wolschke-Bulmahn (Washington, DC: Dumbarton Oaks Research Library and Collection, 1997), 6.

5
Ibid., 6.

6
Thomas Schramme, "Natürlichkeit als Wert," *Analyse und Kritik* 24 (Stuttgart: Lucius & Lucius, 2002): 257.

7
Rolf Peter Sieferle, *Rückblick auf die Natur: Eine Geschichte des Menschen und seiner Umwelt* (Munich: Luchterhand, 1997).

8
Gang Chen, *Landscape Architecture: Planting Design Illustrated* (Irvine, CA: ArchiteG, 2011), 145.

9

Robert Elliot, *Faking Nature: The Ethics of Environmental Restoration* (London: Routledge, 1997), 76.

10

Regine Keller and Diana Huß, eds., *Stadt und Fluss. Innerstädtischer Isarraum*, Landeshauptstadt München (Munich: Landeshauptstadt München, 2010).

11

Hans Carl von Carlowitz, *Sylvicultura oeconomica oder Haußwirthliche Nachricht und Naturmäßige Anweisung zur Wilden Baum-Zucht* (1713), ed. Joachim Hamberger (Munich: Oekom, 2013).

12

A. D. Bradshaw, "Restoration: An Acid Test for Ecology," in *Restoration Ecology: A Synthetic Approach to Ecological Research*, ed. William R. Jordan III, Michael E. Gilpin, and John D. Aber (Cambridge: Cambridge University Press, 1987), 23–29.

13

Stefan Zerbe and Gerhard Wiegleb, *Renaturierung von Ökosystemen in Mitteleuropa* (Heidelberg: Spektrum, 2008), 469.

14

Naturkapital Deutschland-TEEB DE, *Der Wert der Natur für Wirtschaft und Gesellschaft: Eine Einführung* (Munich: ifuplan; Leipzig: Helmholtz-Zentrum für Umweltforschung– UFZ; Bonn: Bundesamt für Naturschutz, 2012), 80.

15

Zerbe and Wiegleb, *Renaturierung*, 9.

16

Landeshauptstadt München, *Der Isar-Plan. Projektdokumentation* (Munich: Landeshauptstadt München, 2011).

17

Landeshauptstadt München, "Beschluss des Bauausschusses vom 27.09.2005, Munich

2005," in Susann Ahn, *Freiraum München: Perspektive, Plan und Praxis: Beteiligungskultur und Beteiligungsverständnis in München* (diploma thesis, Technische Universität München, Munich, 2007).

18

Julia Düchs, *Wann wird's an der Isar wieder schön? Die Renaturierung der Isar in München: Über das Verständnis von Natur in der Großstadt* (Munich: Utz, 2014), 59–60.

19

Ibid., 45.

20

Keller and Huß, *Stadt und Fluss*.

21

Ludwig Trepl, "Es gibt keine kulturellen Ökosystemdienstleistungen," *SciLogs*, accessed October 10, 2014, http://www.scilogs.de/landschaft-oekologie/es-gibt-keine-kulturellen-oekosystemdienstleistungen/.

22

Friedrich Nietzsche, *Die fröhliche Wissenschaft* (Berlin: Edition Holzinger, 2013), 66.

23

Peter Finke, "Landschaftserfahrung und Landschaftserhaltung: Plädoyer für eine Ökologische Landschaftsästhetik," in *Landschaft*, ed. Manfred Smuda (Frankfurt: Suhrkamp, 1986), 266–98; Ian L. McHarg, *Design with Nature* (New York: Wiley, 1969), 77.

24

James Corner ed., *Recovering Landscape: Essays in Contemporary Landscape Architecture*, (New York: Princeton Architectural Press, 1999), 8.

25

Thomas Hauck, *Landschaft und Lüge, Die Vergegenständlichung ästhetischer Ideen am Beispiel von "Landschaft"* (PhD diss., Technische Universität München, 2012), 167.

THE LANDSCAPES OF AIRPORT
TRANSFER—*Sonja Dümpelmann*

Airport design posed a new challenge in the early twentieth century, at a time when it was still unclear how powered aviation would develop and change the world. In contrast to many of their colleagues who were using nineteenth-century train stations as precedents for twentieth-century air stations, in the 1930s, some optimistic avant-garde architects, such as Norman Bel Geddes and Richard Neutra, began conceptualizing the airport as a transfer point rather than a terminal. Neutra's 1930 airport project, "Rush City Air Transfer," catered to "speed and fluidity in the transition from air to ground vehicle," intending to give an architectural to this flowing transition and to the continuity of space and time. Neutra's project relinquished the static monumental entry plaza so typical of many early airports and was based instead on the objective of a "smooth, rapid and inexpensive" transfer of goods and people between different means of transportation.[1] His airport concept was based on the perception of space-time compression, and on the facilitation of movement of people and goods at high speeds. While his "Rush City Air Transfer" project was never built, its underlying ideas are what characterize the architecture and infrastructure of air transportation today. Yet, as any air passenger who has been stranded at airports due to canceled flights, missed connections, or just simple layovers, knows, the increased speed of air travel has also led to slowness and moments of stasis. Thus, while air transportation's objective has always been to minimize the time of transfer between the ground and the air, and one flight and another, the air passenger paradoxically often finds her- or himself stranded, almost motionless, in the logistical zone of the airport that is built for movement. It has been this tension between speed and slowness, or even stasis, and between the actual, geographically situated location of the airport and air transportation's global aspirations, that have inspired attempts to conceive of the airport as a landscape that can make aplace, and that, as a place, can forge local, regional, and national identities. As a site that sits at the nexus between the local and the global, the airport is both a motor and product of the global economy, and the space where flight passengers enter and leave the airspace and are grounded.

More than any other transportation infrastructures, including railroads and train stations, motorways, and even harbors, airfields and airports have been read, understood, and designed as landscapes and distinct environments. The understanding of airports and aviation in general has been closely intertwined with notions of landscape, environment, and ecology, even if the airport has during its evolution been described by many as an anti-landscape, as being obsolescent, and, finally, as a "non-place."[2] In fact, what landscape architects have come to deal with in airport environments is what Tim Cresswell has called on the one hand "a largely ahistorical and non-placebound space of flows" and on the other hand "the rooted and historical space of place."[3] The genealogy of airport landscape throughout the twentieth and into the twenty-first century reveals the airport not only as an expression of glocalism, but also as a site with an oscillating relationship between technology and nature, engineering, and design.

AIRFIELDS

Many early attempts at powered flight were undertaken in environments that provided suitable natural conditions including wind and soft landing areas, such as the ones on the North Carolina coast near Kitty Hawk, where Wilbur and Orville Wright undertook their first short flights in 1903 before they moved to a cow pasture—the first flying field—near Dayton, Ohio. While the cows could be driven into the southern end of the pasture, the one obstacle that remained was a thorn tree in the middle of the field, which was sooner or later found to be an important point of orientation for their first flying maneuvers along the oval flight path. (FIG.1) That technology and nature would, however, ultimately come into conflict on multiple levels was foreshadowed in the simple 1911 map drawing of the Harvard Aviation Field (today Squantum Point Park) that was used for the first time for the 1910 Harvard-Boston Aviation meet convened by the Harvard Aeronautical Society.[4] (FIG.2) The one-and-a-half-mile-long course for the pilots who gathered to compete was marked on the ground by five pylons that signified the turning points. On the map, the pylons were connected by precise straight dash-dotted lines that disregarded the natural land formation, including a creek and the sinuous coastline. Amongst the men responsible for the first aviation meets was Abbott Lawrence Rotch, Harvard professor of meteorology and the first president of the Harvard Aeronautical Society, who combined in his person the close connection between aviation and the scientific exploration of the environment, in particular the atmosphere. Many early balloon ascents in the late eighteenth and nineteenth centuries had been instrumental in the explorations of the atmosphere. At the weather observatory on the Great Blue Hill (southwest of Boston) that he had founded in 1884, Rotch studied the weather, wind, and atmosphere with kites, balloons, and balloon sondes. (FIG.3) Part of his climatological research was geared toward facilitating flight across the Atlantic. Only

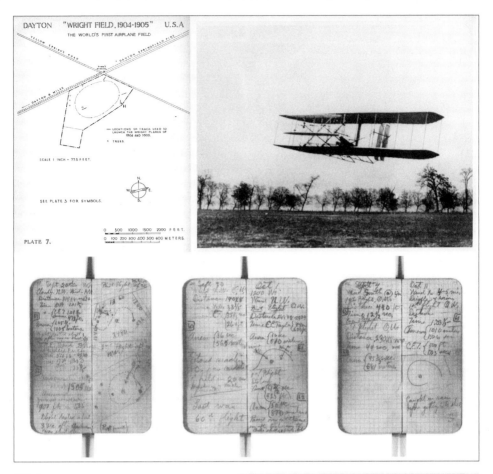

FIG. 1 —

TOP LEFT: Plan of the first flying field of the Wright brothers near Dayton, Ohio, including the thorn tree in the middle.
(John Walter Wood, Airports *[New York: Coward-McCann, 1940]).*

TOP RIGHT: Wright 1904 Flyer II above Huffman Prairie at Simms Station, about ten miles (16 km) northeast of Dayton, Ohio.
Courtesy National Air and Space Museum (NASM 84-2385), Smithsonian Institution.

BOTTOM LEFT, MIDDLE, AND RIGHT: Pages from Wilbur Wright's diary, 1904. Notation of climatic conditions and flight data. The sketches record the respective flight paths on September 20, October 1, and October 11, 1904. Note the round marking of the thorn tree as orientation point in the flight path sketches.
(Diaries and Notebooks: 1904–1905, Wilbur Wright, Wilbur and Orville Wright Papers, Manuscript Division, Library of Congress, Washington, DC).

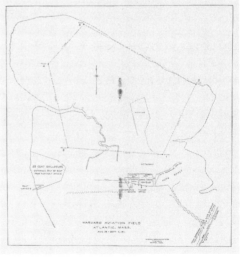

FIG. 2 — Map showing Harvard Aviation Field, 1911.
(HUD 3123 Box 1, Harvard University Archives).

CHART I.

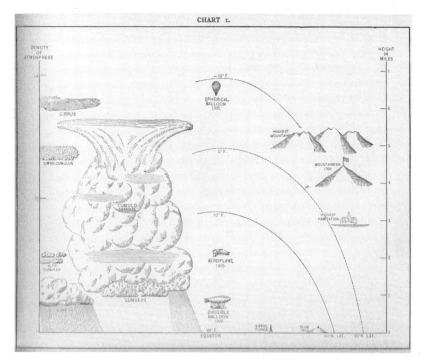

FIG. 3 — Abbott Lawrence Rotch, diagram showing different types of clouds and stations for atmospheric observation.
(Abbott Lawrence Rotch and Andrew H. Palmer, Charts of the Atmosphere for Aeronauts and Aviators *[New York: Wiley, 1911]).*

by ascending into the air was humankind able to learn about the atmosphere and its gases, and only knowledge about the weather, air currents, and cloud formation could further progress in aviation. The development of balloons and planes therefore promoted and resulted from the early atmospheric explorations.

MANUFACTURED SITES

The first sites for airfields were chosen because they seemed naturally prone to allow for the easy takeoff and landing of aircraft. As the engineer Archibald Black reported in 1929, the desirable "natural" conditions were level terrain on open ground, naturally draining soil, "close growth of tough all-year grass," low or evenly distributed precipitation, and freedom from fog and gusty winds.[5] Thus, the first airfields were flat and grassy, measured about 750 by 1,000 meters, and were outfitted on their periphery with simple lightweight buildings. They were often marked by a white circle approximately forty-five meters in diameter and by the place's name in giant letters. A centrally located smoke pot indicated the wind direction. In addition to aeronautical strip charts, the early pilots in the United States studied the small airport maps published in the *Aeronautical Bulletin* that explained the condition and orientation of the respective airfields that they would be using for takeoff and landing. The early sketches of the airfields highlighted hollows, hills, woods and trees, swampland, creeks and rivers,

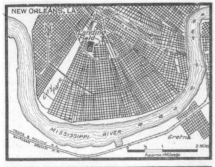

FIG. 4 — Context and detailed map sketches for Peters and Claiborne Ave. Field in New Orleans.
(*Office of the Chief of Air Service, Washington, DC*, Aeronautical Bulletin, *no. 119 [January 2, 1924]*).

roads, power lines, cultivated land, and, in some instances, even the kind of crop grown. (**FIG. 4**) Later *Bulletin* editions also included wind roses that indicated the dominant wind directions. In short, the small thumbnail maps of the airfields and their context and relationship to the nearest city were shorthand for conveying the lay of the land and its environmental conditions.

The development of larger, heavier, and more powerful aircraft demanded that the early manufactured airfields would finally be equipped with concrete and asphalt runways and extensive subsurface drainage systems, and turned into airports that were built more or less following comprehensive designs. The airport infrastructure became increasingly independent from the natural conditions, passing from "pleasant pastoral scenes" where herds of sheep had kept the grass short and the ground compacted, to a site where "[m]en must bring to the…site machines and materials to rectify the frugalities of Nature, and scar the surface with broad, straight deep-laid runways, fell trees and other obstructions that might endanger the fast-moving vehicles of the air." As the British aeronautical engineer Sydney E. Veale commented in 1945, "Modern airports must be man-made."[6] The only thing left, to be determined by nature, was the orientation, length, and strength of the main runway that was to parallel the prevailing wind, which also depended on the elevation above sea level that resulted in varying atmospheric density.

AIRPORT LANDSCAPES

The conception of the airport as a landscape already began in the 1920s when landscape architects realized the opportunity that airport design provided them.

Architects and designers were quick to understand airports as a comprehensive design problem that included the design of the airfield, the terminal buildings, and the hangars, as well as the surrounding open space and planting design. Applying ideas of the American City Beautiful movement to airports, designers in the United States even understood airports to be a problem that resembled the complexity of expansive seventeenth-century French gardens. Many designers conceived of airports as landscapes and cities. In the late 1920s, while engineers were experimenting with the modular design of different runway patterns that could be assembled depending on the airports' growth requirements, architects and landscape architects were embedding these runway designs into the larger landscape. The American architect Francis Keally developed a visionary airport design that positioned a monumental circular landing field into a large ornamental garden that was modeled on seventeenth-century French gardens. The American landscape architect–turned–city planner John Nolen proposed a prototypical airport plan in which the quadrangular airfield and its accompanying satellite town with a street layout based upon a *patte d'oie* resembled the seventeenth-century ensemble of the gardens and town of Versailles.[7]

In the late 1950s, one of the later jetports, New York International Airport (now John F. Kennedy International Airport) in New York City, did indeed implement a design for its International Park, which was mockingly described by the architecture critic Rayner Banham as the "pointless *Marienbad* Allée," modeled on seventeenth-century French gardens.[8] Surrounded by parking lots, approach roads, and terminal buildings, the eighty-nine-hectare International Park stretched along an axis between the International Terminals building and the airport's transparent Central Heating and Refrigerator Plant. It included planting beds and three circular fountains that due to their varying sizes and positions along the axis created a forced perspective.

Like the designs for the early terminal buildings and their interiors, beginning in the late 1920s, increasing care was taken of the design of the outside spaces. In fact, the landscape architect Jacob John Spoon even argued in the early 1930s that "fancy interior or exterior decorations" were not entirely essential in the necessary "beautification" of airports, which too often presented "a repellent scene" with their "patched hangars, irregularly placed, sparce growth of parched grass, cinders and dust." Attention to interior and exterior architectural details of terminal buildings could, according to Spoon, be "eliminated in favor of well designed grounds." While it was important to ensure the functioning of the airport, he considered the "grouping and arrangement of approaches,

FIG. 5 — Interior view of the Transcontinental Air Transport passenger station at Waynoka, Oklahoma, ca. 1929.
Courtesy National Air and Space Museum (NASM 00133605), Smithsonian Institution.

as well as landscaping,...of almost equal importance."[9] However, to calm passengers' nerves and make them feel comfortable and at ease, the waiting rooms in the early terminal buildings were often designed to resemble private living rooms including armchairs, couches, and fireplaces. (**FIG. 5**) Similarly, the designs for the outdoor spaces were often expressions of vernacular modernism, conceived to achieve the same effect and to ground and orientate the passengers in the respective location. Airport landscape designs fostered a local, regional, and even national identity, acting as vernacular counterpoints within the increasingly standardized technological airport environment. In the past, as well as today, they often relate the airport to its surroundings in more or less imaginary ways, attempting to counter the airport's inherent placelessness by bringing local landscape qualities and character traits to the foreground. Thus, airport gardens and landscapes play an important role in the airport's function as a transmitter "for shifting from global to local and vice versa."[10]

For example, in front of the Seaplane Station terminal building of the Santos Dumont airport in Rio de Janeiro, a tropical garden, complete with a water basin holding "rare and typical Brazilian plants" such as Victoria water lilies, was laid out in the late 1930s.[11] The vernacular modernist garden introduced the modernist terminal building that featured art deco interiors. Many designers from the 1920s onwards conceived of the airport as a hybrid landscape with contrasting modernist and vernacular character traits and as an expression of what more recently has been called "glocalism." (**FIG. 6**) In the 1960s, the terminal building at Honolulu International Airport was built surrounding a triangular piece of ground that was designed by the landscape architect Richard Tongg as the

FIG. 6 — Garden in front of the terminal building at the Santos Dumont Seaplane Station in Rio de Janeiro, ca. 1937. *(Civil Aviation in Brazil [Sao Paulo: "Graphicars," Romiti & Lanẓara, 1939], 33.)*

so-called cultural gardens. Divided into three parts, the cultural gardens included a "Chinese Garden," a "Japanese Garden," and a "Hawaiian Garden," thought to represent the various cultures that had shaped island life.[12] The gardens followed ideas that Tongg and his coauthor, Loraine E. Kuck, had expressed in their 1939 book, *The Tropical Garden*. In the tropics, they noted, cultures mingled, and therefore "[design] details from one source do not appear too strange in the other."[13] At the airport, the cultural gardens grounded and introduced the passengers to the islands' culture and nature, regardless of the widespread repression of native Hawaiian customs and culture at the time and the US-Japanese tensions on the islands that followed the Japanese World War II attacks on Pearl Harbor.

AIRPORT SCENERIES

While the airport landscape had to be designed to be experienced on the ground, it also had to accommodate the vertical view. As architects experimented freely with the use of art deco and vernacular styles like Spanish colonial revival in terminal architecture, landscape architects similarly used the first commercial airports as experimentation grounds for new formal expressions that related to both modernist and regionalist agendas. The new means of transportation provided new design opportunities to challenge accustomed forms and perspectives. It gave landscape architects the chance to provide a new vertical scenery for the view from above. In 1930, Ernst Herminghaus created one of the few early modernist landscape designs in the United States for Fairfax Airport in Kansas City, Kansas. Based upon his observation that yellow and orange were the colors most easily detected from the air, and that details were not perceptible to the aerial viewer at high speeds, he proposed planting brightly colored masses of plants. His design for the area in front of the terminal building was based on symmetrically laid out geometrical forms and could be easily identified from the air.[14] Similarly, his American colleague Jacob John Spoon promoted airport landscape designs adapted to the aerial perspective and great heights. Spoon considered the strip of land surrounding the airfield that was at least ninety-one meters wide per requirements issued by the Department of Commerce, the ideal area to turn the airport into an attractive landscape infrastructure. There, hedges that were several meters wide, as well as broad strips of grass, colorful flowers, and white sand, could form appealing geometrical shapes easily visible from above.[15] In contrast to Herminghaus and Spoon, who promoted iconic and graphical designs easily recognized from the air, the German landscape architect Hermann Mattern attempted to tighten the airport buildings' connection to the ground. His planting design for the new Stuttgart airport further stressed the architect Ernst Sagebiel's design intent—partly based upon the concern for air raid protection—to fit the airport's architecture into the landscape and to design a silhouette that would dissolve into the surrounding scenery. The clean-cut, monumental ledges of the long curved visitor terrace were broken up, and thereby "softened," by interspersed shrub plantings. The selection and irregular planting of tree and shrub species adhered to the rural character of the region. Both regionalist ideas and air-raid protection measures led to a landscape design that attempted to blend the airport into the surrounding landscape. During World War II, a variety of methods were used to render airfields invisible. They ranged from the employment of fake mobile hedges and entire dummy houses on rollers that were pulled onto the runways when they needed to be camouflaged against aerial attack, to applying chemicals and paint to grassland and different surface textures to concrete runways.[16]

THE AIRPORT AS PARK

In the early years of powered flight some landscape architects and planners associated airports with public urban parks and considered the airport a part of the park system. As early as 1913, the German landscape architect Leberecht Migge proposed that airfields could become an integral part of a city's open space system. Citizens would benefit from the hitherto unknown excitement and diversion that the incorporation of airfields into parkland could offer. Like open-air museums, amusement parks, and racecourses, airfields—according to Migge—could be assigned to a city's open space management.[17] In the United States in the 1920s, some landscape architects engaged in a lively debate about the siting and management of airports that was led by different professional groups and municipal agencies. Although airports were conceptually understood as open space, not even landscape architects agreed amongst themselves. Some considered airports both recreational and commercial facilities and argued that they should be integrated into the park system and administered by the park departments. As the planners of the Regional Plan of New York and Its Environs stated in the 1920s, one of the advantages of this treatment was that outdated obsolescent airports, often built near or on former parkland at any time could be turned back into "permanent public open space."[18] Other planners and landscape architects drew attention to the dangers of combining recreational park use and air traffic, and pointed out that they were incompatible. Although this opinion finally prevailed, some small airports were indeed built in conjunction with golf courses and public parks. Toledo, Ohio, disregarded the skeptical voices that warned against the security hazard that airplanes would provide to park visitors, and incorporated an airport into its park system plan, locating it in the city's Bay View Park north of the mouth of the Maumee River.

THE AIRPORT AS ENVIRONMENT

Although many of these early elaborations concentrated on the actual airport site, engineers, planners, and designers realized quickly that security and aircraft technology required unobstructed airspace in the zones adjacent to the airport. In fact, airports as early as the 1930s began to be conceived of as the centers of a much larger airport-related environment, not only in terms of the larger national airport and airway system. Noise pollution was already a topic then, and it became apparent that land use surrounding airports had to be regulated to prevent the creation of physical hazards and obstructions in the airspace of the approach and landing paths of planes. Thus, cities in the early twentieth century not only needed to procure and set aside land for future airports, they also had to regulate the adjacent land use. (FIG. 7) Airport zoning was to determine the height of structures, beginning at the airport boundary and extending to a radius of 3.2 kilometers from the ends of the runways. In the United States, the Californian county of Alameda adopted a first airport zoning ordinance in 1928. It required that no obstruction over fifteen meters high should be erected within three hundred and five meters of the boundary of any public airport.[19]

By 1960, when the construction of the first jetports in the United States had begun, architects and architectural critics were criticizing airports as "obsolete" (Rayner Banham), a "parasite appendix [of cities]" (Paolo Soleri), as lacking visual stimulus, and as wasteland (Lewis Mumford).[20] Airports appeared in these critics' eyes as the complete opposite of parks and landscapes. To this effect, Lewis Mumford explained in ironic and dry prose that the words "park and field have taken on new meanings." According to him, park now meant a "desert of asphalt, designed as a temporary storage space for motor cars" whereas "field" meant "another kind of artificial desert, a barren area planted in great concrete strips, vibrating with noise, dedicated to the arrival and departure of planes." For Mumford, parking lots and airports were wasteland that grew "at the expense of parkland around every big city." If this development continued, he argued, the result would be a "universal paved desert, unfit for human habitation, no better than the surface of the moon."[21]

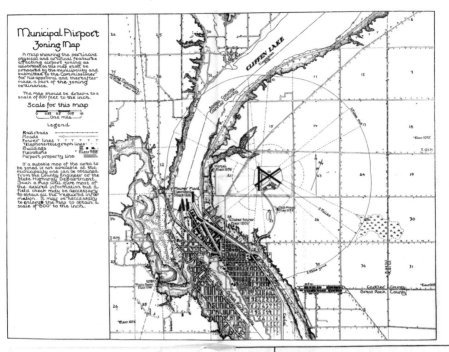

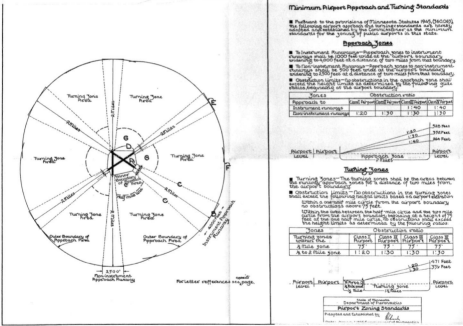

FIG. 7 — Prototypical municipal airport zoning map drawn up for the state of Minnesota.
(J. Nelson Young, Airport Zoning *[Urbana: University of Illinois, 1948]).*

Thus, despite heralding the new jet age, in the postwar years and in the 1960s and 1970s, airports appeared to many as dystopian landscapes, both in environmental and aesthetic terms. The construction of airports began to be subject to environmental impact assessments. In the United States in 1968, the first environmental impact assessment undertaken in the state of Florida prevented the construction of a jetport in the Big Cypress Swamp that would have destroyed much of the Everglades. Only three years later, in 1971, once the National Environmental Policy Act of 1969 had been passed into law, the Federal Aviation Administration declared that the "environmental issue...may well be the greatest challenge to aviation in the '70s."[22] The intention now was to integrate environmental and aviation planning, as well as regional planning. Besides the alleviation of noise, water, and air pollution, and the impacts on land use, hydrology, and wildlife, concern for the airports' visual environment increased as well. A 1972 report for the US Department of Transportation stated that the "undefined amorphous open areas" of airports and the "unimpressive" connections between airports and cities as well as the haphazard development in the airports' vicinity needed treatment. Furthermore, it pointed out that the airport's visual impact on nearby communities could not be separated from the impact of aircraft noise and airport-related traffic.[23] Views toward the city, or characteristic topographical features, as well as toward aircraft and the airside were to be designed "to communicate the experience of travelling by air," and to "reflect some of the individual character and identity of the city or geographic area in which [the airport] is located."[24]

Attempts to counter the perception of airports as dystopian had already been undertaken in the 1960s—for example, by the Manhattan-based architectural and engineering firm Tippetts-Abbett-McCarthy-Stratton. In 1966, they invited the artist Robert Smithson to consult on their preliminary studies and concept plans for the Dallas/Fort Worth International Airport. As a result, Smithson developed what has been considered a key project in the nascent Earth art movement.[25] The airport project provided him with a new scale and a new perspective. He was fascinated with the airport's monumental size and the extent of its runways that, as he pointed out, spanned the length of New York City's Central Park. As the planning officials, architects, and engineers did not fail to emphasize, the airport would expand well beyond Manhattan Island if laid on top of it. (FIG. 8) The ideas Smithson developed in 1966–67 for sculptural interventions on the site were designed for the aerial view from landing and departing airplanes and none required verticality. They included large shallow horizontal glass-covered boxes

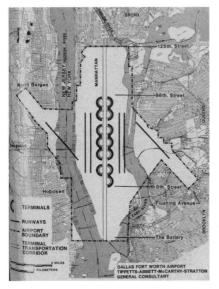

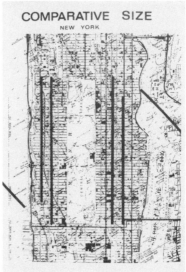

COMPARATIVE SIZE
NEW YORK

FIG. 8 —

LEFT: overlay of plan for Dallas/Fort Worth International Airport and map of Manhattan *(Stanley Cohen, "Dallas/Fort Worth to Open World's Largest Airport this Month," Consulting Engineer 41, no. 3 [1973]: 72–81).*

RIGHT: Robert Smithson, overlay of plan for Dallas/Fort Worth International Airport and map of Central Park, 1967 *(Robert Smithson, "Towards the Development of an Air Terminal Site," Artforum 6 [1967]: 36–40).*

embedded in the earth that contained rows of "yellow fog lights," patterns of large square asphalt pavements and a web of white gravel paths, a vast spiral consisting of triangular concrete panels laid out on the ground (*Aerial Map*), and a proposal for *Wandering Earth Mounds and Gravel Paths* (1967), a pattern of low amoeba-shaped earth mounds between and surrounding the runways.[26]

Through his projects and the works by the fellow artists whom he had invited to participate, Smithson strove to "define the limits of the air terminal site in a new way" and "set a precedent and create an original approach to the aesthetics of airport landscaping."[27] He explained that his "aerial art" inspired by the aerial view, the idiosyncratic site conditions and individual site perceptions replaced the "naturalism of seventeenth-, eighteenth-, and nineteenth-century art." In "aerial art," Smithson contended, "the landscape beg[an] to look more like a three dimensional map rather than a rustic garden."[28] For Smithson the airport was what his fellow artist Tony Smith described as a "created world... without tradition" and an "artificial landscape without cultural precedent."[29]

Yet, already at the beginning of commercial flight in the 1920s, landscape architects and architects had understood the airport as a cultural landscape that was to be designed as a whole, and in detail. Furthermore, architects, landscape architects, and cultural critics, had from the beginning of commercial flight onwards looked in particular toward the large territorial land planning and garden design projects in seventeenth-century France as precedents for dealing with

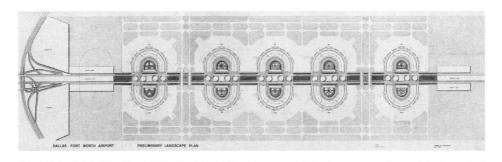

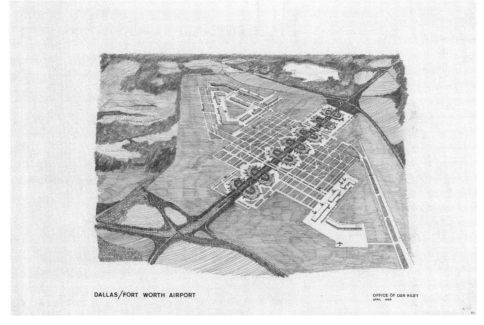

DALLAS/FORT WORTH AIRPORT

FIG. 9 (TOP) — Daniel Urban Kiley, landscape design for Dallas/Fort Worth International Airport, Texas, April 1969. *Courtesy of the Frances Loeb Library, Harvard Graduate School of Design.*

FIG. 10 (BOTTOM) — Daniel Urban Kiley, bird's-eye view of planned Dallas/Fort Worth International Airport, Texas, April 1969. Pencil and black ink on trace paper. *Courtesy of the Frances Loeb Library, Harvard Graduate School of Design.*

the large expanses of the airport landscape. The creation of the first jetports provided designers with new opportunities.

At Dallas/Fort Worth International Airport, the landscape architect Daniel U. Kiley followed Smithson's initial attempts at creating an airport landscape. Kiley had set his own precedent for an airport landscape design at the new Dulles International Airport in Chantilly, Virginia, outside of Washington, DC (1958–1962). In 1968, he produced another landscape design for Dallas/Fort Worth International Airport. (FIGS. 9-10) There, the planners argued that the airport was sited deliberately on land of little ecological and agricultural value.[30] More realistic than Smithson's preceding ideas, yet still too monumental and grand to be realized in its entirety, Kiley's design turned the median of the airport's central highway spine into a sloping axis of monumental reflecting pools.

Fascinated by French seventeenth-century gardens and adept at working on the large scale of the airport, Kiley was an ideal candidate to offer designs for the new jetport landscapes. At both Dulles and Dallas/Fort Worth International he used massed plantings as counterweights to the terminal buildings and access roads, and as elements that further emphasized the vast scale. Plantings and water features were parts of his designs that celebrated the airport landscape and embedded the terminal buildings, access roads, and parking lots into the larger landscape.

At Dallas/Fort Worth the designed rectangular pools are surrounded by double rows of trees. Gridded blocks of trees are planted at the locations of the taxiway bridges that run perpendicularly across the highway. Variously shaped water basins are located in the center of each terminal loop that flank the central highway spine, and the accompanying planting designs consisting of rows, circles, and gridded groves of trees vary from loop to loop. Similar to his design for Dulles International Airport where passengers were welcomed by trees and shrubs blossoming or producing fruit in bright colors that flank the approach roads and Eero Saarinen and Associates's iconic terminal building, Kiley covered the medians of the north-south highway spine at either end with flowering trees. The southern entrance of the highway spine is bracketed by blocks of evergreens, whereas large rectangular areas at its sides on either end are used to grow nursery stock, preparing the airport for the future. Kiley's design accompanied the comprehensive plans that were drawn up between 1965 and 1969 by Tippetts-Abbett-McCarthy-Stratton (TAMS) and the architectural design for the terminal complex by HOK and Hopf & Adler that began in 1968. Like the airport that was built on 7,122 hectares, Kiley's landscape designs were developed with expansion in mind, an expansion that—as the planners announced at the airport's opening in 1973—would ultimately also accommodate the landing of space shuttles.[31] A 1973 brochure issued by the Airport Authority reported that large amounts of ground covering plants, shrubs, and trees provided the airport with a functional and attractive layer that included evergreen live oaks at the entrance of the highway, crape myrtles near the airport center and the "control plaza," and double rows of cedar elm in the terminal area.[32] Although Kiley's monumental designs to turn what Mumford had described as wasteland into functional iconic and attractive landscapes were only partly realized, they testify to an increasing understanding of the airport as a comprehensive landscape and environment in the 1950s and 1960s when the first supersonic jet aircraft connected continents.

THE NEW ROMANTICISM OF AIRPORT AFTERLIVES

In the last quarter-century, changing geopolitics and the increasing mass air travel have resulted in many former airfields and airports being turned into public urban parks. Anticipations in the initial years of commercial flight have therefore come full circle. Often located on what used to be the periphery of cities, the former airfields are today providing large new public open space in urbanizing areas. While their adaptive reuse has provided many city governments with both opportunities and challenges, designers have in many cases embraced these sites as testing grounds for new ideas. Designs for former airfields have been based on the desire to construct or restore ecosystems, and natural and cultural heritage, as in the case of Crissy Field in San Francisco; they have experimented with the application of ecological theories that emphasize the importance of temporal change, self-organization, and indeterminacy as in the case of Downsview Park in Toronto; and given the large size, openness, and horizontality of airfields, some designers have interpreted them as blank slates for topographic and hydrological invention and intervention, as in the case of the Parisian firm OML's plan for Hellenikon Metropolitan Park in Athens. Some designs have sought to integrate urban agriculture and create centers for urban life as in the case of Büro Kiefer's design for Berlin Gatow. They have also provided new models for urban development and for engaging citizens in the shaping of the future urban landscape, as at Tempelhofer Feld in Berlin.

The designs for Tempelhofer Feld and for the Nature and Landscape Park Johannisthal on one of the earliest German airfields southeast of the Berlin city center, besides being the products of complex urban development processes based upon local politics and new urban development paradigms, are also reflective of a new romanticism in landscape design.[33] Büro Kiefer's 1996 design for Nature and Landscape Park Johannisthal turned the core of the former airfield into a nature conservation area to protect a rare biotope type in the region. Humans are not allowed to enter this zone; instead, they are offered a circumferential panoramic path on an elevated boardwalk, as well as a variety of small recreational spaces for ball games and playgrounds along the outer edge of the field. A careful management regimen with a flock of sheep maintains the dry-grass biotope of the core conservation zone, and at the same time provides a rural landscape scenery that resembles imagery associated in Germany since the nineteenth century with the romantic notion of a primordial nature and with an ideal cultural landscape. Furthered by paintings and literary works such as Theodor Fontane's *Wanderungen durch die Mark Brandenburg* (*Walking tours through the*

March of Brandenburg, published in five volumes from 1862 to 1889), dry grass and heathland had assumed an iconic landscape status in the German mind by the early twentieth century. It had also been promoted as quintessentially German, and as a powerful nationalist expression of the homeland by conservative and reactionary garden designers, artists, writers, and art critics who later often sympathized with Nazi politics.[34] After World War II, the imagery of a dry grass- and heathland grazed by sheep, and the romanticism and nostalgia associated with it, was furthered by the establishment of Germany's first nature park, comprising parts of the Lüneburg Heath in which industry and modern agriculture were forbidden in favor of traditional sheep herding.[35] Largely the result of a conservative middle-class critique of industrial society and of health concerns regarding urban life, nature parks were established to provide for controlled "orderly" recreation like hiking, and to conserve landscape scenery for aesthetic enjoyment.[36] The landscape design for the former Johannisthal airfield is therefore grounded both in a national landscape aesthetic and in romantic conceptions for nature conservation and preservation that date back to the nineteenth and early twentieth centuries.

The prized 2011 design by the British landscape architecture firm Gross. Max. for the conversion of Tempelhof airfield was very receptive of the invitation to tenders' requirements that, amongst many other things, asked the designers to pay special attention to the historic remains on the site while developing "new aesthetic visions" and considering the then current "New Romantic style" in the art world as a source of inspiration.[37] This genre is considered a reaction to the increasing mobility of society and the lack of permanent social ties, as well as to the subsequent search for security and intimacy and a yearning for "a paradisiacal, beautiful and fairytale-like state." Whereas the contemporary artists whose work has been associated with this genre often evoked "the abysmal, the uncanny, and the mysterious" hidden behind these idylls, the park designers are not creating an emotionally disturbing landscape.[38] Instead, they are working on and with a site that has a varied and, in part, disturbing history. The park project itself is the outcome of the tension created by the melancholy, nostalgia, and unease resulting from the site's manifold historic significance before, during, and after World War II on the one hand, and by the expectations and desires based upon its big future potentials on the other hand. In the design that has been presented to the public in atmospheric perspectival renderings with a romantic dreamlike haze, produced with the help of layers and filters in computer graphic programs, the designers invoke a vast healthy new park landscape.

This landscape appears to provide space for private contemplation and reflection and for what the art historian Martina Weinhart has described with regards to the New Romanticism as "perceiving the transcendent."[39] The way light, haze, and blurriness are used in some of the images recalls landscape paintings by William Turner, Thomas Cole, Albert Bierstadt, and today's artist Gerhard Richter, and brings to mind pictorialist photography. With the integration of urban farms, and protected dry-grass biotopes, the park design appears as a modern ornamented farm. In fact, the park features and motives also include a ha-ha—a reference to the era of romanticism in garden design—and an artificial rock that is dedicated to two noteworthy Berlin exponents of the romantic era, the Prussian minister and philosopher Wilhelm von Humboldt, and his younger brother, the naturalist and explorer Alexander von Humboldt. The rock that doubles as a climbing school and belvedere also calls to mind one of the key works of German Romantic painting, the *Wanderer Above the Sea of Fog* (1818) by Caspar David Friedrich. As if these references to a romantic worldview did not suffice, Gross. Max. placed the angel Damiel from Wim Wenders's 1987 film *Wings of Desire* on the top of the rock monument in one of their catchpenny renderings. Set in 1980s Berlin, Wenders's film created a counter project to reality by establishing a world of invisible gentle angels who listen to the tortured thoughts of the mortals and try to comfort them. While the film is a meditation on Berlin's past, present, and future, Gross.Max.'s phased park design attempts to build with the past and present, to envision the future. With their design for Tempelhof, the designers, like their late eighteenth-century and nineteenth-century romantic forebears and like the contemporary exponents of the New Romanticism, strive to create "individualized counter-world[s] to [a] disillusioning reality" and attempt to build "a new relationship between the individual and nature."[40] Like in the romantic period, the focus is on the individual and his or her emotions.

The landscapes of air transfer were intended to provide spaces of transition between the air- and landside of airports. They were designed to ground and orientate passengers, thereby intentionally creating a counterpoint to the fast pace of air travel and stressing the airport's geographical locality and cultural context. Architects and designers have attempted to root the new technology that has facilitated the development of a mobile world in a specific locality. These professionals have understood airports not only as transfer stations, but also as localized landscapes, places, and environments that need to be both created and protected. Today parks on former airfields seek to return the land to local social uses, and to embed it into regional ecological networks.

This essay is based upon Sonja Dümpelmann, Flights of Imagination*; and the two exhibitions by the author, The Jetport Landscape and From Airfields to Greenfields: A Genealogy of Airport Landscape, at the Harvard Graduate School of Design, October 31–December 19, 2013. See also Sonja Dümpelmann, "Der Flughafen als Landschaft," in* Ökologie und die Künste, *ed. Daniela Hahn and Erika Fischer-Lichte (Munich: Wilhelm Fink Verlag, 2015), 71–92.*

Notes

1

Richard Neutra, "Terminals?—Transfer!" *The Architectural Record* 68, no. 2 (1930): 100, 104; Norman Bel Geddes, *Horizons* (Boston: Little, Brown, 1932), 79–108.

2

For an elaboration on the ecological and environmental concerns of airports with regards to aviation history in the United States, see Sonja Dümpelmann, "Airport, Landscape, Environment," in *Airport Landscape: Urban Ecologies in the Aerial Age*, ed. Sonja Dümpelmann and Charles Waldheim (Cambridge, MA: Harvard Graduate School of Design, 2016), exhibition catalog.

3

Tim Cresswell, *On the Move: Mobility in the Modern Western World* (New York: Routledge, 2006), 225.

4

Records of the Harvard Aeronautical Society, HUD 3123, Box 1.

5

Archibald Black, *Civil Airports and Airways* (New York: Simmons-Boardman, 1929), 29–30. See also Archibald Black, "Air Terminal Engineering," *Landscape Architecture* 13, no. 4 (1923): 225–38. The word *airport* had only begun to be commonly used at the end of the 1920s when terminal buildings marked the advent of commercial aviation. See Deborah G. Douglas, "Who Designs Airports…Engineers, Architects, or City Planners? Aspects of American Airport Design Before World War II," in *Atmospheric*

Flight in the Twentieth Century, Archimedes 3, ed. P. Galison and A. Roland (Dordrecht; Boston: Kluwer Academic Publishers, 2000), 303. For the use of the words *airfield, airport, aerodrome, airdrome*, etc., see also Wolfgang Voigt, "From the Hippodrome to the Aerodrome, from the Air Station to the Terminal: European Airports, 1909–1945," in *Building for Air Travel: Architecture and Design for Commercial Aviation*, ed. John Zukowsky (Chicago: The Art Institute of Chicago, with Prestel, 1996), 27.

6

S. E. Veale, *Tomorrow's Airliners, Airways and Airports* (London: Pilot Press, 1945), 247.

7

More recently, in 1999, the late cultural geographer Denis Cosgrove compared Heathrow Airport to the landscape of a Georgian estate. Cosgrove used this comparison not only to lay out some morphological parallels between the eighteenth-century landscape garden and the twentieth-century jetport—the size, the open stretches of grass; but also to point out their respective importance as economic engines for land development. On a theoretical level then, studying an airport could, he argued, "recover landscape as a synthetic idea, a flexible concept," and this landscape included social, political, and economic worlds. See Denis Cosgrove, "Airport/Landscape," in *Recovering Landscape: Essays in Contemporary Landscape Architecture*, ed. James Corner (New York: Princeton Architectural Press, 1999), 221–31.

8

See Reyner Banham, "The Obsolescent Airport," *Architectural Review* 132, no. 788

(1962): 253. Banham is alluding to the scenes in
the film *L'année dernière à Marienbad* (*Last Year
at Marienbad*) that were shot in the gardens of
the Munich palaces Schleißheim, Nymphenburg,
and Amalienburg.

9
Jacob John Spoon, "Landscape Design for
Airports," *Parks & Recreation* 17, no. 8 (1934):
267, 271, 273.

10
Sven Kesselring, "Global Transfer Points: The
Making of Airports in the Mobile Risk Society,"
in *Aeromobilities*, ed. Saulo Cwerner, Sven
Kesselring, and John Urry (London: Routledge,
2009), 41.

11
See *Civil Aviation in Brazil: Its Beginning,
Growth, Present State* (S. Paulo, etc.:
"Graphicars," Romiti & Lanzara, 1939), 22.

12
See "Cultural Gardens," Honolulu National
Airport, accessed July 21, 2014, http://hawaii
.gov/hnl/customer-service/cultural-gardens.

13
Lorraine E. Kuck and Richard C. Tongg, *The
Tropical Garden* (New York: Macmillan, 1939), 54.

14
See Ernst Herminghaus, "Landscape Art in
Airport Design," *American Landscape Architect*
3, no. 1 (1930): 15–18; Sonja Dümpelmann,
"Der Blick von oben: versteckte und entdeckte
Landschaft zwischen 1920 und 1960," in *Kunst
Garten Kultur*, ed. Gert Gröning and Stefanie
Hennecke (Berlin: Dietrich Reimer Verlag),
239–64; Sonja Düempelmann, "Between
Science and Aesthetics: Aspects of 'Air-minded'
Landscape Architecture," *Landscape Journal* 29,
no. 2 (2010): 161–78; and Sonja Dümpelmann,
*Flights of Imagination: Aviation, Landscape,
Design* (Charlottesville: University of Virginia
Press, 2014).

15
See Spoon, "Landscape Design," 273–74.

16
See Sonja Dümpelmann, "The Art and Science
of Invisible Landscapes: Camouflage for War

and Peace," in *Ordnance: War + Architecture
and Space*, ed. Gary Boyd and Denis Linehan
(Farnham: Ashgate, 2013), 117–35; and
Dümpelmann, *Flights of Imagination*.

17
See Leberecht Migge, *Die Gartenkultur des 20:
Jahrhunderts* (Jena: Eugen Diederichs, 1913), 7, 35.

18
See Committee on Regional Plan of New York
and Its Environs, *Regional Plan of New York
and its Environs*, vol. 1, *Atlas and Description*
(Philadelphia: William F. Fell, 1929), 371.

19
J. Nelson Young, *Airport Zoning* (Urbana:
University of Illinois, 1948).

20
Reyner Banham, "The Obsolescent Airport,"
The Architectural Review 788 (1962): 252–53;
Paolo Soleri, "The City as the Airport," in
Master Planning the Aviation Environment, ed.
Angelo J. Cerchione, Victor E. Rothe, James
Vercellino (Tucson: University of Arizona Press,
1970), 11–13.

21
Lewis Mumford, "The Social Function of
Open Spaces," in *Space for Living: Landscape
Architecture and the Allied Arts and Professions*, ed.
Silvia Crowe (Amsterdam: Djambatan, 1961), 24,
26; Lewis Mumford, "Die soziale Funktion der
Freiräume," *Baumeister* 58 (April 1960): 324, 328.

22
Federal Aviation Administration, *National
Aviation System Plan: Ten Year Plan 1972–1981*
(Washington, DC: US DOT, FAA, March 1971), 23.

23
CLM/Systems and United States Department
of Transportation, Office of Environment and
Urban Systems, *Airports and their Environment: A
Guide to Environmental Planning: Prepared for the
U.S. Department of Transportation* (September
1972), 183–84.

24
Ibid., 186.

25
For Smithson's "aerial art" and the first earth
works see Suzaan Boettger, *Earthworks: Art and*

the Landscape of the Sixties (Berkeley: University of California Press, 2002), 45–101.

26
To make his aerial art accessible also to passengers and visitors in the terminal, Smithson planned to set up TV cameras that would transmit images of the aerial art outdoors to the indoors of the terminal.

27
Robert Smithson, "Proposal for Earthworks and Landmarks to be Built on the Fringes of the Fort Worth-Dallas Regional Air Terminal Site (1966–67)," in *Robert Smithson: The Collected Writings*, ed. Jack Flam (Berkeley: University of California Press, 1996), 354.

28
Robert Smithson, "Aerial Art," *Studio International* 177 (April 1969): 180.

29
Samuel Wagstaff Jr., "Talking with Tony Smith," *Artforum* 5, no. 4 (Dec. 1966): 14–19.

30
CLM/Systems, Inc., *Airports and their Environment*, A1-137.

31
National Air and Space Museum Archives, F4-824000-01 "Texas, Dallas-Fort Worth IAP." Brochure entitled "Dallas/Fort Worth Airport Opening 1973," 146.

32
Ibid., 60.

33
For a discussion of these and other park designs on former airfields see Sonja Dümpelmann, *Flights of Imagination.*

34
For the use of heathland in nineteenth- and twentieth-century German gardens and art, its

perception and meaning, see Gert Gröning and Uwe Schneider, *Die Heide in Park und Garten* (Worms: Wernersche Verlagsgesellschaft, 1999).

35
For the first German nature park, the Heidepark, see Jens Ivo Engels, *Naturpolitik in der Bundesrepublik* (Munich: Schöningh, 2005), 102–3.

36
For the history of nature conservation and nature parks in postwar Germany see Engels, *Naturpolitik*; on nature parks see in particular pp. 93–154; Sandra Chaney, *Nature of the Miracle Years* (New York: Berghahn Books, 2008), 114–47.

37
Senate Department for Urban Development, *Tempelhof Parkland Open Landscape Planning Competition Followed by a Negotiated Procedure Invitation to Tender* (Berlin, 2010), 25.

38
Max Hollein, "Preface," in *Wunschwelten: Neue Romantik in der Kunst der Gegenwart*, ed. Max Hollein and Martina Weinhart (Frankfurt: Kunsthalle Schirn Hatje Cantz, 2005), 17.

39
Martina Weinhart, "The World Must Be Made Romantic," in *Wunschwelten: Neue Romantik in der Kunst der Gegenwart*, ed. Max Hollein and Martina Weinhart (Frankfurt: Kunsthalle Schirn/Hatje Cantz, 2005), 35–36.

40
See, for example, the artists Justine Kurland, David Thorpe, and Laura Owens; Eelco Hoftman with Kaye Geipel and Doris Kleilein, "Urban agriculture ist ein heikles Stichwort," *Stadtbauwelt* no. 191 (2011): 34.

THINKING LANDSCAPE AS URBANISM
—*Charles Waldheim*

Thinking the Contemporary Landscape asks fundamental questions regarding the intellectual aspirations and appetites of landscape architecture as a discipline and profession. Among the positions and oppositions implied in this project is the relative state of landscape's newfound role in shaping the contemporary city. The recent discourse around landscape urbanism suggests a return to the origins of the field itself. The founders of the "new art" of landscape architecture specifically identified architecture as the most appropriate cultural identity for the new professional. In so doing, they proposed an emergent hybrid professional identity. This new liberal profession was founded in the second half of the nineteenth century in response to the social, environmental, and cultural challenges of the industrial city. In this milieu the landscape architect was conceived as the new professional responsible for the integration of civil infrastructure, public space, and environmental improvement. This origin of the landscape architect in the shaping the contemporary city sheds interesting light on the discourse and practices of landscape as a form of urbanism.

A survey of recent city building initiatives in North America's largest urban centers corroborates a claim of the landscape architect as urbanist. In recent years several North American cities, including New York, Chicago, and Toronto, have articulated a putative landscape urbanist position through a range of projects. Some of these projects deploy landscape as a medium of urbanization and only imply the limits of urban form, while others are explicitly engaged in describing built form, block structure, building height, and setback, in relation to landscape process. In the most legible example, Toronto's waterfront is being reconceived along explicitly landscape urbanist lines.

The city of New York has been among the most important venues for the development of landscape urbanist practices. Following the election of Michael Bloomberg in 2002, the city began a decade of landscape-driven urban development projects of international significance. Many of these projects emerged at the landscape urbanist intersection of ecological function, arts philanthropy, and design culture. The competition for the remediation and reconstruction of Fresh Kills landfill on Staten Island offered an early opening to a landscape architect operating at the scale of urban development. While the James Corner Field Operations commission for Fresh Kills Park (2001–present) focuses on

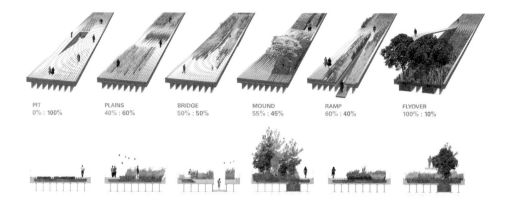

PIT	PLAINS	BRIDGE	MOUND	RAMP	FLYOVER
0% : 100%	40% : 60%	50% : 50%	55% : 45%	60% : 40%	100% : 10%

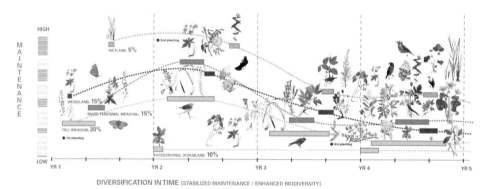

DIVERSIFICATION IN TIME [STABILIZED MAINTENANCE / ENHANCED BIODIVERSITY]

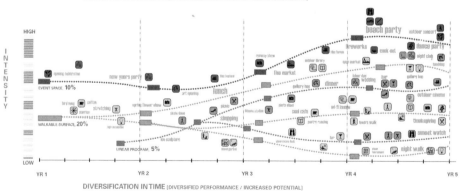

DIVERSIFICATION IN TIME [DIVERSIFIED PERFORMANCE / INCREASED POTENTIAL]

FIG. 1 (TOP) — James Corner Field Operations and Diller Scofidio + Renfro, The High Line, landscape typologies, New York, 2004.

FIG. 2 (BOTTOM) — James Corner Field Operations and Diller Scofidio + Renfro, The High Line, diagrams of diversity over time, New York, 2004.

landscape remediation and ecological function, it is also conceived as a heavily programmed urban space. The park is intended to accommodate ongoing urbanization around the perimeter of its site, while absorbing increasing demands for recreation and tourism. In this early landscape urbanist project the claiming of a park in the public imaginary was as important as the design of a succession process to grow the park over time. In this context, the relatively rare political alignment of Republican leaders in the Governor's Office in Albany and the Mayor's Office in New York produced an equally rare project of public patronage for New York's reliably Republican Staten Island.[1]

At a more boutique and pedestrian scale of landscape architecture, yet more directly implicated in urban development and built form, is Field Operation's collaboration with Diller Scofidio + Renfro and Piet Oudolf for the High Line (2004–present). (FIGS. 1-2) This project was the result of community organization in opposition to a plan to demolish an abandoned elevated freight rail line cutting through Manhattan's lower west side Meatpacking District. While city planners in the previous administration understood the derelict structure to be an impediment to development, the Friends of the High Line advocated successfully for the incoming Bloomberg administration to view it as a potential asset. The Friends funded an international design competition for the site's redevelopment as an elevated landscape promenade, reminiscent of Paris's Promenade Plantée. While the city invested millions of public tax dollars in the design and construction of the High Line, the tax increment return on that funding was reported to be six to one, even through the worst of the economic downturn. Although the project can be described as a work of landscape architecture, the urban implications of the project are equally evident, as the intervention has catalyzed urban development and an intensity of activity equal to the densest urban destinations in North America, yet not through traditional urban form, but rather through landscape. The High Line's particular mix of arts and design culture, development, and public space offers a robust argument in favor of the landscape architect as urbanist.[2]

During the past decade New York has also pursued a range of public landscapes through a variety of planning mechanisms. Among these, the project for the East River Waterfront, Ken Smith Workshop with SHoP (2003–present) is notable. Equally notable has been the development of Hudson River Park by Michael Van Valkenburgh Associates (2001–2012). Across the East River, Michael Van Valkenburgh Associates's Brooklyn Bridge Park (2003–present) offers a mature work of landscape urbanism, convening community, catalyzing

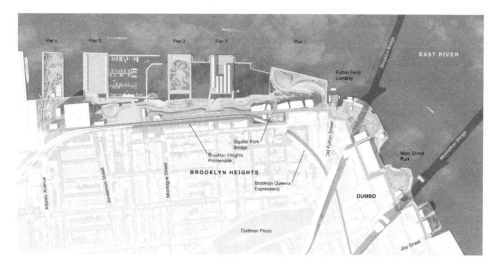

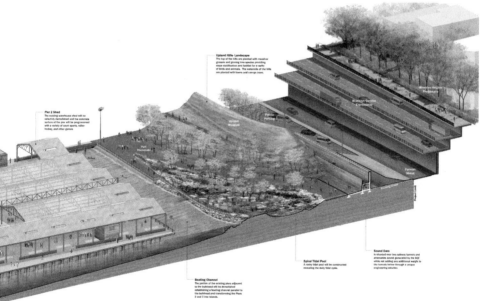

FIG. 3 (TOP) — Michael Van Valkenburgh
Associates, Brooklyn Bridge Park, site plan,
New York, 2014.

FIG. 4 (BOTTOM)—Michael Van Valkenburgh
Associates, Brooklyn Bridge Park, isometric
site section, New York, 2006.

development, and remediating environmental conditions for a newly conceived public realm. (FIGS. 3-4) More recently, Adriaan Geuze/West 8's plan for Governor's Island (2006–present) portends an equally significant confluence of landscape amenity, ecological enhancement, and urban development.[3]

Chicago offers another example of North American landscape urbanist practice. Mayor Richard M. Daley championed a number of highly visible landscape projects coincident with the rise landscape urbanist discourse and practice. The earliest of these projects, Millennium Park, was originally designed by Skidmore, Owings & Merrill to offer an on-time, on-budget faux Beaux-Arts public park over the site of a long abandoned rail yard within Grant Park. Following intervention by several of Chicago's notables advocating on behalf of design culture and the arts, the project evolved into an international destination for design culture. The subsequent hybrid plan juxtaposed the destination landscape of the Lurie Garden by Kathryn Gustafson with planting by Piet Oudolf (2000–2004) with architectural projects by Frank Gehry and Renzo Piano, as well as installations by Anish Kapoor, Jaume Plensa, and others.[4] More recently, Chicago's own abandoned elevated rail line, the Bloomingdale Trail, is being reconceived by Michael Van Valkenburgh Associates (2008–present) as a more equalitarian and diverse equivalent to New York's High Line. Comparable projects for the redevelopment of Chicago's Navy Pier by James Corner Field Operations (2012–present) and Northerly Island by Studio Gang Architects (2010–present) suggest an ongoing commitment to landscape as a medium of the city's public lakefront.

Contemporary Toronto offers the most legible and robust example of the landscape architect operating as urbanist. The postindustrial waterfront of Canada's most populous city is being redeveloped by Waterfront Toronto, a public crown corporation. Waterfront Toronto has commissioned a cohort of leading landscape architects including Adriaan Geuze, James Corner, and Michael Van Valkenburgh, among others, to shape the redevelopment of the city's waterfront. In these projects the public realm and built form of new urban districts are being specified in relation to the recuperation of the lacustrine and riverine ecologies that shaped the city's growth. The first such commission was for Adriaan Geuze/West 8 with DTAH for the development of the Central Waterfront (2006–present).[5] (FIGS. 5-6) Beginning with an explicitly ecological argument for urban form, Geuze's proposal was premiated from among a shortlist of international architects, as the only project that expressed the spatial and cultural implications of fish habitat, zero carbon transit, and spatial legibility. Presently under construction, Geuze's project promises infrastructural continuity, storm

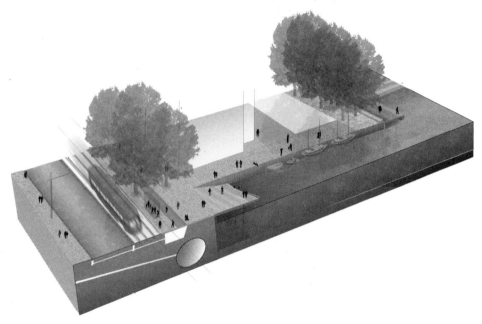

FIG. 5 (TOP) — West 8 and DTAH, Central Waterfront Competition, site plan, Toronto, 2006.

FIG. 6 (BOTTOM) — West 8 and DTAH, Central Waterfront Competition, isometric site section, Toronto, 2006.

water management, and a renewed cultural image for Toronto. At the eastern
end of Geuze's plan, James Corner Field Operations have been commissioned
to design a nearly 1,000-acre public park. Lake Ontario Park (2006–present)
proposes new recreational amenity and lifestyle landscapes in the context of
severely degraded industrial sites as well as several of the most biologically
diverse and attractive bird habitats in the region. In between Geuze's Central
Waterfront and Corner's Lake Ontario Park, the Lower Don Lands are presently the site of an ongoing development effort led by Michael Van Valkenburgh
Associates with Ken Greenberg (2005–present). (FIGS. 7–8) The project for the
Lower Don is the result of an international design competition for the renaturalization of a completely compromised riverine estuary at the mouth of the
Don River, and for the development of new neighborhoods housing up to
thirty thousand residents. This unique program for simultaneously managing
flood control, recuperating ecological function, and accommodating urbanization offers a clear case study in landscape urbanist practice. While several
of the finalist schemes for the Lower Don Lands competition advanced the discourse of landscape urbanism as we have seen previously, the team and scheme
assembled by Michael Van Valkenburgh represents the finest example of the integration of built form and landscape process evident in North America today. As
such, it embodies the promise of contemporary landscape urbanist practice, in
which the landscape architect orchestrates a complex, multidisciplinary team of
urbanists, architects, ecologists, and other specialists toward the reconciliation
of dense, walkable, sustainable communities in relation to diverse, functioning
urban ecosystems.[6]

In recent years East Asia has been particularly fecund for the development of landscape urbanist practice. A number of landscape architects have
been engaged in a range of projects for cities across the region. Many landscape
architects and urbanists have made plans for the redevelopment of Singapore
Bay, as well as for the development of landscape strategies in and around Hong
Kong. Over the past decade, a range of design competitions for sites in Korea
and Taiwan have premiated landscape urbanist strategies for complex urban and
environmental problems.

On the Chinese mainland, Shenzhen is among the most committed to landscape urbanist projects of city building in recent years. The design competition
for the Longgang Town Center offers an international case study in contemporary practices. The proposal Deep Ground, premiated by the Shenzhen Planning
Bureau, was the work of a collaborative group from the Architectural Association

FIG. 7 (TOP) — Michael Van Valkenburgh Associates and Ken Greenberg, Lower Don Lands, plan, Toronto, 2007.

FIG. 8 (BOTTOM) — Michael Van Valkenburgh Associates and Ken Greenberg, Lower Don Lands, aerial view, Toronto, 2007.

School of Architecture Landscape Urbanism unit including Eva Castro / Plasma Studio and Eduardo Rico, Alfredo Ramirez, Young Zhang, et al. / Groundlab (2008–present).[7] (FIGS. 9–10) In their project for Longgang, Castro, Rico, et al., propose a relational digital model through which urban form, block structure, building height, setbacks, and the like, are correlated to desirable environmental metrics as outcomes. Rejecting the competition brief's requirement for an enormous static physical model, the Groundlab team substituted a dynamic relational or parametric digital model capable of correlating ecological inputs, environmental benchmarks, and development targets through specific formal outcomes. The development of associative or relational digital models is at the forefront of landscape urbanist practice, and promises to more precisely calibrate ecological process with the shape of the city. More recently in Shenzhen, the competition for the Qianhai Port City represents an ongoing investment in landscape ecology as a medium through which to articulate the development of the megacity. All three finalist projects by Rem Koolhaas / OMA, James Corner Field Operations, and Joan Busquets, proposed to organize the new town of one million residents first in relation to the recuperation of ecological function and environmental health in the river tributaries flowing to the sea. The premiated project by James Corner Field Operations (2011–present) as well as the other two finalist projects give shape and substance to an otherwise unremarkable urban field as informed through landscape ecology. In this regard all three finalist projects began from a comparable position relative to the watershed and overall urban morphology, before diverging on the question of how best to order and articulate the urban field itself. This symmetry of approach is remarkable, coming from teams led by an architect, landscape architect, and urban planner, respectively.

What do these practices have in common? Collectively they represent the landscape architect acting as urbanist and raise timely and fundamental questions of disciplinary and professional identity for the field. While the various etymologies of the term "landscape" have rightly preoccupied the field for decades, the formulation of "landscape architecture" as a professional identity has received less critical attention in recent years.[8]

Questions of professional nomenclature concerned proponents of the so-called new art since its inception in the nineteenth century. Long-standing debates over the formulation reveal a tension between the disciplinary identity and the scope of work for the landscape architect. Founders of the new field included a diverse array of positions—from those embodying a tradition of landscape gardening and rural improvement through those advocating for

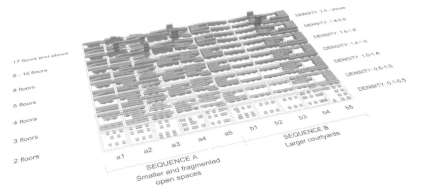

FIG. 9 (TOP) — Eva Castro and Alfredo Ramirez/Plasma Studio and Eduardo Rico/ Groundlab, Deep Ground, Longgang Town Center, Shenzhen, International Urban Design Competition, relational urban model, 2008.

FIG. 10 (BOTTOM) — Eva Castro and Alfredo Ramirez/Plasma Studio and Eduardo Rico/ Groundlab, Deep Ground, Longgang Town Center, Shenzhen, International Urban Design Competition, aerial view 2008.

landscape as an architectural and urban art. Many American proponents of the field held a strong cultural affinity for English practices of landscape gardening. In contrast, Continental practices of urban improvement allied with landscape promised a very different scope of work for the new professional. Complicating matters further was the desire by many for a distinct singular identity, not easily confused with any of the existing professional and artistic categories.

In its American formation this new field was imagined as a progressive response to the social and environmental challenges of rapid urbanization. While there was great enthusiasm for the articulation of a new profession attendant to those concerns, it was much less clear what to call the new profession and its related field of study. By the end of the nineteenth century the available professional identities (architect, engineer, gardener) were perceived by many to be inadequate to new conditions. These new conditions (urban, industrial) demanded a new professional identity explicitly associated with landscape. What did it mean for the founders of this new field to claim landscape *as* architecture? What alternative identities were available to the founders of the field? How do those choices continue to inform the professional purview and intellectual commitments of the field today?

By the end of the nineteenth century, American boosters of the new art of landscape committed the nascent profession to an identity associated with the old art of architecture. This decision to identify architecture (as opposed to art, engineering, gardening) as the proximate professional peer group and cultural lens for the new art is significant for contemporary understandings of the "core" of landscape architecture. This history sheds compelling light on the subsequent development of city planning as a distinct professional identity spun out of landscape architecture in the first decades of the twentieth century as well as debates regarding landscape as a form of urbanism at the close of the century.

In 1857, Frederick Law Olmsted was appointed "Superintendent of the Central Park" in New York. After finding himself without prospects as his forays into farming and publishing had left him in debt, Olmsted eagerly pursued the position at the recommendation of Charles Wyllys Elliott, a family friend and member of the newly created Board of Commissioners of the Central Park. Elliott and the commissioners of the Central Park who appointed Olmsted subsequently awarded him (and his collaborator, the English architect Calvert Vaux) first prize in the design competition for the new park the following year, along a strictly political party line vote. Following their victory, Olmsted's title was enhanced to "Architect-in-Chief and Superintendent," and Vaux was appointed "Consulting Architect."[9]

From the time of Olmsted's first appointment as superintendent in 1857 and through his subsequent elevation to architect-in-chief in 1858, he made no reference to the professional title landscape architect. While Olmsted may have been aware of the French formulation *architecte-paysagiste*, and would certainly have been aware of the English-language antecedents termed by Gilbert Laing Meason and John Claudius Loudon, there is no evidence that Olmsted conceived of the term as a professional identity before his November 1859 visit to Paris. The term emerged only subsequent to Olmsted's tour of European parks and his multiple meetings with Adolphe Alphand at the Bois de Boulogne in November of that year. Associated with the improvements at the Bois de Boulogne, Olmsted would likely have seen drawings stamped "Service de l'architecte-paysagiste" and, more significantly, witnessed the expanded scope of Parisian practice in which landscape gardening was set in relation to infrastructural improvements, urbanization, and the management of large public projects. During his extensive tour of European parks and urban improvements, Olmsted visited the Bois de Boulogne more than any other precedent project, making eight visits in two weeks.[10] Upon his return to New York in late December 1859, every subsequent professional commission that Olmsted accepted for urban improvements included specific reference to the professional formulation landscape architect.

The earliest recorded evidence of the professional title landscape architect in America is found in personal correspondence from Olmsted to his father, John Olmsted, in July 1860. This letter, and subsequent correspondence, refers to the April 1860 commissioning of Olmsted and Vaux as "Landscape Architects" by the "Commissioners for laying out the upper part of New York island." Among those commissioners charged with the planning of northern Manhattan above 155th Street was Henry Hill Elliott, the older brother of Central Park Commissioner Charles Wyllys Elliott, who had originally recommended Olmsted for the position of superintendent.[11] It is likely that the Elliott brothers played equally significant roles in the development of landscape architecture as a profession, one through commissioning Olmsted with responsibility for Central Park, the other through conferring upon him the title of "Landscape Architect" associated with the planning of the extension of the city. The first appointment of a landscape architect in America was not for the design of a park, pleasure ground, or public garden. The new professional was first commissioned with the planning of northern Manhattan. In this context the landscape architect was originally conceived as a professional responsible for divining the shape of the city itself, rather than pastoral exceptions to it.

In spite of his conversion to the new formulation, Olmsted remained "all the time bothered with the miserable nomenclature" of landscape architecture and longed for a new term to stand for the "sylvan art." He groused that "*Landscape* is not a good word, *Architecture* is not; the combination is not. *Gardening* is worse." He longed for specific English translations for the French terms that more adequately captured the subtleties of the new art of urban order.[12] So the question persists, given the long-standing anxiety of conflating landscape *with* architecture, why did proponents of the new profession ultimately choose to claim landscape *as* architecture? Olmsted was convinced that adopting the mantle of the architect would bolster the new field in the eyes of the public, and mitigate against the tendency to mistake the work as being primarily concerned with plants and gardens. It would also, Olmsted argued, guard against the "greater danger" of landscape's potential future "disalliance" with architecture. Olmsted became convinced that the range of study that was called for by increasing demands of scientific knowledge would press the new profession toward increasing reliance on specialized bodies of technical knowledge, and a resulting alienation from the fine arts and architecture.[13]

By the final decade of the nineteenth century, enthusiasm had built for the claiming of a new profession. While many antecedent practices on both sides of the Atlantic predated the founding, the first such professional body, the American Society of Landscape Architects, was formed in 1899. Based on Olmsted's successful advocacy for the French formulation, American founders of the field ultimately adopted the Francophone "Landscape Architect" over the Anglophone "landscape gardener" as the most suitable professional nomenclature for the new art. Based on this formulation, and its claim to practices of urban order and infrastructural arrangement, the profession was first fully embodied in America.

AN OLMSTED IN EAST ASIA

As we have seen, the origins and aspirations of landscape as architecture emerge from very specific cultural, economic, and social conditions attendant to Western European and North American industrialized modernity. The "miserable nomenclature" of landscape architecture has only recently been appropriated for use in the context of East Asian urbanization. While there are many East Asian traditions of landscape gardening, including specific cultural formations in Japan, Korea, and China, none of those cultures have produced a precise equivalent to landscape architecture. Only recently, with the transfer of knowledge on urbanization and design from West to East has the English language formulation "landscape architecture" been adopted for use in China. Not surprisingly, the first professional practice of landscape architecture in China has developed over the past decade precisely in response to the demand for an ecologically informed practice of urban planning.

Kongjian Yu was the first landscape architect to open a private firm in China using the Western model of private consulting practices in design and planning. As such, Yu represents a historical singularity, and is arguably among the most important landscape architects practicing in China today. He has certainly emerged as that for international audiences in the English language over the past decade who have identified him as the Chinese landscape architect of first resort. Yu/Turenscape have leveraged this unique historical position to lobby Chinese political elites, most notably national leadership and mayors, for the adoption of Western-style ecological planning practices at the metropolitan, provincial, and even national scales. The fullest articulation of this aspiration is embodied in Yu/Turenscape's 2007–8 project for a Chinese National Ecological Security Plan. Taken together with over a decade of lectures to the Chinese Ministry of Construction's Conference of Mayors (1997–2007) and the Chinese publication of his influential treatise *The Road to Urban Landscape: A Dialogue with Mayors* (with Dihua Li, 2003), Yu has effectively articulated a scientifically informed ecological planning agenda at a national scale to domestic and international audiences.[14]

Kongjian Yu was one of seven students offered admission to the Doctor of Design Program at the Harvard Graduate School of Design (GSD) in fall 1992. Among his doctoral classmates during this time are several contributors to the discourse on ecology and planning who have gone on to notable academic or professional careers including Kristina Hill, Jacqueline Tatom, Rodney Hoinkes, and Doug Olson, among others. Kongjian Yu was among the first of his generational cohort to have access to doctoral work in the field at Harvard.

The Doctor of Design was organized as a research-based degree, culminating in a written dissertation, but candidates advised by Carl Steinitz regularly entered his landscape planning studios as a part of their coursework. In addition to mentoring from Steinitz, Yu integrated into his course of study the principles of landscape ecology from classes with Richard Forman. He was also immersed in the representational and computational questions associated with aggregating large datasets of ecological information through geographic information systems (GIS).

It was during his doctoral studies at the GSD that Yu integrated Steinitz's rigorous planning methods, Forman's language for analyzing complex landscape matrices, the tools and techniques of digital GIS associated with the Lab for Computer Graphics, and the concepts of game theory. Through this synthesis, Yu first conceived of a national-scaled ecological security plan as a project for China. He developed the concept, methodological questions, representational means, and analytical approach for such a project through his doctoral thesis "Security Patterns in Landscape Planning," advised by Carl Steinitz, Richard Forman, and Stephen Ervin. The thesis included a case study for the ecological security planning of Red Stone National Park in China, but aspired to articulate a methodological approach to planning for ecological security across regional, provincial, and national scales. The thesis embodies a methodological integration of Yu's various influences from Beijing Forestry and Harvard, including the so-called "layer" method of Ian McHarg, the visual analysis methods of Kevin Lynch, the ecological analysis of Richard Forman, and the GIS methods of Stephen Ervin and the legacy of GIS embodied in the Lab through the work of Jack Dangermond and others.

Among Yu's innovations in the thesis was the identification of particular "security points," or "SPs," as identified through the analysis of ecological function as it is impacted at particular thresholds of change in the form of a step function. Recognizing that particular ecological functions can withstand fairly large impacts without proportionate change, but will suddenly change drastically across particular thresholds of impact, Yu's thesis proposes three distinct SPs: ecological, visual, and agricultural.[15] In so doing, he anticipates the conflation of topics associated with ecology, tourism, and food security that his national plan for China's ecological security would embody. Yu's conception of a national ecological security plan for China is therefore not without its precedents in the West. While at the GSD, Yu was exposed to various historical antecedents for regional and national scaled landscape planning through Steinitz's courses, including Warren Manning's 1912 national plan for the United States.[16]

Following the completion of his doctoral work, Yu spent two years as a landscape architect in the Laguna Beach, California offices of SWA. During this time, Yu published a series of journal articles based on his doctoral dissertation.[17] In 1997, Yu returned to Beijing to open his consulting firm Turenscape. Since its formation, Turenscape has engaged in a range of large-scale ecological planning projects, in addition to the national ecological security plan.[18] Turenscape's planning practice, in both its articulation of a national ecological security plan as well as its various regional, metropolitan, and municipal proposals, represent a transfer of scientific and cultural knowledge of historic significance. Beyond their technical efficacy, predictive accuracy, or ease of implementation, the very fact of these plans represents the unique historical circumstances of Kongjian Yu's personal and professional arc. Ironically, the first generation of Chinese professionals trained in landscape ecology and planning in the United States now represent the greatest probability for the renewed relevance of a tradition of planning that has all but been eclipsed in the United States. Over the past decades since the 1978/79 declaration of the "Four Modernizations" in China, the political, economic, and cultural conditions in the United States have trended ever increasingly away from the prospect of scientifically infused spatial planning practice in favor of a neoliberal, decentralized, and privatized economy of spatial decision making. During those decades, improbably, and through the export of higher education in design and planning, practices of ecologically informed spatial planning have found fertile grounds for influencing public and political opinion in China. Contemporary China's unique combination of top-down political structure, centralized decision making, openness to Western conceptions in science and technology, and rapid ongoing urbanization render it uniquely capable of receiving Yu's interpretation of ecological planning strategies devised in the West. Irrespective of its scientific probity or prospects for implementation, the simple fact of Kongjian Yu's proposal for an ecological security plan at the scale of China represents a paradoxical, yet promising return to a long tradition of landscape planning, one on the verge of being eclipsed in the West. It further reinforces the historical claim to the landscape architect as urbanist of our age.

Aspects of this argument were developed in Charles Waldheim, "Landscape as Architecture," Harvard Design Magazine, *no. 36 (Spring 2013): 17–20, 177–78; Charles Waldheim, "Afterword: The Persistent Promise of Ecological Planning,"* Designed Ecologies: The Landscape Architecture of Kongjian Yu, *ed. William S. Saunders (Basel: Birkhäuser, 2012), 250–53; and Charles Waldheim, "Is Landscape Urbanism?" in* Is Landscape … ? Essays on the Identity of Landscape, *ed. Gareth Doherty and Charles Waldheim (London: Routledge, 2015), 162–89.*

Notes

1

See "Freshkills," NYC Parks, accessed
December 31, 2013, http://www.nycgovparks
.org/park-features/freshkills-park.

2

See Joshua David and Robert Hammond, *High
Line: The Inside Story of New York City's Park in
the Sky* (New York: Farrar, Straus and Giroux,
2011).

3

Note: East River Waterfront Esplanade, Ken
Smith Workshop with SHoP (2004–present);
Hudson River Park by Michael Van Valkenburgh
Associates (2001–2012); Michael Van
Valkenburgh Associates's Brooklyn Bridge Park
(2003–present); and Adriaan Geuze West 8's plan
for Governor's Island (2006–present).

4

See Timothy J. Gilfoyle, *Millennium Park:
Creating a Chicago Landmark* (Chicago:
University of Chicago Press, 2006).

5

See "Toronto Central Waterfront," West 8,
accessed December 31, 2013, http://www.west8
.nl/projects/toronto_central_waterfront/;
and "Central Waterfront Design Competition,"
WATERFRONToronto, accessed December 31,
2013, http://www.waterfrontoronto.ca/explore
_projects2/central_waterfront/planning
_the_communitycentral_waterfront_design
_competition.

6

See "Lower Don Lands,"
WATERFRONToronto, accessed December
31, 2013, http://www.waterfrontoronto.ca/
lowerdonlands; and "Lower Don Lands Design
Competition," WATERFRONToronto,
accessed December 31, 2015, http://www.
waterfrontoronto.ca/lower_don_lands
/lower_don_lands_design_competition.

7

See http://landscapeurbanism.aaschool
.ac.uk/programme/people/contacts
/groundlab/ (accessed December 31, 2013); and

http://groundlab.org/portfolio
/groundlab-project-deep-ground-longgang
-china/ (accessed December 31, 2013).

8

Joseph Disponzio's work on this topic has been
a rare exception in tracing the origins of the
professional identity. His doctoral dissertation
and subsequent publications on the topic offer
the definitive account of the emergence of the
French formulation *architecte-paysagiste* as the
origin of professional identity of the landscape
architect. See Disponzio, "The Garden Theory
and Landscape Practice of Jean-Marie Morel"
(PhD diss., Columbia University, 2000). See also
Disponzio, "Jean-Marie Morel and the Invention
of Landscape Architecture," in *Tradition and
Innovation in French Garden Art: Chapters of a
New History*, ed. John Dixon Hunt and Michel
Conan (Philadelphia: University of Pennsylvania
Press, 2002) 135–59; and Disponzio, "History of
the Profession," *Landscape Architectural Graphic
Standards*, ed. Leonard J. Hopper (Hoboken, NJ:
Wiley & Sons, 2007), 5–9.

9

Charles E. Beveridge, ed., *The Papers of
Frederick Law Olmsted*, vol. 3, *Creating Central
Park 1857–1861*, ed. Charles E. Beveridge and
David Schuyler (Baltimore: Johns Hopkins
University Press, 1983), 26–28, 45, n73.

10

Ibid., 234–35.

11

Ibid., 256–57; 257, n4; 267, n1.

12

Beveridge, *Papers*, vol. 5, *The California Frontier,
1863–1865*, ed. Victoria Post Ranney (Baltimore:
Johns Hopkins University Press, 1990), 422.

13

Beveridge, *Papers*, vol. 7, *Parks, Politics, and
Patronage, 1874–1882*, ed. Charles E. Beveridge,
Carolyn F. Hoffman, and Kenneth Hawkins
(Baltimore: Johns Hopkins University Press,
2007), 225–26.

14

See Kongjian Yu, "Lectures to the Mayors
Forum," Chinese Ministry of Construction,

Ministry of Central Communist Party Organization, two to three lectures annually, 1997–2007; and Kongjian Yu and Dihua Li, *The Road to Urban Landscape: A Dialogue with Mayors* (Beijing: China Architecture & Building Press), 2003.

15

Kongjian Yu, "Security Patterns in Landscape Planning: With a Case in South China," doctoral thesis, Harvard University Graduate School of Design, May 1995. Yu makes a distinction between the recorded title of his doctoral thesis and that of his doctoral dissertation "Security Patterns and Surface Model in Landscape Planning," advised by Professors Carl Steinitz, Richard Forman, and Stephen Ervin, and dated June 1, 1995.

16

Carl Steinitz, interview with the author, January 20, 2011. For more on the genealogy of western conceptions of landscape planning that Steinitz made available to Yu, from Loudon and Lenné through Olmsted and Elliot, see Carl Steinitz, "Landscape Planning: A Brief History of Influential Ideas," *Journal of Landscape Architecture* (Spring 2008): 68–74.

17

Kongjian Yu, "Security Patterns and Surface Model in Landscape Planning," *Landscape and Urban Planning* 36, no. 5 (1996): 1–17; and Kongjian Yu, "Ecological Security Patterns in Landscape and GIS Application," *Geographic Information Sciences* 1, no. 2 (1996): 88–102.

18

For more on Yu/Turenscape's regional planning projects, see Kelly Shannon, "(R)evolutionary Ecological Infrastructures," in *Designed Ecologies: The Landscape Architecture of Kongjian Yu*, ed. William Saunders (Basel: Birkhäuser, 2012), 200–21.

UTTERLY URBAN —*Jörg Rekittke*

It is not easy to specify the exact point in time when urban thinkers and designers began to distinguish—in the requisite politically correct manner—between the formal city and the informal city. Beyond doubt, an essential part of pioneering scholarly as well as applied projects was initiated in the 1960s and the 1970s. Chronological exactitude is not crucial for this contribution, and for the purpose of basic understanding we need not to dig much deeper than to what a free online etymology dictionary would do for us. Somewhere at the beginning of the nineteenth century the term *shantytown* emerged. Ostracized as a pejorative, it originates from the Canadian French word *chantier*, meaning "lumberjack's headquarters." *Chantier* in turn has its roots in the Latin word *cantherius*, meaning "rafter" or "frame"—which is still, to the point, in relation to the global and historical majoritarian construction method of informal shelters.[1] (FIG. 1) Informality is not confined to places of poverty, and every city has a formal and informal sector, but when we hear professional colleagues speaking of shantytowns or urban informal settlements, they seldom refer to something pecunious or exaggeratedly desirable.[2] Informal settlements, rather, stand for disputable to miserable living conditions for the have-nots—informally built, perishable, and lacking essential infrastructure.

The Germans found a stunningly pictorial way of interpreting the term shantytown: they tag the neighborhoods of the urban poor *Elendsviertel*, meaning "calamitous or squalid neighborhoods." Almost no exponent of the German postwar generations ever saw such miserable city quarters with his or her own eyes yet all seem to have deeply internalized that the late Mother Teresa dedicated herself and her life to the pitiable people living in the many *Elendsviertel*—slums—of Kolkata. Today the word *slum* makes its career and becomes almost inflationary, pivotally popularized by authors who write bestselling books with titles like *Planet of Slums* and film directors who create blockbuster movies like *Slumdog Millionaire*.[3] Interestingly, while the oldest of informal settlements were the medieval structures of many European cities, today the globalized world community widely seems to agree with the educated view that slums are mainly a problem of the Global South, geographically describing nothing more than what they are no longer allowed to pleasurably call third world.[4] We now are solicited to use the term *emerging countries*, but all this logomachy is of course only tokenistic.

FIG. 1 — The shantytown (*Barackenstadt*) called Freistadt Barackia, Berlin, cleared by the royal police in September 1872. Drawing by L. Loeffler, 1872.
(*Max Ring, "Ein Besuch in Barackia,"* Die Gartenlaube, *28 [1872]: 458–61*).

When searching for a more innocuous explanation of what slums—correctly informal settlements, which are urban neighborhoods or districts that coexist but are not synonymous with squatter settlements and slums—are, the publications of UN-HABITAT appear to be a safe haven.[5] According to the operational definition of the United Nations Human Settlements Programme, a *slum* is an area that combines five essential characteristics: inadequate access to safe water, inadequate access to sanitation and other infrastructure, poor structural quality of housing, overcrowding, and insecure residential status.[6] The congenial character of this definition is constituted by its universal geographical applicability and unwound impartiality. Aside from featuring this quality, the formulation gives us a broad hint that it is rather the urban than the rural environment that is predispositioned for slums.

The problem of overcrowding is, without any doubt, an urban classic. In 2001 an estimated one billion people lived in urban slums; the projection for the year 2030 is a gross number of two billion slum dwellers across the globe, if no significant changes take place—what realists, assumedly, wouldn't put a signature under.[7] The media-stimulated doxology of glittering New-Asian city life with laser shows, fireworks, and popping champagne corks, in Singapore et al., detracts from the ubiquitous but suppressed reverse of the rapid worldwide urbanization process. In the megacities of the Global South, the thing one would call classic *urbanity*—the term *urbanity* originally meant "life in Rome" (*Urbs* meaning Rome), tantamount to refinement, city fashion, elegance, and courtesy—are reserved to the minority of the pecunious caste. The other side of the coin is dominant, shady, filthy, and rather unattractive for the middlebrow as well as the dressed-up, designer type of professional.

Asia dominates the global picture of the shady side of fast urban growth and overcrowding with 60 percent of the world's total slum dwellers.[8] Working on the topic of informal settlements, and doing so in Asia, thus seems to make sense. The significance of Asian cities in this field is unsurprising. In 2001 Rem Koolhaas's Harvard Project on the City released the book *Mutations* and pointed out that twenty-seven of the thirty-three megalopolises predicted in 2015—one year previous to the publication of the book at hand—will be located in the least developed countries, including nineteen in Asia.[9] Informal settlements can crop up everywhere but they particularly catch everybody's eye in veritable big cities.

Such cities are commonly called *megacities* and they exhibit populations in excess of eight million. The very largest megacities in the world, featuring more than twenty million inhabitants, may be called *hypercities*.[10]

The terminology is circumstantial, what matters at this point is the fact that such urban giants constitute contemporary epicenters of urban poverty. It is not hard to guess in what kind of housing type the urban poor are mainly living in such places, they indwell self-built informal settlements. The incredibly versatile and basically tinkered occurrences of informal urbanism are not mishaps, abscesses, or temporary inconveniences in the formal context of very large cities. They are simply natural ingredients of genuinely urban places. Most cities in developing countries are actually economically unsustainable without them.[11] It appears to be coherent that authors with their horizon of experience grounded in the urbanized Global South are especially able to enunciate the sober actuality that the formal sector and the informal sector are two important constituents in a city.[12] They *make* the big city. Many functions in a megaurban environment are unplanned and might even not be projectable. What emerge are encroachments, informal businesses, and informal settlements, which represent and house these missing functions. Those functions are needed and in demand by the low-income masses; thus they reappear even after having been chased off, relocated, or otherwise eliminated in the short-term. The urban informal sector has to be understood as an established function of urbanity, pervasive poverty, rural-to-urban migration, and unemployment. The elimination of these underlying roots seems to be largely unlikely, especially in the context of developing countries.[13]

In 2011, Kim Dovey and Ross King conducted significant research on the ways informal settlements emerge within the spatial morphology of the city.[14] They point out that informal settlements are not entirely unplanned or undesigned, because they are a result of strategic speculative action by those who build and use them, the residents. Dovey and King also emphasize that the vast majority of informal settlements become permanent over time. The researchers found a convincing way of categorizing eight morphological types and urban conditions of informal settlements—out of a potential hundred—representing the major forces at play in informal urbanism: districts, waterfronts, escarpments, easements, sidewalks, adherences, backstages, and enclosures.

In the context of the contribution at hand, we try to see the world through the eyes of an urban landscape architect and will focus upon those categories that embody the enviable urban landscape building skills of the many anonymous informal settlers. These people are unfeigned urbanites, largely without the *freedom of the city*, meaning formal citizenship, but intrinsically urban. In the formal planning context they would represent those who we like to sedate with well-intentioned public participatory processes, when intending to build the formal city and formal urban landscape. Apparently, informal settlers build forms of successful and lasting cities without waiting for well-meant advice from professionals—certainly not from the formally trained design disciplines such as architects, urban designers, or landscape designers. Is this barefaced ostracism of our noble guilds maybe one of the most important drivers for the exigency to assiduously distinguish formal urbanism from informal urbanism? Us and them—we, who so pensively plan urban quality for the people; they, who imprudently knock the city together for themselves? This stance might not be all too far-fetched. It became consolidated knowledge that in the medium term the global growth rate of informal settlements will remain higher than any other form of urban development. All this will happen with or without us. The formal urbanist has to face the keen competition and must accept that it is indispensable to deal with this mighty informal counterpart. Not only that the many informal city builders dare to deliver design work free of charge, they also build in a breathtakingly venturesome and unabashed manner—where a city should and could not be built, according to the imagination of the educated formal designer and urban environmentalist. No waterfront can be too vulnerable, no escarpment too perilous, no easement too forbidding, no sidewalk too crowded, no interstice too narrow, and no backstage location too inapproachable—so as not to engineer a piece of informal dwelling on it.

We may salute these unregistered amateur master builders—they are the ones who use scarce urban land resources to fullest capacity, they reuse every little scrap of material they can find. Eventually they cannot afford to waste anything in an unsustainable way. Relevant research shows that a good deal of the urban poor never succeed in overcoming their financial shortcoming, thus they will not unduly contribute to rising car sales figures, carbon dioxide emissions, rising sea levels, or public health expenditures.[15] Poverty could be mistaken for a pretty ecological lifestyle with a minimum ecological footprint. As it happens, many urban villages built by informal settlers can be thoroughly regarded as quasi ideal, functionally diverse, low-rise, high-density neighborhoods of great centrality, widely car-free and walkable, rather family- and child-friendly and under a remarkable degree of social control—unmatched by any suburban middle-class residential area in this world.[16] Accusations of a sunshine-and-roses attitude or academic cynicism would be mistimed, as long as we limit our reflection

FIG. 2 — A composite of urban waste and natural landscape makes the riverbed of the Ciliwung River, one of thirteen major rivers flowing through Jakarta.
Photo by Jörg Rekittke, 2013.

to the overground parts of such informal city areas and resolutely blank out those things that a formal city builder would hopefully install underground.

Examining informal city environments below the belt will, in contrast, result in a more prosaic view. A large part of the waste and sewage of every description, coming from the informal settlements of the world, does not find its way into the systems of any public utility company. (**FIG. 2**) In the Indonesian megacity of Jakarta, like many other places of the Global South, this cannot even be regarded as a typical issue of the informal part of the city. Superficially, Jakarta looks more *modern* every day, housing more than ten million people and counting, but a coherent sewage system is virtually nonexistent—city wide. Less than 3 percent of the entire city has a serious sewage connection.[17] Each day, more than seven hundred tons of human waste goes directly into the ground or waterways without being processed.[18] Sitting on a gilded toilet seat in a Jakartan five-star hotel, the gentle guest has to be aware of the actuality that all dejecta will most probably end up in the local soil, groundwater, rivers, or sea. To complete the dainty picture, we should not forget that Jakarta's population produces more than six thousand tons of trash a day, of which around 20 percent end up in local rivers, canals, and waterways.[19] Exact figures are irrelevant, and in this case we are just dealing with a single example, one city in one country of the developing world; extrapolating these numbers, we get an uneasy sense of what is really happening out there. All this deficiency is profoundly trivial—not surprising, shocking, appalling, or beyond comprehension. It is utterly urban.

Utterly urban places are challenging *topoi*. They simultaneously display both sides of the urban coin—Beauty and the Beast.[20] They prove to be improper to direct the visitor's view on isolated postcard impressions and accurately marketed flagship localities, because *the other 90 percent* incessantly elbow their way into the picture.[21] This can be reassuring, since it drastically demonstrates that there is more to create than a generic caffè-latte urbanism for the former 10 percent, willingly residing in those *most livable* cities being ranked in the *Monocle* lifestyle magazine or the weekly newspaper the *Economist*. The British weekly claims that the concept of livability would be simple, merely assessing which locations around the world provide the best or the worst living conditions.[22] The top ten collection varies yearly but ever radiates the aura of old friends. In its Quality of Life Survey 2014, *Monocle* ranks Copenhagen at the top, followed by Tokyo, Melbourne, Stockholm, Helsinki, Vienna, Zurich, Munich, Kyoto, and Fukuoka.[23] The *Economist* Intelligence Unit's Liveability Ranking 2013 is headed by Melbourne, followed by Vienna, Vancouver, Toronto, Calgary, Adelaide, Sydney, Helsinki, Perth, and Auckland.[24] Living or working in these destinations doesn't necessitate daily sparring with all too-poor people—informal settlements are rather uncommon and medical facilities unrivaled. What spatial designers prefer to do there is bringing the next waterfront to perfection, building the highest residential tower of the city, region, country, or continent, excogitating freeform shaped museums and going for interior design awards and the like. While that's all right and any kind of moralizing categorically bugs, for all that, it does not require a cynic's midlife crisis to feel saturated with accordant stereotypes.

Herbert A. Simon noticeably imposes on us in a postulating way, reminding us that designing means devising courses of action aimed at changing existing situations into preferred ones.[25] Not only in the urban design context, the achievement of a preferred situation strictly calls for an existing, genuinely problematic situation. It is manageable to change anything, anytime, anywhere, but design action is primarily great if it is needed and makes sense.[26] Read today and by urbanists, authors like Simon and Victor Papanek seem to kick the ball to those corners of the global urban field, which are poorly illuminated by the popular floodlight, yet full of issues that could be converted into something better. Deciding where in this world to start much needed design work is effortless. This is what rankings are good for.

Here are the bottom ten cities, out of 140, in the *Economist* Intelligence Unit's Liveability Ranking 2013: Tehran is only undermatched by Douala, Tripoli, Karachi, Algiers, Harare, Lagos, Port Moresby, Dhaka, and Damascus.

Damascus currently heads our unwritten academic top ten list of cities where talented design students should try to cut their teeth—in throngs. Considered to be among the oldest continually inhabited cities in the world, Damascus was an important cultural and commercial center, located at the crossroads of the Orient and the Occident. Listed as World Heritage since 1979, and as World Heritage in Danger since 2013, the city is currently ground up by the Syrian Civil War, which started when popular protests grew nationwide in 2011.[27] Syrian neoliberal public policies led to heavy inequalities between the privileged centers and deprived peripheries of its cities.[28] As guaranteed in all cities on our unwritten academic top ten list, Damascus sports a growing quantity of informal settlements for the poor, contrasting with gentrifying neighborhoods for the well off.[29] The Syrian Civil War triggered an illegal construction boom, numerous infringements took place in formal zones while in informal zones construction soared. In times of trouble, households tend to divert investment to real estate—no matter what degree of formality it manifests.[30] Urban designers are part of the political landscape, their plans and outcomes can be used as a weapon. In Syria this happens by destroying opponents' houses, bombarding the quarters held by the armed opposition, and by drawing up demolition and reconstruction of specific neighborhoods.[31] War is a tough designer and exacts a good deal of subsequent design work in the course of reconstruction—ideally conducted by professional designers. Nothing prevents us from conceiving an academic postwar studio on Damascus betimes with the proposed working title *Mother of All Cities*.

Dhaka, Bangladesh, comes in second on the bottom ten list—which applies to 2014 as well. The city, like the entire country, continues to face substantial challenges of congestion, poverty, overpopulation, and pollution. Relevant reports periodically affirm that Bangladesh will be among the most affected countries in South Asia by an expected rise in the world's average temperatures, rising sea levels, more extreme heat, and more intense cyclones.[32] This cataclysmal hand— the forces of nature are a mighty designer, just as is war—threatens food production, livelihoods, and infrastructure. Into the bargain, it also comes in second on the total *flood vulnerability index* (FVI), a global ranking of coastal cities for future best and worst scenarios, published by Dutch water specialists from the UNESCO-IHE Institute for Water Education.[33] Thus, Dhaka is yet another pre-destined stomping place for utter urbanists, who accept that urbanity is more than what advertising shows and that the city is constantly built and rebuilt with or without them, formally and informally. Budgets, as well as five-star airlines, will bring everybody there. Here a studio working title for a project could be *Utterly*

FIG. 3 — In Mumbai, a gigantic concrete pipe discharges raw sewage from a prime neighborhood into Mahim Bay. At night the pipe surface becomes an open toilet for nearby slum dwellers.
Photo by Jörg Rekittke, 2014.

Urban Worst-Case. Third on the great bottom list is Port Moresby. Before formulating a potential studio title for this three-hundred-thousand-people-strong city—the many informal settlers not included—we have to look up where it is.

It remains a major task to figure out what kind of projects the informal settlements a fine landscape designer should tackle, in order to avoid doing things that armies of informal builders do anyway. The identification of the right manhole is necessary to avoid capitalist fetch and carry, adding insult to injury or lapsing into petty do-gooder actionism. Focusing on the urban bottom and working bottom-down from there definitely makes sense. The bottom of a contemporary city is neither the ground-floor level of its building layer nor the trivial street or landscape surface, it is the underground ecology and man-made infrastructure that provides essential necessities, first and foremost being vital drinking water for the city residents and users. The second most important function of these widely invisible networks is the controlled disposal of sewage. Together with a functioning aboveground waste disposal system, these are the three most basic parameters that can save the local and wider urban environment from long-term contamination and make civilized forms of urban life and society possible. Unless this basic infrastructure is operational, we will just be dealing with urban forms that are everything but applaudable, sustainable, resilient, etc.

As mentioned before, numerous cities have already been built—without functioning underground infrastructure. (**FIG. 3**) The necessary trenching works will be terribly delicate and dirty at all points. This is not a distress call for the mobilization of civil engineers but rather for what might fall in the category of *urbanism beyond engineering*.[34] Here is the pleading of another landscape architect to an axiomatic shifting of our urban projects with regards to content. In lieu of indulging in our favorite pastime—planting trees, paving the surface and garnishing it with voguish street furniture—we are free to focus on urbanization's back and excreta first. "Shit is the most potent example of urban flows," as Pierre Bélanger puts it.[35] Dirt becomes soil and the landscape profession's basic element always was and always will be intrinsically tied to the different manifestations of soil. Forever, in the past and in the future, landscape and its ecological function was and will be the starting substance of every city development and urbanization process. When urbanization comes about, landscape is used, changed, transformed, exploited, and frequently worn to a nub. Whatever happens to the original landscape in the course of any urbanization process, no matter how positively or negatively, the underlying

FIG. 4 — Changing water levels of urban river floods define a "Horizontal Urban Trim Line" that forces designers to thoroughly focus everything, which lies below, because it is influenced by temporary "river occurrence." Everything above the trim line is less essential, widely substitutable and rather insignificant.
Graphic by Jörg Rekittke, 2013.

landscape—constituted by its manifold parameters and strata—will never cease to exist. It will always be relevant and significantly determine the layout, the function, and the potential of any urban development. Even the most dense, engineered, and affluent city remains closely related to its natural derivation and natural influencing factors. Landscape configuration, climate, hydrologic balance, topography, flora and fauna, and geographic location are, among others, essential factors that can never be completely overridden or neutralized. Landscapes are ceaseless. Their inextinguishability is the most relevant quality of any urban landscape and makes utterly urban places, very large cities where significant portions of the urban environment sprout in total absence of plans, planners, or professional architectural designers, important remits for the landscape profession.

On that score, we had precious opportunities to operate in the megacity of Jakarta.[36] Besides learning to live with an endless number of unsolved and often unsolvable-looking issues, we became admirers of the way the local people cope with the recurrent, cataclysmic tropical floods of fatal regularity. Topography and height matter and not a single design intervention makes sense if it doesn't meet the axiomatic parameters of the local urban water regime. There is a virtual "Horizontal Urban Trim Line" that forces landscape architects to focus and thoroughly design everything below it, and forgives them for disregarding everything above it, because it is comparatively substitutable and rather insignificant—seen from an urbanist perspective.[37] (**FIG. 4**) Like water levels horizontally equalize vast urban environments and the scope of urbanism itself—in Jakarta and other delta cities of the Global South—essential environmental issues like drinking water availability, water quality, sewage treatment, and waste management will equalize the hierarchy of importance in global urban design decision making processes in the future. To even begin to firstly understand and subsequently propose suitable interventions, the utterly urban landscape designer must dig deep—literally.

Notes

1
Douglas Harper, "Shanty," *Online Etymology Dictionary*, accessed March 15, 2014, http://www.etymonline.com/index.php?term=shanty&allowed_in_frame=0.

2
Kim Dovey and Ross King, "Forms of Informality: Morphology and Visibility of Informal Settlements," *Built Environment* 37, no. 1 (March 2011): 11–29.

3
Mike Davis, *Planet of Slums* (London: Verso, 2006); *Slumdog Millionaire*, directed by Danny Boyle (Burbank, CA: Warner Bros./Fox Searchlight Pictures, 2008).

4
Dovey and King, "Forms of Informality"; Manfred B. Steger, *Globalization: A Very Short Introduction*, 2nd ed. (Oxford: Oxford University Press, 2009).

5
Ibid.; United Nations Human Settlements Programme, *The Challenge of Slums: Global Report on Human Settlements 2003* (London: Earthscan Publications, 2003).

6
Ibid.

7
United Nations Development Programme, *Investing in Development: A Practical Plan to Achieve the Millennium Development Goals* (London: Earthscan Publications, 2005).

8
United Nations Human Settlements Programme.

9
Françine Fort and Michel Jacques, eds., *Mutations* (Barcelona: ACTAR, 2000).

10
Davies, *Planet of Slums*.

11
Dovey and King, "Forms of Informality."

12
Akshay Prabhakar Patil and Alpana R. Dongre, "An Approach for Understanding Encroachments in the Urban Environment Based on Complexity Science," *Urban Design International* 19 (2014): 1, 50–65.

13
Ibid.

14
Dovey and King, "Forms of Informality."

15
David E. Bloom, David Canning, and Jaypee Sevilla, "Geography and Poverty Traps," *Journal of Economic Growth* 8 (2003): 355–78.

16
Triatno Yudo Harjoko, *Urban Kampung: Its Genesis and Transformation into Metropolis, with particular reference to Penggilingan in Jakarta* (Saarbrücken: VDM, 2003).

17
Hera Diani, "The Sewage," "Water Worries," special issue, *Jakarta Globe*, July 25–26, 2009, 10–11.

18
Ibid.

19
Kafil Yamin, "The Garbage," "Water Worries," special issue, *Jakarta Globe*, July 25–26, 2009, 12–13.

20
Jörg Rekittke, "Beauty and the Beast," in *Abstracts ECLAS 2011 Conference Sheffield, Ethics/Aesthetics*, compiled by C. Dee, K. Gill, A. Jorgensen, Department of Landscape, University of Sheffield, 2011.

21
Cynthia E. Smith, ed., *Design for the Other 90%* (New York: Cooper-Hewitt, National Design Museum, with Assouline, 2007), exhibition catalog.

22
The *Economist* Intelligence Unit, A Summary of the Liveability Ranking and Overview: August 2013, Toronto Financial Services Alliance, accessed July 22, 2015, http://www.tfsa.ca/storage/reports/Liveability_rankings_Promotional_August_2013.pdf.

23
Monocle Quality of Life Survey 2014, Monocle,

accessed August 25, 2015, http://monocle.com /film/affairs/quality-of-life-survey-2014/.

24
The *Economist* Intelligence Unit: August 2013.

25
Herbert A. Simon, *The Sciences of the Artificial* (Cambridge, MA: MIT Press, 1968).

26
Victor Papanek, *Design for the Real World: Human Ecology and Social Change*, 2nd ed. (Chicago: Academy Chicago Publishers, 1984).

27
UNESCO, *Ancient City of Damascus*. http:// whc.unesco.org/en/list/20; UNESCO, *List of World Heritage in Danger*, accessed March 1, 2014, http://whc.unesco.org/en/danger/.

28
Balsam Ahmad and Yannick Sudermann, *Syria's Contrasting Neighbourhoods: Gentrification and Informal Settlements Juxtaposed*. St Andrews Papers on Contemporary Syria (Boulder, CO: Lynne Rienner Publishers, 2012).

29
Ibid.

30
Valérie Clerc, "Informal Settlements in the Syrian Conflict: Urban Planning as a Weapon," *Built Environment* 40, no. 1 (March 2014): 34–51.

31
Ibid.

32
The World Bank, *Turn Down the Heat: Climate Extremes, Regional Impacts, and the Case for*

Resilience (Washington, DC: World Bank, 2013).

33
S. F. Balica, N. G. Wright, and F. van der Meulen, "A Flood Vulnerability Index for Coastal Cities and Its Use in Assessing Climate Change Impacts," *Natural Hazards: Journal of the International Society for the Prevention and Mitigation of Natural Hazards* (2012), accessed August 25, 2015, http://link.springer.com /article/10.1007/s11069-012-0234-1.

34
Pierre Bélanger, *Landscape Infrastructure: Urbanism Beyond Engineering*, doctoral thesis, Wageningen University and Research Centre, 2013.

35
Ibid.

36
Christophe Girot and Jörg Rekittke, "The Landscape Challenge: The Case of Cali Ciliwung in Jakarta," in "Water and the City," special issue, *Citygreen* 5 (2012): 148–53.

37
Jörg Rekittke, "Being in Deep Urban Water: Finding the Horizontal Urban Trim Line, Jakarta, Indonesia" in *Water Urbanisms East. Emerging Practices and Age-Old Traditions*, UFO Explorations of Urbanism 3, ed. Kelly Shannon, and Bruno de Meulder (Zurich: Park Books, 2013), 80–91.

PART 2 —————

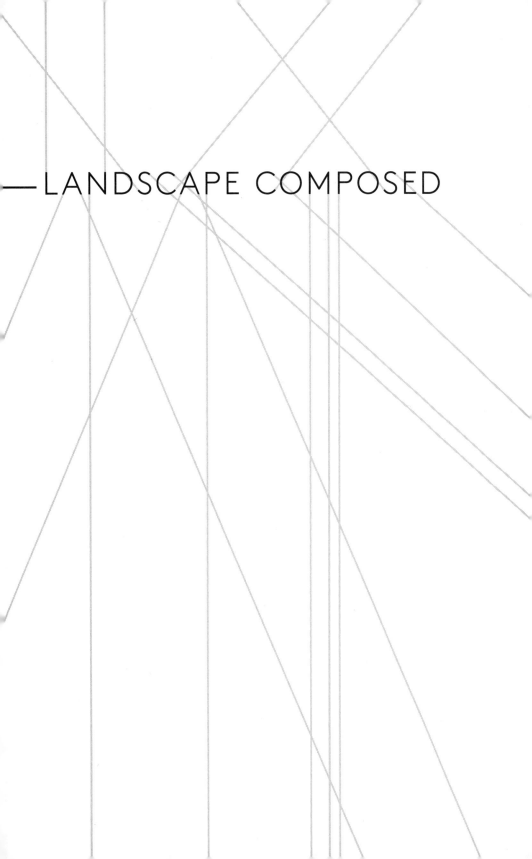

—LANDSCAPE COMPOSED

THE THICK AND THE THIN OF IT
—*James Corner*

A persistent theme in landscape architecture is the apparent tension between the specificity of locale and place (*regionalism*) with the more universal cosmopolitanism of globalization. In this regard, important issues surrounding contemporary urbanization, environment, and culture are foregrounded.[1] However, when viewed from the point of view of design practice, other issues circle around the actual conception and making of projects, and the "how to" of approaching sites and programs in a world both local and global—both native and foreign. Here specific techniques of thinking and doing that help us to approach the reading and writing of sites to produce new forms of work are especially important, particularly those that pointedly address the nuances of site and locality alongside and within an inevitably interconnected world.

The topic of technique in design, and specifically the various methods of working with sites through layers and imaging, underlies some of the most interesting research in the field today. As Christophe Girot has noted:

> The tendency to work through landscape analysis and design in separate layers of information, combined with highly evocative photomontages, has enabled the transfer of an idea of nature from one place to the next without particular regard for the cultural specificity of a place.[2]

The suggestion is that analytical layering has become so pervasive a technique that it easily overlooks local specificity and difference, and leads Girot to conclude that:

> Landscape Architecture will be considerably reinforced with new methods of design, but only if we pay attention to the deeper poetic and philosophical meaning of a terrain and grasp as much about its actual making as its inherent meaning.[3]

Here the emphasis invokes layering, imaging, and making as key techniques of design, but raises questions about universal versus more situational application, as well as representational versus formal work. There is also a critical inference that perhaps once there is too good a technique, too well known and universal a technique, then the more design becomes the same the world over, and the less that design technique is specifically responsive and adapted to local circumstance. Moreover, if a particular place in the world is indeed a uniquely thickened quarry of residues accumulated over time, as in a kind of highly specific stratigraphy or archaeology, then design layering works either to leverage and contribute creatively to that quarry, or to erase, reduce, and overwrite it. Both extremes have positive and negative attributes: the place-bound approach may well result in enhanced meaning and renewed legibility, on the one hand, but also to claustrophobic inertia, nostalgia, and repetition on the other; alternatively, the overwriting approach may well result in novel and emancipated sets of new possibility on the one hand, but also to universalist homogenization and sameness on the other.

To delve a little further into these various possibilities and the various applications of site interpretation and design, let's begin with Girot's assertion that certain techniques in design (specifically layering and photomontage) have become so pervasive that they are no longer helpful in working with local nuances of place. Certainly when one surveys much of the professional work going on around the world today, one can see formulaic uses of layering and imaging as techniques of strategy, composition, and communication. It has become a commonplace from graduate design studios to most professional offices to delaminate and deconstruct the site plan into various systems and typologies. There is also an equally pervasive use of 3-D imaging techniques (computer generated models and Adobe Photoshop renderings—most of which are less spatial than perspectival and scenic, more shape and mood, generally happy and sunny, but increasingly placeless and seemingly could be anywhere). Many of these techniques are driving the production of self-similar, large-scale landscapes and cities around the world—no more shockingly so than in the rapid fire development zones of Asia and the Middle East, with an almost endless self-similarity of urban form and generic green space in a bid to be global, modern, and expedient.

Of course, none of this means that the design methods inherent to plans, layers, photomontage, and visual representation are the root of the problem. The fact that these various techniques can be so easily misappropriated and subject to thoughtless misuse, as if some sort of default recipe or formula, does not render them problematic or obsolete. After all, the plan, and its constituent layers, remains one of the most potent tools we have as landscape architects and urbanists. The plan is what allows us to seriously survey and analyze various site conditions, to organize space and program, to structure surface and material, and to put into play the foundations and physical components of a project. Plans allow us to work and think and build. The plan view, synoptic and extensive, provides a comprehensive vista of a site from above as well as a new projection on that same site—a gossamer veil or sediment that inevitably inaugurates construction. The fact that the plan is inevitably and universally "thin" runs the sure risk of

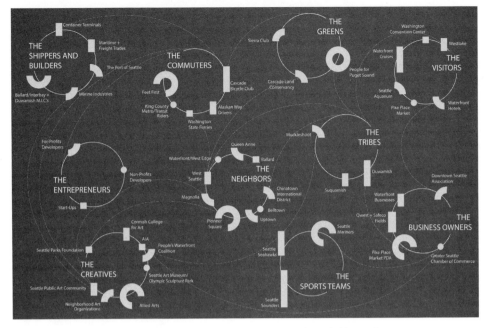

FIG. 1— James Corner Field Operations, "Seattle Agents" diagram of stakeholders and agencies invested in Seattle's waterfront, Seattle, 2012.

superficiality and overwriting, but it is also the most potent device we have for both the analysis and organization of more significant place-form.

Landscape surfaces are, of course, never as impossibly thin as the plan might suggest; landscapes have depth, accumulation, and profile. Their surfaces are sectional, textural, slow, and weighty. They are geographically highly specific and irreproducible outside of context. They are materially thick, in terms of geology, soils, hydrology, layers of foundations, and construction. They are temporally thick, in terms of complex interactive ecological processes as well as inevitable changes in state and relationship over time.[4]

Landscapes are also culturally thick, in terms of cultural modes of relationship to the land, cultural histories, stories, uses, values, and desire. North Dakota is radically different from New York, just as Hanover is not the same as Beijing or Bangkok. The differences are material, ecological, temporal, and cultural. Similarly, any project has its own context, its own material, temporal, and cultural profile, typically with many contested issues amongst competing stakeholders, viewpoints, and agendas, leading to layers of ideological dynamic and discourse. (FIG. 1)

Thus, one obvious attribute of a plan-layering technique is the parsing out and separation of all of the various layers of information that are specific to a particular place and project. Such a method aids with the analysis and understanding of otherwise super complex and overwhelming situations, while at the same time helping to communicate that same complexity to others, effectively facilitating broader participation and decision-making moving forward. This was the basis of Ian McHarg's famed "layer cake" of analytical maps, intended

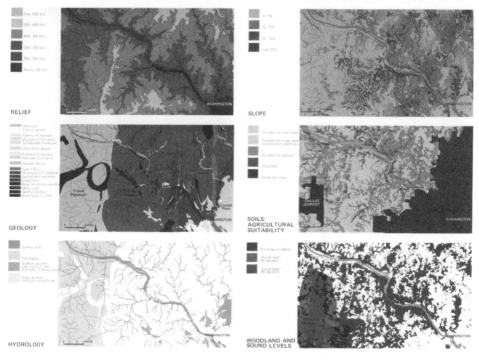

FIG. 2 — Ian L. McHarg, analytical layer maps, 1976.

to provide a rational accounting and understanding of the functioning and values of a particular landscape as a basis for subsequent planning initiatives.[5] (FIG. 2)

This use of layering to deconstruct and inform understanding is one virtue of plan analytics. However, there is also significant value to the other extreme of plan abstractions: the plan as an autonomous tool, with its own inherent set of rules and possibilities that can actually unfold alternative organizations and understandings.

If in the McHargian case, the plan analytic layers are deferential to place-specific information, the more abstract "play" with the plan parameters introduces a more "foreign" influence, an "outside" viewpoint that renders the same information in fresh and novel ways. The best example of this is Buckminster Fuller's invention of the Dymaxion projection, a technique of unfolding a map or plan in varied ways to literally deconstruct and reconstruct new sets of relationship.[6] Abstract, thin, and foreign, this device exercises enormous power upon how a highly specific situation might be viewed differently. There is nothing passive or secondary in this case but more a hyperactive form of effectively enriching, enhancing, and thickening the surface with new possibility and insight. So here we see how abstract, seemingly thin layers can ultimately "deepen" and "thicken" new alternative futures from past histories. They don't simply describe but also transform.

Similar notions of thickening a place through design layering may well resonate with many European landscape architects, especially those for whom traditions of region, terrain, site, locale, place, culture, palimpsests, and history have been central concerns for a long time now. What is less clear in this tradition, however, is the precise role of abstraction and what I shall call *foreignness* in the design process. In particular, the specificity of form, geometry, and material—what I'll call the *format*, both operational and figural—is absolutely key to defining just how productive a design will be. There is nothing natural or innate about the formation of Rome, or Versailles, or Central Park—all are elaborate and "foreign" abstractions, made and forged from specific codes of format. If an abstract format resonates with the site, amplifies and actualizes potentials, and creates new opportunities (as did Sixtus's plan for Rome, for example, centered around surrounding topographic features), then we can say that the originally thin layer will ultimately thicken and deepen a site in newly productive ways over time. Alternatively, if a format fails to resonate or adapt to a particular site or place, then it is inevitably superficial and short-lived, a mere formal pattern, an overlay with little agency or effect.

LAYERS IN INTERACTION

This idea of "layers in interaction" is useful if we first separate the base site layers from the new layers of the project. Let's begin with the notion that any existing site has an inevitable thickness, as in a complex of ecological and cultural histories and interrelationships. This might be Sébastien Marot's notion of a "sub-urbanism"—the place-specific substrates that shape, steer, and guide a particular locale.[7]

With regard to these substrates, there are various methods of design that help a landscape architect become better "grounded" in a particular place—ranging from activities such as walking, interviewing, sketching, photographing, and reading, to analytic research through measuring, inventorying, mapping, charting, and recording. This is an anthropological and ethnographic approach, if you will, with landscape architects finding ways to immerse themselves in and better understand another place, a place with which they are neither familiar with nor a native to. What the outside visitor is trying to dig through is the local "thickness" of a place—its ingrained aura, history, value, and meaning for those who most directly live there.

Whereas the visitor is always trying to better understand a local place and culture, there is always an inevitable *outsideness*—an estrangement that leads not only to a kind of alienated objectivity ("looking at" rather than "being in"), but also to unavoidable influences and affects upon the place itself. Thus, research and analysis inevitably conditions and affects their very subject; there is no innocent or objective eye. There will always be a thin veneer of deposit, seemingly abstract and foreign effects that are significantly transformative nonetheless. In spatial design terms, this import may take the form of alternative readings, geometries, measures, graticules, and foreign materials—organizational and physical formats that both are born from a place and also extending it toward new horizons.

In those same terms, this thickness can take the form of surveys, measurements, notes, sketches, photographs, maps, and analytical diagrams and layers. More experiential impressions might be documented in drawings, collages, and creative writing. Taken together, all of this research culminates in a rich and robust description of a place, allowing the outsider to step a little more delicately on the ground, and to be a more informed and credible authority. However, none of this work suggests what the designer might actually do, what it is that they might envision or propose or create. The action of doing and making change is inevitably somewhat foreign—maybe "embedded foreign" (as in an embedded agent) but foreign nonetheless. Design requires invention and transformation, not simply the repetition of descriptive data. The designer ultimately has to take the next step—envisioning the new overlay, the thin subtext that will shape the next chapter in a site's history. This new overlay can range from being incredibly sensitive and respectful of existing site substrates (Marot's "sub-urban") to being wholly new, autonomous, and overwriting structures (Marot's "super-urban" as exemplified in both Bernard Tschumi and OMA's programmatically layered plans for Paris's Parc de la Villette, for example). Perhaps there might also be a third option here, a combination or hybrid between both "sub-" and "super-" layer—a morphed amalgam, created from both inside and outside. Another way to describe this range or spectrum of approaches to site design might be to use the biological analogies of *species*, *hybrid*, and *clone*; this sequence ranges across a gradient from site dominant to foreign dominant.

SITE AS SPECIES

By analogy, a site or place is a kind of species—it has its own genotype, topology, and code (both ecological and cultural). It looks and acts a particular way, and is distinct from other species, or places. As a species, such a place essentially thrives through modest adaptation and maturation. It persists and is more or less consistent over time, though not without its phases and chapters.

We know these places well—centuries old mountain villages and countryside hamlets; old cities such as Venice or Rome; the great parks of Paris, London,

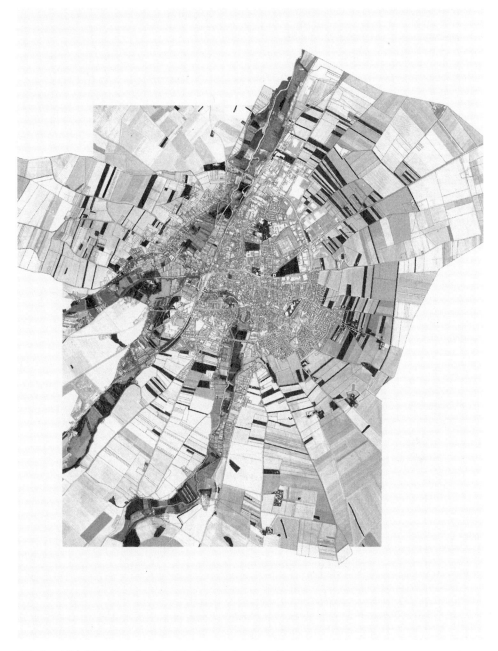

FIG. 3 — Michel Desvigne, Issoudun District Plan, Issoudun, France, 2005.

or New York. These are thick places, thickened over time, but in a more or less congruous or sympathetic way, essentially building more of the same, with only minor adaptation. And these are places that can either continue to mature and thrive, or, like any ecosystem, begin to decline and atrophy: think of Detroit, for example, once a burgeoning and successful urban fabric, now depleted, exhausted and looking for some form of renewal.

As a professional group, landscape architects tend to be innately sympathetic to site as species. They believe in site specificity and slow emergent forms of change. It is in their training (with such a huge investment in site analysis) as well as their ethos (believing in the importance of cultural and ecological continuity).

A landscape architect such as Michel Desvigne, after Michel Corajoud and others in the French school, might be so respectful as to practice a kind of site reincarnation, literally building again the traces of a landscape though substituting their material and function. This is a kind of plastic surgery, or improvement through the reappropriation of existing features. The site-species is revitalized through the injection of new material into its veins. The site is amplified and accelerated through further speciation. (FIG. 3)

Of course, the extent to which this kind of trace marking has any real agency or effect in economic, social, or ecological transformation is not always so clear. The story and the reinterpreted meaning of a landscape's "look," and its conservation, is often more important than the actual socially transformative dimension. Can such a method be seen as little more than an aestheticization of land-use pattern?

Certainly, deeper layers than just pattern are unfolded in McHarg's famous "layer cakes" that delaminate a host of natural and cultural inventories. These deconstruct the highly specific layers from the bedrock up through the soil and vegetation and up to the atmosphere and the climate. They reveal the co-dependency and interaction between each of the various material systems at work in a given place. They describe the bones, veins, and interrelational structures that undergird the metabolism of a place—and of course contemporary digital techniques can do this to an even greater extent. McHarg's method not only describes these interactions but accords value to their relative importance to the sustenance of the ecosystem. Some things could easily be changed or adapted through design; other things need to remain. It is a very powerful technique as it not only records and values resources but also reveals codependent and systemic interrelationships, establishing a deeply informational framework for subsequent planning and design. The sum of the parts is greater than the sum of the whole. The layers in interaction are more fundamental than any composite plan, a plan that is in any case formally inchoate and unstructured. It is less about formal pattern than informational and systemic process.

The limits of this method—as with all work devoted to sustaining the species—is that when it works well there can be such a strong undercurrent of intense place-form and rational coordination that everything works beautifully, but there is always the risk of habit, convention, and staleness. Without innovation or more radical (and perhaps much needed) transformation, the place form can easily fossilize, losing both relevance and effect. Without some injection of newness in the system, something foreign, the species ceases to adapt or evolve, leading to inertia or atrophy. Regulations governing how the countryside or public urban spaces should look and function often smell of a kind of sentimental heritage provincialism, wherein the implied scenic value of the "look" of a place overrides real changes in economy, function, or social exchange. In a sense, the original thickness of the place thins, softens, and congeals when the real work of meaningful transformation is held back.[8]

SITE AS HYBRID

So let's now consider a second variation—hybridization, or the overlay of something new onto something old to create a copresence that is both familiar and new. In the hybrid, crossbreeding and grafting creates a new animal, without erasing the origin of the different parents. (FIG. 4)

Now certainly the previous technique of site speciation is very familiar with landscape architects, but so too is the hybrid. Here the new layers of design are intended to *interact* with the existing ground to create a new synergy. George-Eugene Haussmann's Paris is a very good example, except for the fact that the new boulevards erased a good deal of the original fabric—but nonetheless, there is a seaming and a grafting at the scale of the city that interweaves the new with the old, radically transforming and renewing Paris for the modern age. (FIG. 5)

A different example might be Peter Latz's much-acclaimed Duisburg Nord in Germany, where new layers of access, pathway, and hydrology literally overlay and intersect the existing ruins of the former blast furnace site. It is a kind of a collage, but one where the new layer, the thin and delicate foreign import of pathways and waterways, revitalizes and renews the original and weighty base. As a hybrid, the creative reuse of old structures and abandoned functions toward new social ends is fantastic. And as an organism, the park still continues to grow and evolve—it is intentionally an unfinished and indeterminate work, aimed at continual adaptation. (FIG. 6)

Landscape surfaces are particularly good at assimilating the new layers of a project. The forces of nature can eventually subsume even the most brutal overlay, as the environment affects what survives and what doesn't. A hybrid overlay may very well take the form of collage—a collage wherein the distinction of new with old, or the distinction of the various constitutive parts, is self-evident.

FIG. 4 — Dogbird hybrid, 2012.
Animal morph by humandescent.

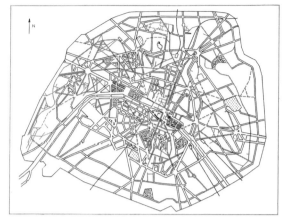

FIG. 5 — Overlay of Georges-Eugène Haussmann's new boulevards on the fabric of Paris, 2010.
Drawing by P. Couperie.

FIG. 7 — Obamabush morph, 2012–.
George W. Bush into Barack Obama video morph by PhakeNam.

FIG. 6 — Duisburg Nord, Germany, 2011.
Photo by Mark Wohlrab.

FIG. 8 — James Corner Field Operations and Diller, Scofidio+ Renfro, The High Line, new paved layers overlaid and blending with existing organic layers, New York, 2004.

In Giuseppe Arcimboldo's famous paintings of faces composed from fruits and vegetables, one sees both the face and the vegetables simultaneously—both are vivid, equally separate though uncannily united. Alternatively, a hybrid overlay may take the form of montage—a melding of one into the other, with no trace of construction, overlay, or graft. The original sources blend seamlessly into a new and strange entity. (FIG. 7)

At Duisburg, the original collagic juxtaposition has now been assimilated with time to become more of a naturalized montage. We now have a wholly new and integrated organism, both melancholic and interactive. Over time, the once collagic layers have symbiotically fused to become one system, one garden, with no trace of seaming. In a similar manner, Humphry Repton's technique of painting and overlaying "before-and-after" views effectively "morphs" a site into a new (but still familiar) arrangement. It is a site-specific hybridization of a locale reshaped according to painterly codes of scenic improvement. The beveled copper Claude glass does much the same thing—distorting and displacing the captured scene while at the same time reimaging and re-presenting it. Along the same vein, contemporary computer digital modeling techniques can allow for radically integrative overlays of forming, pleating, shaping, molding, and morphing.

In the case of the High Line, the key concept was the formation of a new filleted surface, layered over the existing railbed landscape. This new combed, integrated surface allows water, air, and grasses and flowers to bleed and grow through the seams and openings. The old original becomes assimilated into the new. Neither erased or overtaken, nor simply reproduced and copied, the design has achieved a new synthesis. Layers both old and new are refreshed and renewed through reconstitution and hybridization. (FIG. 8)

SITE AS CLONE

The final and most aggressive form of overlay might be likened to the clone. Neither original species nor hybrid form, the clone is an autonomous, universal type that can be replicated almost anywhere. It is a dominant—overtaking a site with its own strident logic.

The grid is perhaps the organizational geometry par excellence for potentially cloning the entire world. Useful for land division, measurement, plotting, demarcation, property allocation and development, the grid undergirds the structure of many cities and landscapes, especially in the United States.

The US Land Survey is a relentless overlay of thirty-six-square-mile quadrants, each with a genetic code for multiple scaling reductions to quarter-acre

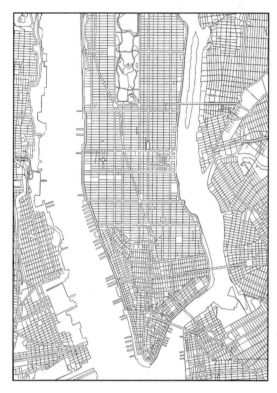

FIG. 9—
"Commissioner's Plan for
New York, 1811," redrawn.
*Museum of the City of
New York.*

lots. The grid is a clonal organism, growing, expanding, spreading—sometimes good (when it enables productive new uses), and sometimes bad (when it erases history and culture, as it did with much of the Native American Southwest, for example). And yet, in most cases, the land inevitably bleeds back, seeping up through the overlay to evolve new formations specific to place and circumstance. Even the most autonomous overlay eventually yields to time and natural process.[9]

The Manhattan grid is especially interesting. Initially an instrumental tool for simply governing property ownership and development speculation, the grid became a highly effective device for enabling a city to take shape—and to take shape in a surprisingly highly variegated way. Almost every block is the same only in plan map form—the actuality is that every block is different in terms of built grain, scale, and materialization. An otherwise monolithic and homogenous cloning technique catalyzed the creation of an extremely heterogeneous mix of spatial types, uses, and social groups. (FIG. 9)

Forestry management grids, under and over planted in phased layers over time are another example of a highly systematic but autonomous organizing system—a clonal system growing and breeding difference, variety, and complexity over time.

The grid as an enabling framework, an organizational tool to set things in motion, remains exceptionally powerful today—although sometimes its organizing function as a thin operational framework for development is over-taken when it is literally concretized monolithically as distinct from many small independent multiple accretions over time. The endless repetition of houses in developer sprawl, or Chinese housing towers cheek by jowl, exemplify the worst of rapid-fire cloning. Formulaic replication overwrites local variation and denies the kind of effervescence that occurs when free multiples can creatively respond and adapt over time.

The point here is that while cloning may seem to be the most foreign and aggressive of all approaches toward site and place, there can be merit in these autonomous systems when they are actually deployed productively as an open system, allowing for the breeding or generation of new and productive condi-tions over time. In this regard, the grid has already been cited, but two other oft-cited examples would be both the Tschumi and the OMA layered plans for the Parc La Villette. Here these very simple, universal organizational frameworks are used to grow a new site—to breed program and event over time, creating if you will a new thickness and sediment while erasing the old. Marot has called this a kind of "super-urbanism"—indifferent to site and focused more on the capac-ity of the new format to transform use, habit, and program.[10]

It is important to note that the misfitting of the layers here; the fact that the layers do not register or fit together compositionally is an important ingredient in the requirement that these systems promote mix and diversification. They are engendering machines—each layer breeding its own program component, which when overlaid creates a rich and unpredictable mix of interactions—a potential hypertext, in which all sorts of indeterminate events and readings are possible. The layers here are an attempt to turn program into a dynamic ecology, and it is indeed an ecological technique of structuring for diversification processes. After all, each layer is autonomous on its own, but becomes wholly implicated and con-comitant with other layers once fused. This is not at all unlike McHarg's ecological layers, or indeed how many ecologists would describe ecosystem dynamics today.

So here we have cloning techniques producing a kind of dynamic thick-ness over time, having very little to do with site, locale, and place, although—arguably—producing their own site, locale, and place in time. The original 2-D base deepens and thickens to grow its own milieu, which one day may very well appear as native and naturalized.

These various geometrical, organizing layers, like the grid or Haussmann's boulevards, are all primarily architectural in technique. They assume a tabula rasa (no site per se) and deploy 2-D geometry solely in the service of allocating

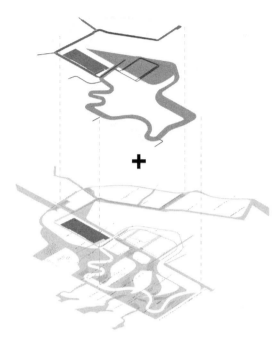

FIG. 10 — James Corner Field Operations, Downsview Park, Toronto, Canada, organizational layers, 1999.

opposite:
FIG. 11 — James Corner Field Operations, Fresh Kills Lifescape, site layers, 2004.

overleaf:
FIG. 12 — James Corner Field Operations, The High Line, New York, 2011.
Photo by Iwan Baan.

space to program. This is their strength. However, landscape is fundamentally different from the fixed surface of paper or concrete—it is thick, ecological, alive, dynamic, slow, and weighty. The geometries that bring life are not necessarily there to just merely demarcate surface but more to dig deep and articulate the processes that flow across that surface.

This deeper sense of digging into the site underlay Field Operation's proposal for Downsview Park, Toronto, in 1999. Here is the development of a series of organizational layer systems that are designed to produce a new living ecosystem—effectively building soil, retaining water, and growing habitat on an otherwise ecologically bereft windswept plateau. The layers are wholly coordinated with the base conditions of the site, but at the same time the plan wholly erases and reconfigures the place toward new ends. There are two key layers—one soft for the through-flows of water and organic materials, and one more formal, a thick earthwork loop for activities and programs—each with additional embedded layers that describe the actual landscape construction required to build the new surfaces, from subterranean hydrological cells, to new soil layers, to new earthworks and planting layers. A complex but orderly topology is created as a kind of groundwork for processes of occupation and growth to take root. (FIG. 10)

Similarly, at Fresh Kills, a closed landfill with barely any living soil or biodiversity, the task of the layers is to build a new thick surface over time—an ecologically engineered surface that will self-colonize and grow and adapt. Rather than a designed plan composition, the design focuses upon the various methods around which a new park may begin to take shape, flexibly and adaptively over time. The design is staged as a sequence of growth and maturation phases, with

LAYERS OF FRESH KILLS **lifescape**

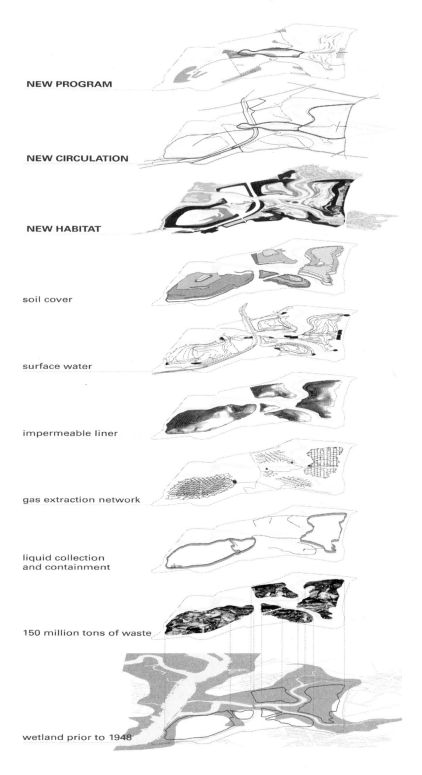

NEW PROGRAM

NEW CIRCULATION

NEW HABITAT

soil cover

surface water

impermeable liner

gas extraction network

liquid collection
and containment

150 million tons of waste

wetland prior to 1948

one stage setting the conditions for the next. The layer stack shows the multiple engineered layers of the landfill—some that exist and must remain as part of the engineered layer, and some that can be imported and made to build the new soil structure and planting communities. (FIG. 11)

The form, geometry, and operational format of these techniques and layers are super precise and important for how the park is ultimately designed as a sequence of stages. They do the same thing as many of the other layering types I have quickly reviewed except there is a lot more emphasis upon the work they are intended to do—their productive and engendering capacity to actually grow and build a new landscape, both ecological and programmatic. I would argue that this approach is more a considered combination of the site species, the hybrid overlay and the clonal agent. Time and agency are the key dynamics, deepening ecological time in the landscape medium as opposed to strictly urban planning or architectural techniques.

Similarly, as noted earlier, the High Line is conceived and constructed from layers—some concrete and inert, others living and dynamic. It is first a projection, an invention, and then a very precise and specific design detail, each formal component designed with a role in mind. Even though there is inevitably representational content (the High Line after all has such a deep story, culture, and impact), the primary functions of the layers are primarily conceived to do work, to transform. The emphasis is upon surface articulation and its thicker construction as an amalgam to produce new effects. New geometries and techniques produce new formats with new potentials that may have sufficient agency to grow, breed, and support new life and activity. (FIG. 12)

CONCLUSION

With the myriad challenges of creatively working with sites in a cosmopolitan world, the thick and the thin of it will not be resolved in this short essay. But it is important and worthwhile to conclude with this provocative if not brash suggestion: that the typically European concern for the thickness of sites, place and locale, and their parallel concern for the thin design layer as carrying primarily representational content, differs significantly from what I might call a more US-based landscape urbanist approach that places the emphasis on the transformative, catalytic, and performative effects of that thin layer, especially ecologically in depth and dynamic.

The strength of the former is the deep respect accorded to site and place—how it deepens culture through memory, hope, and desire; whereas the strength of the latter is the emphasis upon performance—how it deepens through work and productivity, through what it effectively instigates, breeds, and produces. Perhaps this comparison characterizes the broader differences, the strengths and the weaknesses, between Europe and America throughout the past century to the current day.

Notes

1

Such themes were outlined in Kenneth Frampton's seminal essay "Towards a Critical Regionalism," in *The Anti-Aesthetic: Essays on Postmodern Culture*, ed. Hal Foster (Seattle: Bay Press, 1983; repr., New York: New Press, 2002); but have also been developed with specific regard to landscape in much of John Dixon Hunt's writing on issues of site, genius loci, and placemaking.

2

Christophe Girot in his notes for the conference "Thinking the Contemporary Landscape," Hanover, Germany, 2013.

3

Ibid.

4

"Thickness" is a compelling notion in landscape architecture, and has been elaborated upon by Stan Allen with his description of the "thick-2D" in Stan Allen, *Points and Lines: Diagrams and Projects for the City* (New York: Princeton Architectural Press, 2001), and more ethnographically by Clifford Geertz in his *The Interpretation of Cultures* (New York: Basic Books, 1973).

5

Ian L. McHarg, *Design with Nature* (New York: Wiley, 1969).

6

R. Buckminster Fuller and Robert Marks, *The Dymaxion World of Buckminster Fuller*, (New York: Reinhold, 1960); and James Corner, "The Agency of Mapping," in *Mappings*, ed. Denis Cosgrove (London: Reaktion Press, 1999).

7

Sébastien Marot, *Sub-Urbanism and the Art of Memory* (London: Architectural Association, 2003).

8

W. J. T. Mitchell, ed., *Landscape and Power* (Chicago: University of Chicago Press, 1994).

9

James Corner and Alex MacLean, *Taking Measures Across the American Landscape* (New Haven, CT: Yale University Press, 1996).

10

Sébastien Marot, "Sub-Urbanism Super-Urbanism: From Central Park to La Villette," in *AA Files* 53 (London: Architectural Association, 2006).

BREAKING GROUND: A RETURN TO TOPOLOGY

—*Christophe Girot*

When speaking about the conception and making of a landscape, it is important to understand the thinking modes, the discourses, and the techniques that are applied in the course of the design and growth of a project. The current trend promotes new landscape forms under the banner of ecological design, which tends to enhance the effects of globalization over local cultural specificity. This trend comes short of convincing that it has the only infallible method and discourse for landscape design.

Landscape is all about nuances in the reading, writing, and creating of a particular ambiance and space. It is about embodying the myth of our relationship to nature, reinventing each time a particular posture and sentiment toward the world. Landscape operates first and foremost as a strong imageable and poetic reality. The techniques of design, therefore, also condition the results of a particular discourse; thinking a landscape as a set of discrete analytical layers as opposed to a single body and terrain affects both the way one approaches the physical realm and how one deals with it and decides a course of action.

The design method calling for a systematic delamination and deconstruction of landscape through a series of layered site plans invites a generic form of imaging that looks pretty much the same from one continent to the next. Mapping overlay has become so standardized, placeless, and banal that it may bring one to question what it is the images are actually depicting in the first place, and to what intent? If renders are no longer linked to the study of the physical terrain at hand, but rather to the replication and representation of established ideas about some moralizing landscape green imported from elsewhere, then what can the intrinsic cultural values of such a project be? Normative separation of landscape information in systemic layers through mapping gives a certain kind of reading about landscape, yielding results that are both specific and general—local as well as "de-territorial."[1] The method has the merit of clearly itemizing information, which then becomes readily available for a programmatic deductive decision-making process, but has the disadvantage of propagating a universal approach to landscape analysis to the detriment of other kinds of readings and inventions. A landscape is as much about differences in language and poetic expression as it is about the scientific assessment of a place. In other words, a sandwich of ideas, however appetizing it may seem, will never replace a fully crusted loaf even though both are made of bread. It is undeniable, however, that the method approaching landscape design through layers and imaging has yielded some of the most significant projects in the last half century, and if this method has been working for so long, then why challenge it in the first place?

There is reason to plead resistance to a single formulaic approach to landscape design gone global, which tends to use planar delineation and deconstructed layers to explain and interpret each and every landscape in a form of dissected reality. It betrays, more often than not, a lack of understanding of landscape as a body and as a cultural whole. As in medicine, one can either heal through dissection and ablation or work on the body and organism in its entirety. Both approaches are indeed valid, but not necessarily to be reconciled. If one dissects, one has to sew back together again, but if one works directly on the inherent force of a full body, it is the body itself that tends to its repair. The question of how we address local circumstance in a design simply cannot be left aside; it is of the essence and vital in the success of any project. The universalism claimed by the layered approach in landscape analysis and design fits well with rapidly growing cities and peripheries where cultural specificity is all too often set aside. An alternative to such a unilateral approach, topology would be a way to enter a project physically, knowingly, and locally.[2] A landscape can only be properly interpreted and designed when a proven understanding of the terrain and its physical properties has taken place. It is precisely the manner in which we apprehend a place that is at stake. If we accept as premise that a landscape is always the bearer of a clearly identifiable type, one that has grown into a culture over time, then a call for newness must always be related to type in order to make a place more significant, acceptable, and comfortable. A topological approach to landscape design invites for variations on a type; it is not about pure invention, but rather about reinterpretation through a given trope. A shift in trope determines how far a landscape type can actually drift apart from its origins without being disfigured.

Design methods have always been at the root of the problem in landscape architecture and related fields. One can read Christopher Alexander's *The Timeless Way of Building* with far more pleasure and lucidity than his overly prescriptive and stifling *A Pattern Language*, which attempts to establish axiomatic truisms to be applied to designs worldwide.[3] Landscape architecture should first and foremost be an invitation to topological intelligence and the art of terrain modeling, a practice that is currently opposed to blind and repetitive 2-D mapping methods. Ian McHarg's layered plan technique, first presented in his

<blockquote>
FIG. 1— Atelier Girot, point cloud section of Zimmermann Garden, Brissago, Switzerland, 2012.
</blockquote>

landmark book *Design with Nature*, has evolved into a questionable universal design method.[4] It was originally meant as a tool of analysis at the very large landscape regional scale, through mapping overlays of geology, hydrology, infrastructure, soil, and vegetation one could fully analyze and assess the given potential of a site. As such, the method still works well at the regional scale for impact assessments and zoning plans and helps provide a strong normative framework in future urban developments. But it is the transfer of this method to the design field that opens up a broad series of interrogations. How, for instance, can one design a landscape project without a physical terrain model of the existing site? Is it really possible to design just by using plans in layers coupled with artsy photomontages and "ecological" renders that all look alike? The question is not to deny mapping its role and place in design, but simply to say that it is lacking a fundamental dimension in physical modeling that is seldom taught in schools.

The 3-D landscape model informs us more about various physical terrain conditions than the plan; in the case of point cloud models, a site is illustrated through multiple transects and elevations that enable a far better study and understanding of the physical features of a place. (**FIG. 1**) Mapping is well adapted to organizing a program across a given site, but it misses out on the fundamental physicality of the world. The plan is useful in mapping out ideas and sketching up schemes and variants, but it cannot test the surface of a terrain and act upon it ideas that translate into design. It is, in fact, quite limited in terms of thinking and building landscape space; a point cloud terrain model, on the other hand, enables one to enter at full scale in the textured reality of a site and invites us to make careful topological reflections and examinations. Mapping is quite literally the projection of an idea in plan, whereas modeling needs to be more comprehensive and inclusive in its testing of the physical viability of that same idea. It is worthy to note that the plan was not always used as a tool of landscape design. Back in Renaissance, baroque, and early picturesque times a landscape was done with chains, poles, and ropes, and the help of range finders on-site. The overall plan was only drawn thereafter once the landscape had been made. Most early geometric and curvilinear landscape projects were traced, modeled, and tested directly on-site; some used triangulation whilst the others applied tangents on elliptical foci. The recovery of this direct physical relationship with the ground (traces notwithstanding) is what is at stake when speaking about a topological approach to landscape design.

Landscapes have always been the complex product of typological exchange between regions and local cultural invention. The fundamental difference in language and religion between cultures has never been a barrier to type, for each region acts as a specific biotic and climatic trope bringing inflection to the manner in which the type is transformed and interpreted. For instance, the evolution from the desert Maidan with its sun baked dusty courtyard in front of a mosque in a Persian caravanserai to the lush open green square of an alun-alun facing a Kraton Palace in the jungle of Central Java shows how a type can maintain its formal essence, in this case the square void as microcosm, while adapting to the changing culture and climate. The arid sands of the Persian desert become a lush lawn cut out from the jungle, and the walled square archetype in the desert become a green square framed by a dense forest canopy. The shade under the tent pole in the desert is replaced by dappled shade under twin trimmed sacred banyan trees. In spirit both places remain similar, although in essence their climatic and material tropes are diametrically opposed.

It is precisely this sense of adaptive renewal and invention that needs to be encouraged yet again today, in which we can learn to accept a varied range of tropes within a given type of landscape. This range allows for rites to be set in similar topologies, yet with marked differences expressing various traditions, stakeholders, and imperatives that can help forge anew the face of our rapidly evolving world. Landscape theory is not so much about unilateral ideological repetition and staunch, not to say positivistic methodological assertion, but much rather about topological appropriateness and mindful adaptation. Topology is not about lamenting nostalgically about some long lost nature of the origins or genius of place to be preserved under a glass bell, nor is it about glorifying some fictitious "critical regionalism" meant to brand a particular architectural provincial clan; it is more simply and directly about bringing specific and proficient answers to the design of a particular place.[5]

Ever since the first ritual meeting grounds were made at Avebury five thousand years ago, on the chalk hills of Wiltshire in England, there has constantly been the need to adapt terrain for the purpose of humankind. (FIG. 2) Thus, landscape architecture has always proceeded to modify and alter surfaces for the

FIG. 2— Avebury, Great Britain.
All photos by Christophe Girot.

purpose of society. Some archetypes have remained and been modified by various tropes, but the fact is that today few landscape architects intervene topologically anymore; this capacity has been handed over more to engineers and architects. Topology is about the mastery of the tools of physical transformation and construction on a terrain. It is not necessarily opposed to a conceptual approach but rather works as a strong physical complement in design.

Taking the case of topology further, landscape architecture has little to do with inventing new forms of landscapes at each generation; rather, it focuses on best practice and the improvement of well-established types. When J. B. Jackson shows us a picture of a forest clearing and a farm in the American West, little separates that picture from one of a forest clearing with a farmhouse chalet in Switzerland.[6] The two cultures have only a remote linguistic tie to each other, but the forest clearing as operative landscape type still prevails through both regions and times. Times do indeed change, but landscape types remain and evolve for a good reason. New York City's Central Park, for instance, is a combination of two archetypes blending a vast walled urban garden with a series of open forest clearings from within. The same could also be said of the early Dutch Beemster Polder in North Holland, which influenced the development of the Jeffersonian grid two centuries later. (**FIG. 3**)

What kind of intelligence stands behind the history of form giving in landscape architecture? And how culturally specific can a landscape culture actually be? The late Michel Corajoud brought forth a strong argument in favor of cultural difference and deference during his years teaching at the Versailles School of Landscape Architecture. He remarked that the transfer of landscape constructs from one culture to the next was probably one of the most difficult, if not impossible tasks to achieve. One could react strongly against this conjecture, which smacks of ethnocentrism, particularly to those that have studied in America and have been taught rules of environmental planning and landscape ecology that are meant to be applicable in any given situation around the world. If we are actually challenged, not to say threatened, by the hurdles Corajoud claims still exist between different regional and cultural landscape entities, where do we find the answers to these very legitimate conceptual interrogations?[7] Forms can often be understood as an oversimplification of things in landscape architecture. The French Formal Garden, for instance, sought to push our world into a rational mold where things were asked to fit into a rigid framework, the fact that it could

FIG. 3 — Road in the Beemster Polder.

neither add nor ingest other levels of complexity doomed it to failure in subsequent periods of history. But working more specifically on the shaping of forms and surfaces on the land, there is clearly such a thing as cultural specificity, the way a type is set in place differs in the manner that cut and fill are balanced as well as the art in which drainage is conducted. It all pertains to a realm of topology—call it local culture, if you will.

Topology should be an essential part of landscape architectural education to help foster conceiving and assembling a design that is both pertinent and specific to a particular place. Landscape is not about the fabrication of some piece of intact wilderness in the middle of a suburb, but about the making of a piece of nature, albeit symbolic, that is both useful and culturally significant to society. Nor are landscapes pure whimsical inventions of the moment, but rather consistent reinterpretations of established types that vary and adapt according to trope. What was invented in a place like Central Park in the mid-nineteenth century was the transfer of a habitual topology that corresponded to an ancient landscape archetype, with its trope displaced at the heart of a modern city. There is almost no abstraction in Central Park; the language used to depict the landscape is borrowed in fact from traditional sources and archetypes dating back to earlier periods of history. It is rather the topical juxtaposition within a city of a vast rectangular park that operates a leap in scale and heightens the contrast in the urban environment. A more recent park, the Parc de la Villette, built in Paris in the 1980s by the architect Bernard Tschumi, tried to reinvent itself completely as an abstract system freeing itself from type by proposing an elaborate design consisting of plan overlays based on the theory of points, lines, and planes developed by the Bauhaus artist Wassily Kandinsky.[8] Unlike the overlay system developed by Ian McHarg, which reverted to the mapping of environmental analysis, Tschumi's approach claimed to open the door to an entirely new form of design with the overlay technique. It became a widespread method taught in schools, heralding an entirely new brand of design projects abstracted from context and landscape form. The Parc de la Villette distinguished points of activity, from lines of movement and open fields and planes. (FIG. 4) The "park of the twenty-first century," as Tschumi claimed it to be, resulted in a mitigated collage of deconstructed fragments expressing layer upon layer of abstract concepts with no clear relation to site. Although the design plan overlay method continued to be taught at schools, the park itself was never reproduced as a model thereafter because

FIG. 4 — Bernard Tschumi, Parc de la Villette, Paris, France.

it failed at creating a new landscape type, and something clearly identifiable as landscape for the modern city. The Parc de la Villette instead provides a contemporary deconstructed space best suited for large cultural events; in this sense it is far removed from the contemplation of any sort of nature, albeit symbolic.

TOPICAL LANDSCAPES

What makes each landscape unique is a combination of the existing physical and natural features framed by strong cultural indicators, where history transcends and meets the local terrain. The sound grounding of a project in a particular place depends mostly on the capacity of the designer to recognize what is topical and unique to the place. The cultural weight given to a particular project over natural features depends on the degree of abstraction required, but it also appeals to the level of belief in nature that is at hand in society. These factors vary strongly from one culture to the next and from one generation to the other. The Shinto Sanctuary at Ise in Japan confers godly meaning to the spirits of the trees; the Jingu Shrine dedicated to the woodland goddess Amaterasu Ōmikami is framed by tall and timeless Hinoki trees that have been revered there over millennia. The place located in a bend of the Isuzu River is considered so sacred that it has been preserved from any kind of urbanization, but the nature embodied by these tall stands of trees and the wooden altars where people clap and pray is the product of centuries of human care. Through all the maintenance and worship, it became not so much a natural forest stand than a sanctuary of nature for people. In the Cedron Valley below the Mount of Olives in Jerusalem, the landscape stands here for major human and spiritual events past, present, and to come; the setting as burial ground is a place of desolation turned almost to desert with only a few scattered cypresses and olive trees reminding us of our presence on earth. Topical meaning here is eternal and belongs to the three monotheistic religions that inhabit the place. The topical can also transgress religion and enter the realm of the profane, it can break ground in new ways, adding or even inventing meaning outside a given tradition, but it is always grounded in a culture and language that confers deeper meaning to things.

When working on a landscape design in situ one is always breaking ground, digging, hauling, planning, and moving all kinds of soil and materials around. The art of breaking ground has always been at the very heart of landscape design, whether through the use of Theodolites as in the case of Humphry

Repton, Graphomètres as in the case of Le Nôtre, Lancy machines as in the case of Vignola, back to the Roman Groma for the Cardo Decumanus, and beyond. Each landscape epoch has been supported by the surveying technology of its time to attain the most accuracy and the best possible results on site. Topology is about accepting full physical and cultural immersion into a site through the advanced capabilities of a geographically positioned point cloud terrain model. Whether this translates into a better design depends entirely on the designer's poetic capacity to grasp a landscape in essence as a whole.

There exists no failproof method in topology, since it relies on the designer's capacity of judgment. Beyond the explicit physical properties of a site, topology always poses the question of the cultural limitations given to a designer, of the language and concept of nature that are at hand in society and that he or she has to bear and promote. The inherent limitations and risks pertaining to a layered approach to landscape design is that it systematically yields an answer to the question asked even when the designer is mostly ignorant or unfamiliar with the environment at hand. The method also presents the added risk of providing only a rudimentary ready-made moralizing ecological answer to a sometimes far more complex human and cultural environment. This is where the necessity to compliment this layered analytical method with an informed 3-D approach to site modeling and design becomes most evident. Present-day surveying techniques inherited from engineers deliver extremely precise 3-D point cloud models of sites that are remotely known. The terrestrial laser scanner (TLS) and the 3-D geographically informed point cloud model that it generates is the latest of these inventions and it is going to transform our approach to landscape design entirely in years to come. These models describe the spatial and physical properties of a place with a spatial accuracy within centimeters. There is also an extraordinary aesthetic and experiential quality linked to these models that can be scaled both within and without a site at will; this adds considerably to the physical description of landscape space and has become a very significant complement to more conventional forms of analysis and notation in design. The 3-D model confers much more control and authority on a site under investigation, where each slope and every surface and level can be considered, modified. and tested virtually. The faculty to navigate in and out of a terrain in geographically informed 3-D makes all the difference in both the approach and resolution of a design. For one thing, looking at a landscape as a full physical body to work upon provides an entirely different reading, understanding, and mode of design than a conventional 2-D layered mapping method. (**FIG. 5**) It places the designer

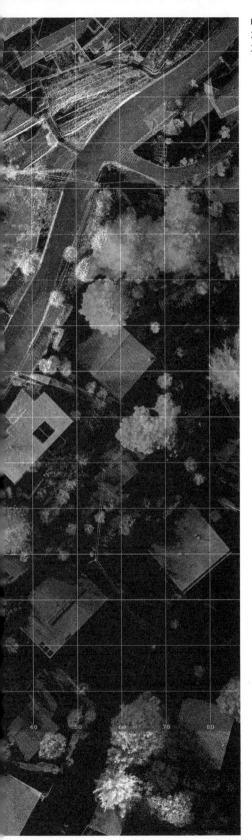

FIG. 5 — Atelier Girot, point cloud plan of Zimmermann Garden, Brissago, Switzerland, 2012.

at the heart of a virtual site and helps recognize landscape from a differentiated and subjective viewpoint. Moving within a point cloud model creates an entirely different reading of site, adding relationships and a value between things that are of a completely different order. It introduces in fact the notion of perceptual relativity in design, which is quite different than conventional modes of planning and perspectival imaging.

The contemporary point cloud model can also be an invitation to imagine a landscape in its fuller dimension, by testing various physical suggestions and inventions virtually in situ. It does not guarantee in itself good design, but provides a much better and informed vision of place. How each individual designer pursues a specific design choice results from a complex set of inclinations and decisions based on a combination of site conditions, program, and individual intuition. Coming back to the Parc de la Villette project there is an obvious lack of physical approach to design in the conceptual 2-D layered method that it promotes.[9] Despite an extremely strong discourse in plan, the project fails both in space, scale, and time to convert what it pretends to have in layers into a tangible and convincing landscape body; it works rather like an abstract collage. The paucity and limitation of this design overlay method becomes here patent, for what works brilliantly in theory and rhetoric falls short of reality on this difficult peripheral terrain in Paris. A landscape can only work as an invention if it acknowledges the type it is derived from, the high fragmentation and juxtaposition of different geometric shapes has led to an incongruous coagulum of forms at the Parc de la Villette, where the greater order of things in the park itself remains unclear. In any topical approach to landscape design, the clarity of surface topology and complementarity of scales is of the essence.

THE LANDSCAPE AS BODY

Topology reaches far beyond the reading of a landscape in stratified layers, and moves rather toward a composite reading of terrain as a single body and surface, thus bringing disparate elements and epochs back together. A designer that comes to a place for the first time comes with a cultural baggage of his or her own and is often blinded by preestablished ideas and conventions. The limitations of a given culture in reading others is difficult to accept and probably the most humbling of things. Returning to Michel Corajoud's conjecture there certainly exists a tangible cultural framing to our own reading and understanding of landscape. Being a complete foreigner to a land can sometimes be an advantage, but in most instances it isn't, and there are serious doubts as to whether any landscape tradition is exportable from one country to the next, from one language to the other, from a particular region to the next without careful consideration and meditation. How can an archetype gradually transfer from one culture to the next by exerting a significant shift in trope? This is particularly remarkable between the early Ming gardens of China and the Zen gardens of Japan, as well as between the artificially wooded gardens of Renaissance Italy and the subsequent picturesque gardens of England. The fundamental shift in landscape spirit and expression in these two comparisons is clear, although the garden types remain roughly the same. Any invention in landscape architecture needs a starting point that is by definition local and not global. In addition to cultural differences there also exist shifts in topography, climate cycles, and modes of urbanization that seriously challenges assertions about a global approach to landscape architecture whether ecological or not.

A systems approach to site planning is indeed important in the early stages of project analysis, it helps identify conflicts of interest as well as resources and is a powerful tool that enables the formulation of precise environmental policies. The approach can embrace vast environmental questions at a regional scale and can nurture a project by identifying the potential services provided; but it cannot become a substitute to creative design by giving in to formulaic answers with regard to form giving. It is a fallacy to believe that we are now able to promote a global landscape culture capable of responding to ecological trends worldwide. Such formulas inevitably come short of many local needs and expectations. It reminds one of the stylistic transfers that occurred earlier on with the English Garden style in Australia, which proved to be completely wrong for an entire continent. The very idea of transposing some triumphant pastoral landscape onto the parched and overgrazed inland hills of the capital Canberra proved the inherent limitations of such a literal landscape import. Both the McHargian overlay method and topology would have decried the Griffin Plan for the Australian capital because it spoke against any climatic and biotic reality. But the lobby in favor of "autumn color and coolness" in this very arid place had the last word. We now find kangaroos gathering and mating on the putting greens of the capital's golf course. A unilateral approach to global ecology would for instance like to claim the planting of a dense jungle on the location of a Javanese alun-alun under the pretext of environmental legitimacy but it would in a single stroke eliminate centuries of a strong societal relationship to a symbolic form of nature. The sum of the twin banyans standing in the middle of this open green square describes a powerful microcosm that cannot be simply replaced by biomass. The star landscape architect may in certain circumstances be confronted with such choices locally, and may be well advised to take into account these hidden cultural dimensions with great caution.

Topology is about working on the reappropriation of a site by making sense of its prevailing landforms and traces. The work need not be nostalgic; it must simply act on a landscape as a living body with intuition, empathy, and feeling, taking the marks and scars on a particular terrain as essential elements of the composition and understanding of a place. It would be wrong, however, to categorize topology as a rekindled form of genius loci, which praised all existing traces indiscriminately as things of eminent significance. Design requires a sense of discernment, and this school of genius loci of the 1970s and 1980s often led designers to embrace de facto a site in a completely uncritical way. Christian Norberg-Schultz's notion of genius loci was often misinterpreted and changed into a very confining, not to say claustrophobic, glorification of past features, where no overwriting or design change on a site even seemed conceivable.[10] Such a mindless conservation of all traces good and bad cannot be the point of departure of a project.

Topology acts on a terrain through eminent selection, tackling critically the very substance of a place. It looks carefully at terrain and ways of appropriating and channeling natural phenomena that occur there. Topology is local, and powerfully so in its determination to design, because it has the ability to deal physically in 3-D with terrain. The manner in which we apprehend and deal with landscape is immanent and topologically quite different in its approach to problem solving. For instance, carving a road against a given terrain at constant slope has a name in French: *plein jalon* meaning "full bearing." Entire landscapes and cities were assembled in France according to this simple rule of planning a regular surface at constant slope. This topological principle, inherited from the Roman notion of *clinamen* explained in Lucretius's writings about epicurean physics, gives in turn a specific quality and direction to the ground we tread upon.[11] An entire system of movement can be set in a landscape according to this simple rule conferring tremendous unity and power to a place by giving it a particular topological feel. This may indeed qualify what Corajoud referred to as a culturally rooted and specific act.

THE SITE AS BODY

We have entered an age, call it Anthropocene if you will, where landscape architecture now seems to be taken as the primary maker and healer of nature. But this new branding of the profession essentially into a proactive conservationist role, leaves the path wide open for other professions to take over large-scale projects that involve not only natural processes, but also cultural factors and urban infrastructure. We don't need unilateral landscape methods today—what we need is a very specific and clearly rooted approach to each particular case. It behooves us, in this highly digitalized age, to enter the realm of 3-D thinking appropriately. The point cloud model is the perfect way to familiarize oneself with the intricacies of a given site. Work on the massive artificial landscapes of the AlpTransit Sigirino Mound in Ticino, Switzerland, would not have been possible without the mastery of such tools. (FIG. 6) Thanks to this method, we were able to work in a physically integrated way with the site, solving difficult topological problems on this grafted body of fill.

Almost every site we deal with bares traces of past human events and disturbances in the natural order of things. No site is in fact virginal, and this is what makes a place significant as it varies and evolves through time, beliefs, and events in history.[12] Landscape design is all about the intention to create a strong symbolic form of nature, inducing forms capable of reconciling a broad spectrum of processes and intentions. The question is with what kind of intelligence and what kind of tools do we tackle such a delicate selection? The design choice that is made in the end needs to confirm and show how all factors old and new, natural and cultural, interact together in the physical realm. This has now become possible, and one could of course argue that good landscape designs have long been made prior to the appearance of point cloud models, and that there is, therefore, no real need for landscape architecture to enter the digital and geographically informed age of tomorrow, pleading that the layered design approach in itself suffices.

One of the best examples of a layered ecological design is most certainly the Schöneberger Südgelände project in Berlin. (FIG. 7) There, the subtle artistic layering of an elevated wooden walkway on top of a pioneer "ruderal" layer of vegetation, itself growing out of the rubble of an old bombed-out rail yard, sets an absolutely unique landscape precedent. Add to this the factor of time and decades of undisturbed spontaneous natural growth of seedlings of all sorts in between the railroad ties and we have all the ingredients of a very original "ecological" design. The elevated walkway was done in order for the visitors not to disturb the ground layer healing from the upheaval beneath their feet. The ground at the Schöneberger Südgelände is essentially composed of ballast, brick and mortar, rusted steel, and decaying wood ties that produce a terrain vague aesthetic with an extremely complex microtexture and topography of its own. The experiment as such was unique to the historic conditions of postwar Berlin,

FIG.6 — Atelier Girot, point cloud model of Sigirino Mound, Canton Ticino, Switzerland, 2003–.

particularly the way the imbricate details of the site such as contorted Siberian birches growing through the ballast of long abandoned tracks or rare ferns and ivy pushing their way through heaps of rubble in building foundations created a wonderfully desolate and romantic aesthetic of decay. It is therefore no surprise that such projects, set in the very peculiar landscape context of postwar Berlin, inspired many subsequent projects up to the High Line in New York, which itself is rather a stylistic reinterpretation of the genre than a spontaneous ecological experiment on rail tracks per se. (FIG. 8)

The High Line addresses the social ecology of Manhattan, with its unquench-able thirst for nature, in a trend that has promoted this abandoned elevated rail-road to an incredible landscape icon in recent years. The attentive design for the new promenade done by the office of James Corner Field Operations, combined with the outstanding horticultural talent of Piet Oudolf, has produced one of the most resounding successes of the last decade.[13] What is most interesting in the case of the High Line is not so much the "ecological" choice of plants displayed along the promenade that are meant to resist throngs of visitors that come by each day, but rather the specific experience of walking on this elevated path where visitors glide nonchalantly over the old Meatpacking District of Lower Manhattan on a perfectly crafted and designed surface. Unlike the example in Berlin, with its very rough microtopography, the High Line presents a smooth paved topology that frames perfectly the clean ballast with new railroad ties free of creosote and other contaminants designating new planting areas. The High Line leaves no room for spontaneous plant growth, which ironically enough was the absolute credo of the German ecologists monitoring the old abandoned rail yards of Berlin. Unless the High Line is left to its own botanical demise, the new landscape layer added on top of the old cast iron bridge structure will never resemble nor merge with the old, it is indeed a separate layer suspended above the streets of Manhattan, acting like an overlay that would not have reached the ground.

The matrix upon which our cities stand is essentially cultural and engineered; even the most natural of rivers are forced to twist and bend to comply with our cities and landscapes. The history of the Mississippi River, for instance, is a tragic succession of systematic and often unreflected encroachments on a natural

FIG.7— Natur-Park Schöneberger Südgelände, Berlin, Germany.

FIG. 8 — James Corner Field Operations, The High Line, New York.

domain. As with countless other rivers, the constructs at hand no longer match the natural forces at play. There is no reason why the next generation of projects on the Mississippi should not be directed by landscape architects trained with an averted knowledge of topology. The case of the Mississippi calls for adaptive solutions, where controlled flooding of vast acres of land should become the rule and not the exception. But who is going to hold on to the rein of such a proactive topological project if not the landscape profession? Who will lead the multidisciplinary teams and propose highly politicized solutions in this age of drastic environmental changes? As with many large-scale topics, it is clear that groundbreaking technology provided by geographically positioned point cloud models is going to revolutionize the way we work and think a project together. And it is the task of schools to foster such interdisciplinary collaborations through innovation. There is a great future ahead for topology to develop and mature in the field of landscape architecture and it is only a matter of time until it becomes the main tool of best practice. Topology should not be taken as ideology, we can all become topologists siding for certain reasoned design choices be they formal or process-oriented. Robert Smithson was once quoted as saying, "Nature is indifferent to any formal ideal."[14] It is therefore our role to impregnate a place with more meaning and respect. We need to learn how to respond to the physical qualities of a place with confidence, leaving behind the crotches of some overly cerebral graphic overlay system as we design. Topology can reconcile the act of form giving with processes in a comprehensive way by testing things in the physical dimension, and simulating events over time. Progress has been made that even enables design projects to be embedded into geographic reality. The 3-D GIS base opens a broad range of alternative possibilities for teams that can make the appropriate choices and difference.

In the case of work done by ETH students on the Ciliwung River in Jakarta, design models of an entire fluvial neighborhood were run through flood simulations to test the validity of each scheme. The results of such simulations actually sent some of the teams back to the drawing board. The point cloud method opens up an array of possibilities that will help reposition landscape architecture at the heart of major engineering projects to come. The ecological design methods that have been developed over the last decades are now being pushed into a physical dimension that will no longer necessitate thinking landscape in layers, but rather as a whole body. Topology will teach us how to use a site model that has been generated by a combination of TLS, Light Detection and Ranging (LIDAR), and drones. Through that method base material will either be added or subtracted—carved in and carved out, displaced and replaced in real time. Design will no longer rely on a simple before-and-after picture to test and demonstrate some landscape change; the point cloud model will provide the base for that change itself. Its coordinates will enable the precise assessment of quantities such as ground, built fabric, water, and vegetation, not to mention air currents, sound, and temperature. It will become a tool where design can be induced and tested repeatedly in order to refine a variety of parameters and options.

The challenges of our times call for the best possible tools of design— tools that are readily equipped to help us conceive the most appropriate solutions to come. For most of the challenges involving environmental change, contamination, erosion and waste there exist no ready-made solutions to lean upon. It is precisely by testing and reiterating new approaches to virtual reality that landscape architecture will best define the potential future of a site. The artificiality of the landscape that we deal with today has never been so great. From the Fresh Kills waste dump by Field Operations to the Sigirino Mound by Atelier Girot, it is ironic that we are asked to act "naturally" on such profoundly disturbed sites. A lot of the work in topology will remain heuristic and empirical for years to come. For instance, it has required more than ten years of testing and monitoring to determine exactly the proper mix of compost to aggregate the artificial vegetative layer of the Sigirino Mound.

The tools and methods of topology are universal and catching on worldwide, but the approach and agency proper to each place will remain determinant and unique. Our work will not only be precise, but also culturally sensitive to each case. Topology will no longer juxtapose old and new in distinct layers, but rather work them together in a binding whole. The case of the garden of the Villa Zimmermann in Brissago in Ticino shows how topology can work with the microtopology of a garden, binding seamlessly the very local scale with the regional scale of the Lago Maggiore. In this project done with surgical precision, century old dry walls are kept in continuation of new walls built for residential comfort. The slope is so steep there that it imposes a terraced topology—a landscape type as old as the first landscapes made by humankind on the hills of Judea. The terraced type is derived from the dual necessity of providing some flat terrain for cultivation, dwelling and leisure as well as to insure structure and drainage to a site. There is no new idea in a terrace, only continuity in purpose and intent. It is a universal landscape type that is always readapted to the local conditions of geology and hydrology. Some of the most exquisite and delicate landscapes we know are comprised of hanging terraced gardens, and when their purpose is sound, they are explicitly cultural, ecological, and natural. There should be a clear reason for breaking ground topologically, one that serves a purpose with clarity and intent, one that can be understood as the best expression of humankind irrespective of the faith and culture it portrays.

We live in a world of complete artifice where form giving, technique, and performance of a landscape come together under the banner of topology. The artificial nature that future generations will inherit from us will certainly evolve, but it is the proper form and ground given to these new natures that will matter most in the end. We are entering a period of change in environmental conditions that is as important and consequent as that which occurred ten thousand years ago at the onset of sedentary civilization. We are now working on the layers of detritus and rubble of past generations that will significantly influence our natural futures. It may very well be that our landscape types will need to be reconsidered and even reinvented for the occasion.

Notes

1

James Corner, "The Agency of Mapping: Speculation, Critique, and Invention, 1999" in *The Landscape Imagination: Collected Essays of James Corner 1990–2010*, ed. James Corner and Alison Bick Hirsch (New York: Princeton Architectural Press 2014), 196–239.

2

Christophe Girot, Anette Freytag, Albert Kirchengast, and Dunja Richter, eds., *Topology: Topical Thoughts on the Contemporary Landscape.* Landscript 3 (Berlin: Jovis, 2013).

3

Christopher Alexander, *The Timeless Way of Building* (Oxford: Oxford University Press, 1979); Christopher Alexander et al., *A Pattern Language: Towns, Buildings, Construction* (Oxford: Oxford University Press, 1977).

4

Ian L. McHarg, *Design with Nature* (Garden City, NY: The Natural History Press, 1969).

5

Kenneth Frampton, "Towards a Critical Regionalism: Six Points for an Architecture of Resistance" in *Anti-Aesthetic: Essays on Postmodern Culture*, ed. Hal Foster (Seattle: Bay Press, 1983), 16–30.

6

John Brinckerhoff Jackson, *Discovering the Vernacular Landscape* (New Haven, CT: Yale University Press, 1984).

7

Michel Corajoud, *Le paysage c'est l'endroit où le ciel et la terre se touchent* (Arles/Versailles: Actes Sud ENSP, 2010).

8

The book by Wassily Kandinsky *Punkt und Linie zu Fläche. Beitrag zur Analyse der malerischen*

Elemente was first published by the Verlag Albert Langen in Munich in 1926. Engl. *Point and Line to Plane*, trans. Hilla Rebay (Mineola, New York: Dover Publications, 1980).

9

Christophe Girot, *"Learning from La Villette" Documents* 2, no. 4/5 (Spring 1994): 31–41.

10

Christian Norberg-Schulz, *Genius Loci: Towards a Phenomenology of Architecture* (New York: Rizzoli, 1980).

11

Lucretius, *On the Nature of Things: De rerum natura*, trans. Anthony M. Esolen, (Baltimore: The Johns Hopkins University Press, 1995).

12

Christophe Girot, "Four Trace Concepts in Landscape Architecture" in *Recovering Landscape: Essays in Contemporary Landscape Architecture*, ed. James Corner (New York: Princeton Architectural Press 1999), 59–67.

13

James Corner, "Hunt's Haunts: History, Reception, and Criticism on the Design of the High Line, 2009" in *The Landscape Imagination: Collected Essays of James Corner 1990–2010*, ed. James Corner and Alison Bick Hirsch (New York: Princeton Architectural Press, 2014), 340–61.

14

Nancy Holt, ed., *The Writings of Robert Smithson* (New York University Press, 1979), 119.

LAND MOVEMENT—*Kathryn Gustafson*

There are many ways to think about how we create landscapes and how we feel in them. In this short essay I would like to go through where I came from, as this explains in great part how I do things today. I hail from a high pla-teau in Washington State, where there was no water beyond the edge of the river, and so no vegetation whatsoever in the great expanse of the desert. But despite that fact, these are still some of the most beautiful mountain landscapes I can remember—and as the sunrise and the sunset move through them, they become extraordinary sculptures of light and matter. I was raised in Yakima, Washington, considered by some to be the apple capital of the world. And what you find in this landscape at the foot of Mount Adams are bright green patches of irrigation—you can see the hand of man, and how he has come to change completely the natural desert, normally comprised of sagebrush (*Artemisia*) with silvery earthy beige tones. (**FIG. 1**) As I was growing up, it was important to understand the edge of irrigation, the technical threshold where it stopped and became wilderness. The Army Corps of Engineers created many of the original canals in the 1940s. Water was brought in from dammed rivers from the Cascade Mountains, and this is how an entire desert valley was transformed into a verdant agricultural valley. Is this sustainable? Is that good? The irrigation that has been going on for decades grows absolutely beautiful fruit. But, if you look at the Columbia River Basin, it is obvious that too much water is taken out for irrigation. So, no, this is not sustainable, but it has helped me understand the preciousness of water as I grew up—and showed me how land and water form a body together.

I then went to New York City to study fashion, which was all about cloak-ing the body. It taught me how the body fits and moves within that cloth, and how it captures light and turns alive. After that I moved to Paris, France, where I worked for a while in the fashion industry until I decided to change fields and began to study landscape architecture at Versailles. There I discovered two masters of landform and movement. The first was André Le Nôtre, who designed Versailles, amongst other places, and who was a genius at manipu-lating depth, levels, perspective, and the way that one actually moves through space. His work is about a pure geometry of illusion set within the scenography and sequence of a landscape. (**FIG. 2**) He is the master of French perspective and always remains in control of what you perceive. When you look at his creations,

FIG. 1— Landscape at the foot of Mount Adams, Washington State, United States.

FIG. 2— André Le Nôtre, Garden of Versailles, France.

FIG. 3— Jacques Sgard, Parc de Vincennes, Paris, France.
Photos by Kathryn Gustafson.

you are convinced that he even manipulated a piece of sky to make you believe that you are going up into it, as if there was nothing left to reach beyond that point. Le Nôtre shows control over not only the design of a landscape but also the way people move through it. The second person that taught me is Jacques Sgard. He trained Michel Corajoud, Alexandre Chemetoff, and myself, among others, in the art of landscape design. He is the absolute master of grading the curve. He marries form, vegetation, function, and art all into one piece of terrain. (**FIG. 3**) His landscapes can be understood as constructed pieces of nature that contribute beauty to cities, and create places that people can use, love, and remember.

Two other big influences in my design life are Isamu Noguchi and Dennis Oppenheim. Noguchi produced a model for a New York City park that he never built; alas, but the model shows all the refinement of his talent and craft. And not many people may know the artist Dennis Oppenheim today, but I have always found him fascinating. There are several pieces done in the 1970s that mix conceptual objects with exquisite landform. His work on the body in the land is expressed in such pieces as *Parallel Stress* (1970), *Identity Stretch* (1970–75), and *Waiting Room for the Midnight Special (A Thought Collision Factory for Ghost Ships)*, 1979. The talent with which Oppenheim marries conceptual inventiveness with sensual landform is just amazing—these are very abstract works of art, but there is a unity in them that turns them into a great piece of landscape. These are small crafts or boats that move your ideas around, and then you get into them and they spin you out and nurture you.

LANDSCAPE MODELS

I constructed my first landscape model in 1978. After training in art and going into fashion, I then came back to working with clay when studying landscape architecture. My first built landscape was the Morbras project (1986), an agricultural stormwater management piece where a lot of ground needed to be moved and shaped. We moved 300,000 cubic meters of earth around a site to create a retention pond. (FIG. 4) We were invited to work on-site as landscape architects to save money, and to avoid removing the soil off the site to be dumped on some landfill. The client wanted us to sculpt and form the land artistically, by modeling the fill soil in a creative way. We only had five months to do the design work, while the construction work was halted for the rainy season. This was the first large-scale earthmoving experiment that I did and learned many lessons from it, the first being the preeminent role that the small clay model played throughout the design and construction process.

The other piece done during the time of my Paris office is the Shell Petroleum Headquarters (1991), where we proceeded to design an abstract landscape on top of buildings that were completely covered with plants, including a four-story underground garage (FIG. 5) The project used the land movement of the artificial topography to tell a symbolic story—the story of the Shell Petroleum Company. What do they do? They go into the rock; they pull out the fluid; they refine the fluid, which delivers energy. So the landform is really intended to evoke what Shell *does*, and turns it into an iconic entry for their headquarters in Rueil-Malmaison.

We also worked on some difficult infrastructure sites in the city of Marseille, a virtual engineered mess leftover by highway construction in the late 1960s. We had a one-hundred-meter rise that went straight up the hills, with areas where the natural pine forest grew. It was located on the Highway A7, which cuts through Europe, beginning in Amsterdam and ending in Marseille. The other highway crossing runs laterally from Nice to Barcelona, and is located in an agricultural plain. How the two opposite topographies met had to be resolved through landscape form. The regional authorities were digging a tunnel elsewhere in Marseille, and had over one million cubic meters of earth they wanted me to place in this space. At the same time, they wanted a sculptural entry to

FIG. 4 — Kathryn Gustafson, Morbras Meeting Point, France, 1986.
Photo by Amyn Nasser.

FIG. 5 — Kathryn Gustafson, Shell Petroleum Headquarters, Rueil-Malmaison, France, 1991.

Marseille. The result was meant to be both an economical and cultural solution. We also had to integrate stormwater management for all the adjacent freeways in the sector; the highways generate impermeable surfaces, which need to be properly managed in case of rainstorms. This was back in 1993, at the beginning of a new type of ecological awareness. Difficult issues, such as managing vast quantities of fill, required a different process of understanding and different sets of technical solutions. When you need to put in that much soil, how then do you structure it and hold it? The drawing in figure 6a shows walls that are eight meters high, and how the fill comes in between, resulting in a water basin for the storm water management of the entire area. But I understand this work first as a sculpted piece, where the technical requirements become the sensual forms that I give them. The first model is always done in clay.

The first time Wolf Prix of Coop Himmelb(l)au saw this model, he said, "You have got to digitalize it." And I asked, "How? What does that mean?" He told me to use a program called, "formZ." To which I replied, "Okay, what do I do?" I had a small inheritance from my grandfather—I spent it in three days. I bought the computers, hired a tutor, and did this entire project digitally. So that was the first formZ model that I ever did. Now all the models are digitized, but I still create them by hand first in clay. From the clay they are then molded in resin or rubber, and from there they are poured in plaster, and then scanned in 3-D. A model from 1993 shows in volume how much water was actually coming off the roads. (FIG. 6b) The columns were set on a given horizontal line, so that when the water filled up the basin area you would see the watermarks and could actually understand the volume of the water that was flowing off the freeway surface. This allowed people to better grasp just how impermeable the land had become. During the design process we considered the site, with its local rock, and vegetation, before pulling that unifying language through the whole piece.

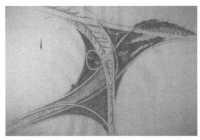

FIG. 6a (TOP) — Kathryn Gustafson, drawing of freeway interchange Les Pennes-Mirabeau, near Marseille, France, 2003. Drawing.

FIG. 6b (BOTTOM) — Kathryn Gustafson, model of freeway interchange Les Pennes-Mirabeau, near Marseille, France, 2003.

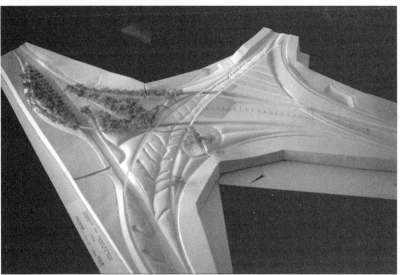

The watermarks were meant to show just how much stormwater got captured, before it seeped back and percolated into the natural water system again. In this sense it marries a conceptual and artistic approach with some early ecological concerns. This is an interesting project because you can never actually walk into this freeway landscape; it is lost among all the on-ramps and off-ramps, and so is a totally visual and sculptural experience that you get to enjoy for about ten seconds as you drive by. This brings another consideration into account; that of the eye of the observer. The actual speed at which people perceive landscape is really important. Is it a walking speed? Is it a driving speed? Is it a bicycle speed? Understanding just how much our vision can capture at these various speeds has become a new imperative and necessity in our profession.

For the Venice Architecture Biennale 2008, Aaron Betsky asked us to design a Paradise Garden. I made a small model entitled *Towards Paradise*. (FIG. 7a) The project, which blends landform with a large suspended white drapery, is about understanding the intimate scale of what people can walk through and experience as landscape, albeit reduced in form. (FIG. 7b) The actual dimensions of this land and air piece are eighty-five by forty-five meters; and depending on where you walk and how the wind plays with the suspended drapery, you are never in the same space. The control of space in design is one thing, but the continual

FIG. 7a (TOP) — Gustafson Porter/ Gustafson Guthrie Nichol, model of Towards Paradise, 11th International Architecture Biennale, Venice, Italy, 2008.

FIG. 7b (BOTTOM) — Gustafson Porter/ Gustafson Guthrie Nichol, Towards Paradise, 11th International Architecture Biennale, Venice, Italy, 2008.
Photo by Grant Smith.

transformation of that same space over time through the effects of light and wind brings forth also a completely different dimension and understanding of space. In *Towards Paradise*, you can walk into the space, walk around the sensual land-forms, or hide by lying down in the center. I call this hiding space the "place du prince." The *place du prince* is usually the place in a theater where you have the best sound and view. In this landscape, it is a sort of womb-like landform space where no one can find you. People can actually settle in this very private location, and watch the clouds fly by.

The Culture Park Westergasfabriek project in Amsterdam (1997–2004) began with sketches and then a clay model—and a difficult model to do, because the area is one kilometer long and very flat. (FIG. 8) The park also had a tremendous amount of pollution that we could not move off-site, and the polluted soil had to be placed and compacted within the lower layers of the terrain profile. We collaborated with Ove Arup Engineers in London. While Neil Porter and I worked on this model, they were calculating the volume of polluted soil that we were moving around the site. We were in Seattle at the time and would send them images and sections of the model to show how much earth we had been able to incorporate into the site that day. The Arup engineers would then do calculations, and we would wake up in the next morning to their messages of "More,

FIG. 8 — Gustafson Porter, Culture Park Westergasfabriek, Amsterdam, The Netherlands, 2004.

more, you have got to put more earth in there." There was a rail line up on one of the dikes, and we artificially raised all of the area along it. We then finalized the grading with a "life layer" above the compacted contaminated material, so now the park surface is safe.

I also like working with big models because I can *feel* where I am in space and can wander creatively around. The Westergasfabriek is a big and generous urban open space, and you can really appreciate it in the model. You can feel how the open space and landscape all of a sudden starts to turn in and fold in on itself. This I can only do with a model; I still don't know how to do that in a computer. What I truly love about a model is that it does not lie to you. It looks at you —if you have not solved a problem between two points, it will tell you. Usually, you know intuitively how to do a grading plan at any point with a clay model, but with a 3-D model and computers, you can easily forget that sensory dimension and loose touch. There are also times when computer models are incomplete and do not help the creative process—all of a sudden you have a wall in front of you and you see it on the screen, but there is a hole in the digital model, and everything goes down that black hole into infinity. With the physical model I can look at the space as a microcosm, put my little people there, and can ask: Is it too big? Is it too small? Does it fit? Does it feel right? When you build after having followed a handmade model, it is exactly what you thought it was going to look like. I think it is because you have touched it and sensed the space you are making with your own hands. Within the model of the Westergasfabriek, you can virtually go into one particular area of the project that is really intimate, where there are waterfalls; it does not look like much at first, but it actually communicates a lot of delicate nuances. Once built, the landscape space radiates a feeling that pulls you in, and, as you look around, you find other spaces that were present in the model that also contribute to this consolidated feeling. When you start deriving plans, and forming pathways from the model, you fully recognize the spirit and feeling you were trying to create. Everything in this landscape comes together as one sculpted piece, and then people use it the way that you imagined—and everything fits and resonates! So, in the end, with the simple means of a handmade model and a lot of creative intuition and experimentation, you have created a place that has turned into what it was supposed to be.

You do not always have to do big things; you can do little things—things that will also change how somebody experiences and walks through a space. We worked with the RFR engineer Henry Bardsley on these huge pylons for the

FIG. 9 — Kathryn Gustafson, model of EDF
pylons, France, 2002.

International Pylon Design Competition launched by Electricité de France in
1995. I made the pylon out of wire and clay, because it is customary to my way
of working. (FIG. 9) I played with all those sensuous forms, and shaped it out of
dry plaster. Henry touched it and exclaimed, "Oh my God, Kathryn, it is going
to break on me." What he said to me next made a lot sense, and it is why I worry
about computer-generated pieces that more often than not seem so immaterial.
He said, "Kathryn, you have to use the material for your models that has the
same properties as the material you are going to finally build in. For this model
you used a pourable material. It is a moldable material—it is like your body, it
is organic, it has water." And so the fact that I used this pourable material to
represent something that actually had to be made out of steel meant that it was
very difficult to produce. If I had used the correct material for the model, then
we would have come up with a form that fit, but that was far from the case. What
I worry about with computers is that when I see all the triangulations, they look
like steel to me; they do not look like soil. And I do not quite know how one
translates one into the other, and how to actually build with this when you cannot
build with that. Do you see my dilemma?

You probably know that the Diana, Princess of Wales Memorial Fountain
(2004) in Hyde Park, London, was made completely digitally, but I still started
with a clay model. (FIGS. 10a–c) Some say that the landscape profession does not
embrace the digital the way architects do, but I disagree completely. We do
everything in Rhino and Grasshopper, and everybody in our offices is com-
puter-trained; they know how to run the machines and the programs, but that
doesn't necessarily make them good landscape architects and designers in the
end. For that matter, the biggest problem I still have with the digital world is
that as a designer, the 2-D world you look at and work with on the screen does
not embody the space that we experience out there in the landscape. Your brain
cannot actually see in 3-D. I use formZ, and can manipulate the 3-D software, but
I get completely lost. I get lost in that computer, where the endpoint is its own
internal logic. I cannot figure something out in terms of landscape design and
form giving if I cannot touch it; and this is certainly one of the things that has

FIGS. 10a–c— Gustafson Porter, model of
Diana, Princess of Wales Memorial Fountain,
London, 2004.

helped me the most. For that reason, I believe in relating to physical models and
sensual land movements—when creating with a model you see the path of sight,
and feel what you actually physically experience when you are there. How does
your mind differ from your path of sight? In other words, as you move through
space, what are you actually *feeling, perceiving, and deciding?* There is something
commendable about how we get into these computational processes, and how
abstract conceptual thinking and advanced intellectual postures in artificial intelligence and design are produced. But in the end, where are you? What are you
building? And what are you truly experiencing in the landscape? This is the only
thing, for me, that really matters.

THINK LIKE A KING, ACT LIKE A PEASANT: THE POWER OF A LANDSCAPE ARCHITECT AND SOME PERSONAL EXPERIENCE—*Kongjian Yu*

This text relates my experience as a landscape architect in China. It should be understood in the context of the country's concentrated political system and in the transitional time of the technocratic society. I do not intend for it to be read as me blowing my own trumpet to a small audience from the very small and sometimes—or, perhaps, often—powerless profession that we call landscape architecture. But if my personal experience is valuable for my colleagues, professionals, and academics to understand the potential power of this profession, such a risk is worthwhile.

1.0 KNOWLEDGE IS POWER AND INFLUENCING THE INFLUENTIAL

First of all, knowledge is power. The world now faces multifaceted challenges, including ecological and environmental degradation, water and food security, and the depletion of energy and mineral resources. All of these challenges take place within the landscape and are closely associated with the practice of landscape architecture. I was shocked, when I went back to China in 1997, to see the dramatic changes that were happening at that time, when urbanization was just beginning to pick up speed. Consequently, massive changes to the landscape were underway. Hills were leveled, wetlands were filled, and rivers were channelized and lined with concrete. Not only was the natural landscape affected, but so too was the human landscape. Heritage buildings and entire villages were being wiped out to develop new city districts and urban infrastructure. I was surprised to find that decision makers and professional planners and designers were simply ignorant of the physical and social impacts of these changes. They were certainly not aware of the issues of food security, air quality, and climate change that are now at the forefront of today's discourse. Even discussing sustainability was a luxury at a time when "development is the hard truth" (Deng Xiaoping's famous motto). In China, the urban ills suffered by many industrialized countries in the early and mid-twentieth century were once joked about as the fruits of capitalism, but over the last decade they have become major issues within the country. It was within this wave of optimism and ignorance that I established myself as a fighter against the trend—a risky position to take. But this counter-movement was gradually empowered by the increasing environmental awareness among decision makers in urban areas, who, unfortunately, soon began to experience and suffer the effects of ecological and environmental degradation.

1.1 DO NOT TRY TO INFLUENCE THE "EXPERTS"

It is ironic to note that trying to influence or challenge the views of established "experts" is usually difficult and can easily make one a lot of enemies. This is the mistake I made when I began: by trying to criticize the misconceptions and practices in landscape architecture and urban planning, I created a huge wave of controversy and backlash. Back in 1998, shortly after I returned to China from the United States and saw the misguided practices taking place in the cities, I wrote a series of articles in the *Journal of Chinese Landscape Architecture* criticizing the City Beautiful movement in Chinese cities, which favors cosmetic landscaping and urban design.[1] Rather than the "little feet" aesthetics of a wasteful ornamental landscape, I called for "big feet" aesthetics that favor productive, ecological landscapes.[2] I suddenly became a "public enemy" in the landscape gardening profession. A group of well-established and respected academics organized and wrote articles to launch a collective attack on me and, furthermore, I was criticized at meetings held by the Chinese Society of Landscape Architecture, from which I was eventually expelled for being rebellious of the "glorious tradition of Chinese Gardens."[3] My firm, Turenscape, was not able to pass the evaluation (by expert committee) for landscape practice for about fifteen years, although it was definitely the largest and arguably the best practice in China.

In the fields of urban and land-use planning, indiscriminate urban planning methods and strategies have recklessly destroyed cultural and ecological assets. In response to this, I proposed an approach called "negative planning" in 2002 as a counterstrategy to address the ecological degradation and chaos of city planning in China, particularly in large, metropolitan areas. When it comes to dealing with issues brought up by rapid urban development, the conventional "population speculation–land use–and infrastructure layout" approach has been, in my opinion, proven invalid. It is largely responsible for the "chaotic situation and degrading ecological conditions" in Chinese cities like Beijing, Shanghai, and Guangzhou, as well as the loss of cultural and spiritual landscapes. Negative planning is an ecological planning methodology that prioritizes the planning of EI (ecological infrastructure), and tries to provide land use and urban planning with a solid ecological basis.[4] It was based on Ian McHarg's book *Design with Nature* and landscape ecological studies.[5] Again, as one may expect, this was incredibly controversial. My keynote speech at the 2007 National Planner's Conference was forcibly withdrawn due to objections from established planning authorities. I was then called upon to stop the publication of my book *The Negative Approach*, and letters of accusation from experts and academics were sent to the Ministry of Rural and Urban Construction. I was criticized as someone disrespectful to fellow professionals in the planning fields.

This may sound terrifying and even unbelievable to many, much like the Cultural Revolution during the 1960s and 1970s, but this was the reality of the profession. Thankfully, they were not considered to be political issues but "conflicts among the professionals." I have to say that the hostile environment against innovation and dissenting opinions is actually quite common in professional circles. One of main reasons may be that the Chinese society is primarily a technocracy, in which decision makers are selected based upon how knowledgeable and skillful they are in their field. The technocratic officials, whose knowledge is obsolete, try to secure their authority through the power of administration and are thus afraid of being told that they might be wrong. So, to gain power, one has to turn directly to the administrative or political power. This system has undergone change in recent years as more and more professional administrators, rather than technocratic officials, have come to power at different ranks.

1.2 TALK TO MAYORS

Soon I began to understand the underbelly of the technocracy, and turned to influencing those who have solid administrative and political power and are young, but not necessarily "experts." I lectured at the Mayors' Forum operated by the central Chinese government, made trips to individual cities to speak to mayors directly, and also lectured to ministers, all thanks to my academic reputation and my Harvard degree. So far, since 1997, over one thousand mayors, ministers, and their deputies have listened to my lectures in the past seventeen years. In 2003 my colleague Dihua Li and I published the book *The Road to Urban Landscape: A Dialogue with Mayors*, which was based on my numerous lectures.[6] The book became a bestseller and has since been reprinted fourteen times, and I have sent out thousands of copies to mayors, a position that is usually reelected every four years. In this book I sharply criticized the wasteful, destructive, and cosmetic urbanism that was a fever in China at that time, and pointed out the multifaceted ecological challenges that Chinese cities are facing and will have

FIG. 1 — Yu lectures to ministers from various ministries including the Ministry of Water Resources, Ministry of Land Resources, Ministry of Agriculture, Ministry of Housing and Rural and Urban Development, and the Ministry of Environmental Protection in 2002.
Photo courtesy of China National Library.

FIG. 2 — Yu lectures to mayors and officials of all ranks from the Party Secretary and city mayors to the township leader in Guanzhou City along with over three thousand officials of all ranks in 2013.
Photo courtesy of Guanzhou Municipal Government.

FIG. 3 — Yu (second from right) is able to convince the mayor (first on right) to make an order to stop and adjust the ongoing ecologically destructive river channelization project on site (Kaiyuan City, Yunnan Province, 2010).
Photo courtesy of Kaiyuan City Government.

to face in the future. On the other hand, I called for learning from the Western countries in their experience of urbanization; I brought up the need to plan and immediately build an ecological infrastructure across the nation, and for that an alternative planning and design philosophy, namely the negative approach, is necessary.[7] This battle has proven to be a great success, which is due to the fact that the young generation of Chinese leaders, at various levels, are quite open and are willing to make changes. They are at the forefront of urbanization, making them the first group to be aware of the serious ecological problems.

I use the term *mayor* in reference to the top decision makers in the city, which also means the Communist Party secretaries (Shuji) of individual cities, who are ranked higher than the mayors in China. Although the political circle is extremely competitive in China, the nontechnocratic administrative officials are not competitors for professional power as in the case of technocratic intellectuals, and, as a matter of fact, innovative solutions give politicians the power to change their cities, in an era of furious competition between cities for speed and image. Being appreciated by the mayors and high-ranking decision makers in individual cities afforded me tremendous privilege. I was frequently invited by the mayors to lecture to officials of all ranks under his power, from the township level to the top municipal level. I was privately escorted on tours of the city to assess rivers, streets, and even individual buildings, which sometimes produced immediate effects. In cities such as Guangdong's Zhongshan City, Zhejiang's Taizhou City, Jiangsu's Suqian City, and others, I was able to convince the mayors to halt ongoing river channelization projects immediately on site or adjust ongoing construction.

Because of my reputation among mayors, the top authority, I have been able to easily avoid any direct conflict with the technocratic officials, who still hold on to obsolete knowledge and practices, particularly those in the urban planning department, hydrological engineering department, and landscape departments, which are under the direct control of the mayors. I am able to bypass the system that protects the power of individual departments, such as the flood controlling code, the ornamental landscaping code, the stormwater management codes, etc. (FIGS. 1–3)

1.3 MAKE A PROPOSAL TO THE PRIME MINISTER

In a concentrated power system, an individual official of any rank can be considered the king of his administrative territory. While the mayors are powerful in making decisions regarding the landscape in their municipal area, they are unable to break through national policies such as land use and land ownership regulations. The top authority of the nation has always been the most powerful agent of landscape change. The first king in China was the legendary figure King Da Yu, who was able to lead the Chinese people to divert major drainage systems and control flooding, dividing China into nine prefectures and changing the flood-plagued territory into a productive and inhabitable land. More than 2,250 years ago, Emperor Qin Shi Huang was able to build a national highway system that linked the whole nation under his rule and created the Great Wall of tens of thousands of miles. About 1,500 years ago, the Emperor Yangdi of the Sui Dynasty was able to direct his subjects to build the Grand Canal extending 2,000 miles across five major drainage systems in East China and linked South China with the north. In modern times, the power of the "king" is no less significant. In the 1950s and 1960s, Mao Zedong called his farming people to learn from Dazhai Village to build terraces in mountainous areas, making every farmer in China construct terraces, claim agricultural fields from wetlands and lakes, and cut trees to burn for steel production. These policies changed the national landscape in a disastrous way in only a decade. More recently, in the 1980s, Deng Xiaoping initiated the opening policy and stated that "development is the hard truth," prioritizing rapid urban development and encouraging individual villages to start their own industries. The results of these policies are visible in the land-scape we see today in urban and suburban China.

In 2006, after two decades of urbanization, the central Chinese government decided to make a campaign to build the New Socialist Countryside. It was per-haps the greatest opportunity to fix the landscape, as opposed to continuing to degrade ecosystems already damaged by the relentless pace of urbanization and development. I was extremely concerned, and I knew that only the power of the "king" or "emperor" could make a difference in China—the power of the pres-ident or the prime minister.

On the eve of the Chinese New Year in 2006, I drafted a letter to Wen Jiabao, the prime minister of People's Republic of China. In this letter, I commented that for the last two decades, China had virtually ruined its cities (old and new), but its rural area is still vast and remains relatively healthy, rich with ecological and cultural heritage of thousands of years. I pointed out that the New Socialist Countryside movement is very likely to destroy this valuable heritage and the ecological system that has sustained the rural Chinese society for millennia. In order to avoid this potentially catastrophic result, I suggested a negative planning approach, meaning planning and building a National Ecological Security Pattern and Ecological Infrastructure Concept at all scales to identify and protect the ver-nacular cultural and ecological assets, which would become the baseline for the massive development campaign. As an example, I also pointed out that the Grand Canal is a typical cultural and ecological infrastructure that needs to be protected as a whole system for its multiple ecological and cultural services, such as regional water regulation, biodiversity protection, its function as a national recreational corridor, and cultural infrastructure that strengthens the Chinese identity.

Surprisingly, two weeks later, I received feedback from the prime minister's office and was called upon to explain the National Ecological Security Pattern and Ecological Infrastructure concept. Soon afterward, I was called upon by the Ministry of Environmental Protection to make a National Security Plan for the whole nation, because "the prime minister needs this plan," and "we want it as soon as possible, the deadline is one year after!" This is, of course, an impossi-ble task, but we were able to make a quick and rough plan at a national scale to provide a framework for more detailed plans at the regional and local scale to be done later by others. As a pilot project of National Ecological Security Pattern planning, we were allowed to access all available data from government depart-ments. We organized a team of thirty professionals and doctoral students who

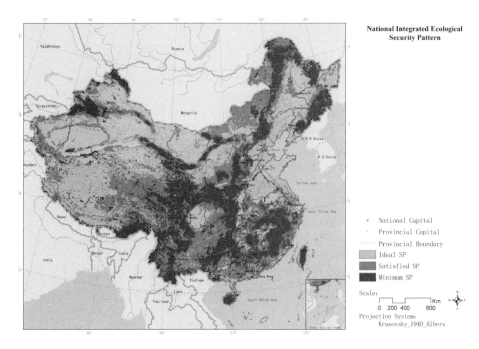

* National Capital
- Provincial Capital
Provincial Boundary
Ideal SP
Satisfied SP
Minimum SP

Scale:
0 200 400   800 Km
Projection System:
Krasovsky_1940_Albers

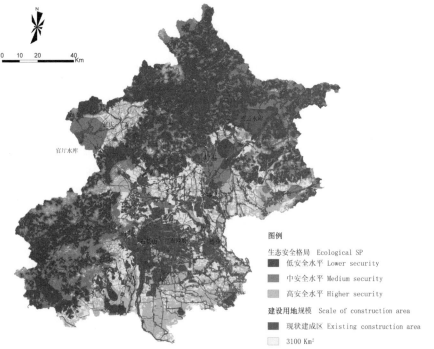

N

0   10   20   40 Km

图例

生态安全格局 Ecological SP
低安全水平 Lower security
中安全水平 Medium security
高安全水平 Higher security

建设用地规模 Scale of construction area
现状建成区 Existing construction area
3100 Km²

FIG. 4 (TOP) — The National Ecological
Security Pattern.
Kongjian Yu/Peking University.

FIG. 5 (BOTTOM) — The Regional Ecological
Security Pattern for Beijing and Urban
Development Scenario.
Kongjian Yu/Peking University.

working day and night, developing the National Security Pattern Plan by early 2007. This plan and the method of negative planning approach were a major basis for the National Functional Zoning. By 2011, negative planning and the ecological security pattern approach had become the official Methodology Guidelines of the National Land Use Planning and the National Land Use Zoning (Ministry of Land Resources), and have been applied in many municipal plans and land use plans (including Beijing, Shenzhen, Chongqing, and Guangzhou). By the time of the Eighteenth National Congress of the Chinese Communist Party in 2012, building an ecological security pattern across the nation, together with Teach for China (Měilì zhōngguó, meaning, literally, "beautiful China"), had become one of the five major agendas for the new central government. (FIGS. 4-5)

2.0 ACT LIKE A PEASANT AND SHOW THE POWER OF EXAMPLES
2.1 LEARN FROM THE PEASANTS

At the beginning, during my lectures to mayors and ministers, I was asked: looking at these depressing, degraded ecological situations, do you really think that healing the land is at all possible with your way? By then, I had recognized my weakness as a professor trying to influence the influential. I had to show my own power as doer, and prove that what I said was doable. Soon after, in 1998, I established my firm, Turenscape. The name literally means "dirty man" or "rural bumpkin." I understand that healing the ecological system at the national scale need simple, replicable and inexpensive solutions, not self-indulgent ornamental design or artistic form. Beautiful, ecologically sound and culturally sensitive solutions are the necessary characteristics for these solutions.

No matter how powerful King Da Yu, Emperor Qin Shi Huang, Emperor Yang of Sui, Mao Zedong, Den Xiaoping, or our contemporary prime minister were, the king has to depend on his people, the farmers or the peasants. It is actually the individual peasants who changed the landscape envisioned by the king. The pond-and-dike system in the Pearl River Delta in South China, the rice-paddy-and-dike farming system in the Yangtze River Delta in China, and the terraces that covered the numerous mountains in Southeast Asia, are all regional and even national landscapes that have been created by individual peasants. It is the transscale characteristics of the farming techniques that have intrigued me and inspired me to build the national and regional ecological infrastructure. We have to learn from the peasants who little by little have transformed the national landscape in a sustainable way. Some of the key principles that peasants follow in their survival strategy include:

—Dependence on the limited resources available in the immediate environment

—Dedication of minimum effort to achieve maximum harvest

—Commitment to the sustainable use of resources inherited from ancestors and necessary to the welfare of the descendants

—Retention of human scale in farming as the work is done manually so that fields, paths, and rows are built around human reach and movement

Some of the key techniques by peasants that are wisely used to transform the landscape in a meaningful way include "making friends" with nature and adapting to natural processes and patterns: employing cut and fill to create suitable habitats for crops and balance the earthwork, irrigating the fields using natural gravity, fertilizing using waste to enclose the nutrient cycle, and growing for the purpose of harvesting.[8] Through these simple methods, habitats are created using minimum investment, the natural processes are sped up instead of slowed down, the nutrient cycle is weaved into the production process, and any piece of land becomes productive but not consumptive. Eventually, productive and sustainable systems are created to provide holistic ecosystem services including provision, regulating life support and making the landscape spiritually meaningful and beautiful. If we can incorporate the peasants' approach into contemporary landscape practice to build ecological infrastructure, we can make the king's vision of national and regional ecological planning a reality.

2.2 THE POWER OF EXAMPLES

The power of example is infinite. While the research team under my leadership at Peking University focuses on the research-based national and regional landscape planning, envisioning the ecological infrastructure and eventually reporting to the top authorities at various levels of government, the practice of Turenscape focuses on designing and building demonstrative projects that aim at solving multifaceted ecological problems. All of these projects apply peasants' techniques and wisdom that are low cost, low maintenance, and replicable at different localities, and can be integrated across different scales.

2.2.1 MAKE FRIENDS WITH FLOODS

Aiming at demonstrating an alternative solution to flood control in order to counter the conventional hydrological engineering of concrete damming and channelization, Turenscape's first project with this ecological solution is the Yongning River Park, built in 2003. This project virtually removed the concrete embankment and recovered the riparian wetland, contrary to the advice of hydro-logical engineering experts and turning the engineering codes upside down. As was discussed earlier on, I was able to convince the mayor, and the power of the mayor was then transformed into the power of the ecological solution proposed by the landscape architect. This demonstrative project has proven to be a great success: not only did we create a beautiful, floodable riparian park for the local residents, we showcased an alternative flood management solution, which was eventually designated as a good example of ecological water management by the Ministry of Water Resources, attracting many mayors from other cities. The success of the first project was followed by a second project commissioned to Turenscape after the Yongning River Park, which continues to transform another longer section of concrete river into ecologically healthy riparian greenway, was built and tested successfully for eight years. The idea and tactics of making friends with floods have been replicated in many projects by Turenscape, including the most recent Yanweizhou Park in Zhejiang's Jihua City, where the waterfront land was designed as a floodable park adapting to the monsoon climate.

2.2.2 UTILIZE GREEN SPONGE TO SOLVE URBAN INUNDATION PROBLEMS

Almost all Chinese cities suffer urban inundation problems during the monsoon season. In 2012, seventy-nine people drowned in the city streets and in the outskirts of Beijing. Engineers were called upon to design thicker drainage pipes and implement stronger pumps, but this solution cannot solve the problem of inundation due to the climate of concentrated rainfall, which not only is beyond any capacity of the pipe system, but also worsens the water-shortage problem and the drop in groundwater. Turenscape demonstrated the "Sponge City" alternative through a series of projects in different cities in China. In these demonstrations, a simple cut-and-fill technique was used to create the "green sponge" to retain and filtrate storm water, as was showcased in the Qunli Stormwater Park. Based on the tested experiment, it was revealed that if 10 percent of the total area is designed as "green sponge," the urban inundation problem can be solved, with only one third of the total cost of a normal park. Based on Turenscape's experience, I sent out letters to the most powerful authorities, including President Xi Jinping and the Secretary of Beijing City, calling for building hydroecological infrastructure and a water-resilient city (Sponge City for short). The terms *green sponge* and Sponge City have now become nationally accepted, after President Xi Jinping and premier Li Keqiang used them to describe their vision for a better city. (FIG. 6)

Photo by Kongjian Yu.

FIG. 6 — Utilizing green sponge to solve the urban inundation problem. Qunli Stormwater Park, Haerbin, Heilongjiang, China, 2010.

overleaf:
FIG. 7 — Go productive demonstrating agricultural urbanism. The Shenyang Jianzhu University campus, 2004.
Photo by Kongjian Yu.

2.2.3 GO PRODUCTIVE IN DEMONSTRATING AGRICULTURAL URBANISM

In the past decades, urbanization has taken over more than 10 percent of the fertile land in China. Only 10 percent of China's terrestrial area is arable land, which feeds a population of 1.3 billion; food security is a top national priority. How to solve the conflict between urban development and grain production presents a big challenge. One of the keys lies in agricultural urbanism: while a great amount of fertile land has been claimed for urban development, almost 40 percent of this urban territory is actually used as green space, typically ornamental green space that consumes a considerable amount of water, energy, and chemicals. Using peasants' techniques and rules, much of the urban green can be turned into productive land again and an alternative urban public green can be developed by integrating production with urban functions. The peasant rule of growing for harvesting can become "urbanized." One of the earliest projects by Turenscape is the Shenyang Jianzhu University campus, which has now become an iconic precedent for urban agriculture. It has been duplicated in many projects across China, fundamentally changing people's mentality about the aesthetics and functions of urban green. (FIG. 7)

2.2.4 LANDSCAPE AS A LIVING SYSTEM TO CLEAN THE WATER

In China, 75 percent of the surface water is polluted. While water treatment plants are built to clean the sewage and industrial wastewater, the nonpoint pollution is almost impossible to be cleansed by the water treatment plants. At the same time, the 75 percent surface water pollution is primarily caused by eutrophication, nutrients from agricultural fields, and household waste, which would have been the peasants' treasures for farming practice. Reconnecting the broken nutrient cycle can be an alternative solution for cleansing river and lake water. One of the most visible demonstrative projects of landscape as a living system is Houtan Park, built for the 2010 Shanghai Expo, which still operates well today. Through the cut-and-fill technique, terraces were built to turn the flood control dike into wetland terraces covered with productive crops and wetland plants that remove the nutrients from the water. This living landscape was able to turn the poor fifth-grade water into clean water of third grade. The observed data shows that three hectares of constructed wetland, 1.7 kilometers long, can produce 2,400 cubic meters of clean water daily, enough for five thousand people to use as non-potable water, meanwhile creating habitats for native biodiversity and a pleasant public space. Now, we have been commissioned to replicate this model at a large scale of hundreds of hectares in projects like the Liupanshui Minghu Wetland Park (built in 2012, winner of the ASLA Award), and even at thousands of hectares to create water remediation farms to clean the eutrophic water in Taihu and Dianchi Lakes, two of China's largest lakes (a project in the planning phase). In Kunming, the designed water remediation farm is made of eight patches, altogether 246 hectares, which together with surrounding ecologically designed landscape, is expected to produce 0.83 million cubic meters of clean water every day. (FIGS. 8-9)

2.2.5 LET NATURE DO THE WORK TO REMEDIATE CONTAMINATED SOIL

Brown fields are a major issue in the world, and particularly in China, due to the unwise management of the land during industrialization and urban development. Soil remediation is a very expensive and challenging process in the creation of usable public green space. In the Qiaoyuan Wetland case in Tianjin, Turenscape applied the peasants' technique of cut-and-fill to create diverse habitats by collecting and retaining rainwater, which changed the soil's pH value and initiated the self-regenerative process to improve a habitable landscape for native plant communities and wildlife in the middle of the city. With minimal costs and low maintenance, the otherwise hostile brown field was transformed into a lush green

FIG. 8 (TOP) — From the constructed wetland, aquatic plants like *Ceratophyllum demersum* are collected as feed materials for pigs or domestic birds, to close the nutrient cycle in the way that peasants do.
Photo by Kongjian Yu.

FIG. 9 (BOTTOM — Slow Down: Liupanshui Minghu Wetland Park, 2012. The park expands over one square kilometer.
Photo by Kongjian Yu.

FIG. 10 — Let nature do the work to remediate contaminated soil. The Qiaoyuan Park, Tianjin City, 2008.
Photo by Kongjian Yu.

space loved by the urban residents. This technique has been replicated in many larger projects designed by Turenscape. (**FIG. 10**)

2.2.6 A REGENERATIVE SOLUTION TO TRANSFORM INDUSTRIAL HERITAGE

In the past few decades, Chinese cities have been undergoing a dramatic transformation from industrial workshops into postindustrial residential and commercial cities. Industries were relocated to industrial parks or bankrupted, leaving tremendous amounts of industrial brown field and "ugly" industrial factory structures. The most common solution for this is simply wiping out all of the factories and building new cities from ground zero. During this process, the people lose their connection to their cultural heritage, and the city loses its stories and history. Featureless, brand new high-rise buildings dominate the city skylines. Inspired by Peter Latz's and Richard Haag's works, Turenscape showcased the "preserve, reuse, and recycle" approach in designing the first postindustrial park in China back in 1999: the Zhongshan Shipyard Park (completed 2001), which became the landmark project in China.[9] For the first time ever, a landscape project designed by a Chinese firm won an ASLA Award. In order to have the design approved, the author fought for one year against the controversial forces from the experts of traditional landscape gardening both locally and nationally. In one important evaluation meeting that called in over one hundred Chinese gardening experts, all but one expert objected to my original design, nearly killing the "preserve, reuse, and recycle" concept. A traditional new garden was proposed to replace my design. Again, I finally won the battle by successfully convincing the young mayor and the director of the Urban Planning Bureau, who made the final decision to approve the design. This park is now celebrated by the locals as well as visitors from around the nation, and accommodates thousands of wedding couples who use the "rustic and messy" landscape as a background for photographs.

2.2.7 MINIMIZE INTERVENTION TO TRANSFORM NATURAL ASSETS INTO URBAN PUBLIC SPACE

Overwhelming urbanization has left very limited ecological assets in urban and rural China. The question of how to both save the valuable natural assets and urbanize the environment for people to enjoy comfort and artful design is a big challenge. For the past seventeen years, Turenscape has followed the peasant's rule of using minimum effort to maximize the benefits from landscape design. One example showcasing this principle and technique is *The Red Ribbon* in Qinhuangdao City, Hebei Province. Against a background of messy nature along the riparian habitats, a red bench made of fiberglass winds through various native plant communities and adapts to the unleveled terrain. This 500-meter-long bench integrates seating, lighting boardwalk, and the natural environment together into a single piece of landscape installation. Its construction cost was even less than the design fee, but has tremendously changed the otherwise inaccessible riparian corridor at the urban periphery, and attracts visitors from the city and beyond. *Condé Nast Traveler* named the *Red Ribbon* project as one of the New Seven Wonders of the World in 2008, and the minimum intervention strategy has become a well-applied strategy by Turenscape and other firms in China.[10] The power of the project is more obviously seen through the 400 percent increase of the real estate values near the park and the new pride and cultural identity that the park has given to the city.

These seven examples of projects and solutions can be taken as design modules aimed at specific challenges that China and the world at large currently face. Although each individual design has its own unique artistic features, they are all low cost, low maintenance, replicable, and easily integrated into a holistic landscape at all scales. Like peasants who work individually on their land for the purpose of survival but eventually transform the global landscape, these replicable contemporary landscaping modules might be used to transform the landscape trans-scales and heal the globe we are inhabiting today.

CONCLUSION

Landscape architecture has, for a long time, been identified as the descendent of ornamental gardening—creating a paradise for entertaining and pleasure making within exclusive walls or fences. This essay, on the one hand, tries to rediscover landscape architecture as the art of survival, closely integrated with kingship. It is made clear that landscape architects are the direct descendants of King Da Yu, who was able to make friends with floods, envision the whole territory of his kingdom as a paradise using rules and measures to investigate and plan, make wise use of the land for agriculture, and select safe places to build cities for his people. This was the essence of landscape architecture, combining the art of survival and the leadership of the king.

This paper also tries to recover the authentic meaning of landscape as a "Peasant and His Land," which has been disappearing since the first day that "landscape" (*landschap*, in Dutch) became "a picture depicting scenery on land" by artists in Europe in the sixteenth and seventeenth centuries, or even earlier in China during the fourth century. During this process, "my or our land" has become "his or their land"; the relationship between a peasant and his land has evolved into the one between the urban elite and visual object; the land for survival has been replaced by a landscape of "aesthetic disinterestedness." The quality and beauty of the landscape has been detached from the notion of a holistic land system for living and survival, and has now become the high-art landscape designed exclusively for the pleasure of the urban elite. Aside from that, during the process of industrialization, the multifunctionality of landscapes has been either oversimplified for monocultural production economies such as modern mechanical farming, or substituted by highly controlled engineering in the form of gray infrastructure (to control water, treat sewage, etc.). The serious ecological degradation in today's urban environment is largely due to this separation and disinterestedness. It is time to reclaim the lost meaning of landscape: peasant and his land, to rebuild and to heal the living system of the earth.

Given this mission, landscape architecture, more than any other profession or discipline, should take on responsibility in healing the earth, by adopting two strategies: thinking like a king and acting like a peasant. We, the landscape architects, have to reposition ourselves as the kings—the good kings—who are aware of the degrading ecological environment in our territories and the survival challenges facing *Homo sapiens*, and be able to think big and envision a global, national, and regional landscape as an ecosystem, as well as regulate and change this system effectively through a workable infrastructure—ecological infrastructures that can secure sustainable ecosystem services for the survival of humanity. Landscape architects should be able to work like peasants and follow the rules of survival, including making friends with natural forces, making minimum investments to maximize outcomes, and obeying the basic land ethics of keeping the land sustainably productive. And, they should be able to transform the landscape by using simple and replicable techniques such as cutting and filling, irrigating, fertilizing, and growing for harvesting, which will incrementally create the envisioned ecological infrastructure at a regional and global scale.

Being able to think like a king and act like a peasant will empower landscape architects to bridge the grand vision at the global scale to the working modules at the local scale. It is a reinterpretation of well-known motto for a sustainable world: "Thinking globally, act locally."

Notes

1

Kongjian Yu and Ji Qingping, "China to Learn From the International 'City Beautiful Movement,'" parts 1 and 2, *Journal Of Chinese Landscape Architecture* (2000): 1:27–33, 2:32–35; Kongjian Yu and Mary G. Padua, "China's Cosmetic Cities: Urban Fever and Superficiality," Landscape Research 2, no. 2 (2007): 255–72.

2

Kongjian Yu, "Beautiful Big Feet: Toward a New Landscape Aesthetic," *Harvard Design Magazine* (Fall/Winter 2009): 48–59; Kongjian Yu, "The Big Feet Aesthetic and The Art of Survival," *Architectural Design* 220 (November/December 2012): 72–77.

3

Kongjian Yu, "Challenges and Opportunities for the Development of Landscape Architecture Profession in China," *Chinese Landscape Architecture* (1998): 1:17–21.

4

Kongjian Yu, Dihua Li, Han Xili, Liu Hailong, "On the 'Negative Planning,'" *City Planning Review* 9 (2005): 64–69; Kongjian Yu, Sisi Wang, Dihua Li, "The Negative Approach to Urban Growth Planning of Beijing, China," *Journal of Environmental Planning and Management* 54, no. 9 (2011): 1209–36.

5

Ian McHarg, *Design with Nature* (Garden City: The Natural History Press, 1969); Richard T. T. Forman, *Land Mosaics: The Ecology of Landscapes and Regions* (Cambridge: Cambridge University Press, 1995); Richard T. T. Forman and Michel Godron, (New York: Wiley, 1986).

6

Kongjian Yu and Dihua Li, *The Road to Urban Landscape: A Dialogue with Mayors* (Beijing: China Architecture & Building Press, 2003).

7

Ibid.

8

Kongjian Yu, "Creating Deep Forms in Urban Nature: The Peasant's Approach," paper presented at Nature and Cities: Urban Ecological Design and Planning, Austin, Texas, February 28–March 1, 2014, sponsored by the Lincoln Institute of Land Policy, Cambridge, Massachusetts, and the School of Architecture, The University of Texas at Austin, proceedings in press.

9

Mary G. Padua, "Industrial Strength: At a Former Shipyard, a Park Design Breaks with Convention to Honor China's Recent Past," *Landscape Architecture Magazine* 93, no. 3 (2003): 76–86, 107.

10

"Condé Nast Traveler Names 7 Modern Architectural Wonders," *USA Today*, March 25, 2008, accessed August 25, 2015, http://usatoday30.usatoday.com/travel/destinations/2008-03-25-seven-architectural-wonders_N.htm.

NEXUS: SCIENCE, MEMORY, STRATEGY
—*Kristina Hill*

Since antiquity, memory has been called the mother of all wisdom.[1] But science has been said to gather knowledge faster than society gains wisdom.[2] Where is the wisdom in landscape architectural design and planning, when it claims to draw on scientific theories? Is it possible that the use of ecological theories in design strategies could be incompatible with the importance of memory and culture?

Literature provides cautionary tales about the reliance on either science or memory. Mary Shelley's 1818 novel, *Frankenstein; or, The Modern Prometheus*, refers to the dangers of scientific experimentation in the absence of compassion. It was written during the exceptionally cold, wet summer produced by the 1815 eruption of Indonesia's Mount Tambora, which led 1816 to be known as Europe's "Year Without a Summer."[3] Shelley's proud but unwise scientist, Dr. Frankenstein, creates a living creature he expects to find beautiful and instead finds abhorrent. Frankenstein cannot feel love or sympathy for his creation; in revenge, the creature murders Frankenstein's wife, family, and friends.[4] With regard to memory, Arthur Miller's play *The Crucible* (1953) tells a story of memory run amok. Miller turns the American colonial era witch trials into a narrative about the destructive capacity of prosecution that relies on false memories, without evidence—and without compassion. (FIGS. 1–2)

I refer to these works of fiction for two reasons: First, they point to the shortcomings of using either science or memory as inspiration for action, since both can leave humans vulnerable to disasters born from a lack of compassion. Second, these narratives argue for a greater reliance on wisdom, restraint, and caring for others as a superior foundation for action. The methods of the sciences and the fallibility of human memory can both create flawed cultural practices prone to subversion by politics and prejudicial beliefs.

Jean-François Lyotard claimed that narratives fall into two different categories: the "petit" and the "grand."[5] The petit narrative takes its validity from how convincingly it is performed, in unique instances and by unique individuals. The grand narrative relies on an accepted universal validity, and can only be "true" to the extent that more people believe it is true than believe it to be false. Political philosophies and religions fall into the latter category of the grand narrative. In contrast, the cultural practices of empirical scientific observation, of recounting memories, and of proposing designs could all be seen as petit

FIG. 1— Frontispiece of Mary Shelley's *Frankenstein* (London: Colburn and Bentley, 1831) by Theodor von Holst. Steel engraving, 3.9 x 2.8 in. (9.93 x 7.10 cm).

FIG. 2— This unattributed illustration of the Salem witch trials appeared in 1876, in *Pioneers in the settlement of America: From Florida in 1510 to California in 1849*, by William A. Crafts, published by Samuel Walker and Company, Boston.

narratives because they are only valid and compelling if they are performed well by trusted individuals.

Science, storytelling, and design are all performances, all cultural acts that draw on multiple epistemologies. From an external viewpoint, science may appear to generate grand narratives like the narratives of politics and ideologies. But these are popularizing overlays, superimposed on a set of petit narratives that generate conditional knowledge. Practicing scientists are encouraged to be intensely skeptical—to be filled with creative doubt that leads to new questions that can only be answered by extensive, repeated empirical observations; artists whose work challenges and triggers memories can help generate critical reinterpretations of past meanings. Perhaps we exaggerate the existence of conflict between the practices of science and of art because we are unfamiliar with them as sources of intensely specific petit narratives. One could argue that the supposed differences are themselves an element of a familiar grand narrative about human knowledge, which needs to be unpacked and reexamined for our time.

In my own work, I have participated in large- and small-scale scientific research efforts, worked with complex design teams, and led a public agency with a $2 billion budget that was created as the result of a political movement. In each effort, my colleagues and I were challenged to engage in different ways of reasoning—from careful skepticism to intense political advocacy. After those experiences, I am convinced that the representation of landscapes and proposals for landscapes have the greatest potential to express something significant about what it means to be human in our time.

My argument here is that science offers us as much in these activities as art, through the scientific practices of empirical observation and the generation of creative metaphors. Scientific reasoning is as essential as memory in the design and planning of landscapes because we cannot afford to ignore either the evidence obtained through systematic observation, or the moral context and emotional consequences of our proposals.

FLOWS AND ARMATURES ACROSS MULTIPLE SCALES

Part of the challenge presented to me in writing this piece was to provide examples of the scientific theories that inform my design work. In order to do that, I should note that it is rare for any practitioner to apply theories directly from science in a design or planning case. Principles that guide application are more often derived from practice than from theory, although in situations requiring new approaches, science-based designers may try a risky approach that emerges directly from a theoretical concept as a way of constructing a full-scale experiment. By observing flows and processes, and interpreting sites as places of nexus among flows, we have been able to identify designs that provide multiple benefits and increase the diversity of life in urban systems.[6]

Over the last 125 years since Frederick Law Olmsted designed Boston's Emerald Necklace, ecological designs for urban systems have been based on an understanding of water as a concentrating flow. Water flows with different amounts of energy and volume across landscape surfaces and through the three-dimensional mélange of rubble, rock, pipes, and soil, concentrating materials and organisms. Water gathers as it moves, and everything it carries is concentrated downstream. To understand the spatial and temporal patterns of this flow, ecological design and engineering rely on theories of ecology, hydrology, and geology—along with mathematical theories of probability and possibility (expressed as different types of categories, discrete and graded, and different rules for reasoning).[7]

In Europe and the Americas, and increasingly in Asia, the use of water as an organizing system for cities has become a dominant practice for the protection of public health and safety. As the theories of landscape ecology became increasingly important to the subfields of biology over the last seventy-five years, the fundamentally hierarchical analytical approaches of hydrology have been extended to the study of ecological communities. Hierarchy theory has proposed ways of studying the interactions among flows and landscape structures that allow these complex relationships to be understood across different geographical scales.[8] It was developed in its contemporary form using information theory, and is now

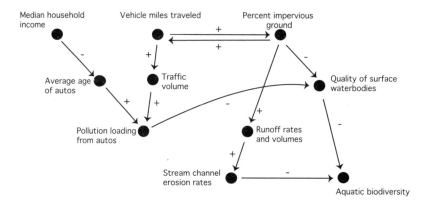

FIG. 3 — An urban ecological system defined by correlations, and represented hierarchically. Network relationships represented in a signal graph can reveal hierarchies of influence. Here two social variables (household income, vehicle miles traveled), and one physical design variable (percent impervious ground) are represented through their correlations with multiple ecological variables. Plus (+) signs indicate positive correlations, and minus (-) signs indicate negative correlations. Arrows indicate hypothesized relationships of influence, based on the correlations.
Diagram by Kristina Hill, 2015.

used in ecology to represent the ways in which information (genes, biological signals, etc.) are transmitted across spatial scales. Designers have long used it intuitively when working with water systems, which are spatially hierarchical. Since the 1990s, ecological designers have used hierarchy theory to identify and prioritize flows within landscape patterns, so that some can be reinforced and others can be altered. Hierarchy theory allows us to prioritize the conservation or creation of particular features that support those flows when they are desirable as part of a regional pattern of system behavior, and to remove or reduce them when they are not, resulting in tactics of intentional "system pruning." (**FIG. 3**)

For example, when plans are developed to improve water quality and reduce destructive flooding in urban streams to allow more diverse uses and communities to coexist, hierarchy theory reminds us that local problems are really regional problems. The nutrients, metals, petroleum products, and heat energy that in high enough concentrations create pollution come from many individual roofs, streets, and parcels of land, along many different flow paths. In that maze of flow paths, are all of them equally important as conduits? Are all sources consequently equally important? If not, can designers alter some and not all source areas, and reduce the pollution or flooding with less cost and effort? Hierarchy theory provides a framework for thinking about spatial and temporal strategies in altering a hydrologic system, producing consequences for ecological processes and human health. This example represents an application of theory to organize practical experience and ask new questions, to avoid being driven by "best practices" in a repetitive way and instead to consider the possibility of "next practices."[9] (**FIGS. 4–5**)

FIG. 4 — Urban stormwater in box culverts.
Photo by darkday.

FIG. 5 — Salmon at the underwater dome at the Seattle Aquarium. Fish and other aquatic organisms are affected by the hierarchies of water systems as pollutants are concentrated at different points in the pattern of water flow, at the same time they can be agents of nutrient redistribution as in the case of adult salmon traveling from marine systems to freshwater streams.
Photo by Melissa Doroquez.

Theories of biodiversity and ecosystem function (BEF) provide a different type of example.[10] A long and fascinating history of different theories of classification has produced today's concept of the biological species. Conventional "best practice" is to design in ways that increase or conserve the diversity of species (i.e., the number of species and the evenness of their population sizes). But research over the last couple of decades suggests that at the ecosystem level, it is the functional diversity of animals and plants that increases performance— not the species diversity, per se. According to this theory, if we are designing a wetland to maximize the improvement of water quality, we should choose plants that have different functional roles—whether or not they are different species. We might choose cultivars with different heights or stem patterns, root lengths, or leaf shapes in order to capture more nutrients or slow the movement of the water as much as possible, so that it will drop its sediment load. Adding more functional goals (providing food for specific birds, or increasing the population of specific soil organisms, for example) makes this design problem much more difficult to optimize. But again, applying this theory—which was derived from field observations, not from an a priori normative position—allows me to question the rote application of best practices and focus on insight and innovation.

At the landscape scale, with all its complex interactions, biodiversity is still the best proxy for functional diversity. But it is interesting to consider whether accelerated climate change and other stressors may produce functional adaptations more frequently in the future. If so, perhaps our legal system—with its focus on protecting species—should be redirected to protect trait diversity instead, producing the functional diversity that can lead to higher productivity in ecosystem services. As a policy issue this is an open question, but as a design issue, these theories create opportunities for immediate application. Most biological scientists believe a period of mass extinction is likely to occur in the near future as a result of both the speed of climate change and the extent of urbanization.[11] On the other hand, there are already examples of rare species that have become more common as a result of the combination of environmental change and biological trait adaptations.[12] We could temper the "fundamentalism" of biodiversity conservation by investing public funds in long-term plans to support functional biodiversity instead of what may be expensive, short-term efforts to save individual species.

Perhaps the biggest change in ecological design is the emerging focus on conserving underlying processes, instead of emphasizing the restoration of historical patterns or the conservation of characteristic species. The goals of science-based "optimization" have fundamentally shifted. In the nineteenth and twentieth centuries, the primary goal was to keep the environment clean for human and ecological health. In the late twentieth century, the goal shifted to "sustainability" with the intention of creating landscape patterns that would incorporate disturbances and be resilient, meaning they would recover quickly from events like fires and floods. In the twenty-first century, the goal of optimization has been changing again. This time, the goal is to maintain the underlying processes of water flows and biotic dispersal patterns that will allow new groups of species to coexist with humans that will presumably be better adapted to future climates. The recent application of the concept of "operational landscape units" to coastal adaptation is an example of this shift in the goals of ecological design.[13]

As ecological design becomes focused on identifying and conserving or restoring significant underlying processes, hierarchy theory and theories of biodiversity and ecosystem function will continue to be important sources of principles for practice. Designers may look less at the long-term history of a place as

a guide to maintaining biodiversity, and use it more to identify hierarchical processes that could accommodate future biodiversity—with a greater emphasis on
interactions among ecological traits as the source of ecosystem functions, rather
than species per se. We will need to identify significant spatial patterns and flows
that might be called *armatures*, in the sense that many processes depend upon
them. These armatures can be expected to allow transfers of ecological information across spatial and temporal scales, and may include obvious structural
components such as rivers and topographic features, along with less obvious
spatial phenomena such as salinity and temperature gradients in regional aquatic
systems. It is the nexus of these armatures with the processes that they influence
that we will seek to manipulate through design and planning strategies, while
regional climates change around us.

INTELLIGENCE, COMPASSION, AND STRATEGY

Aesthetic experience has also been explicitly addressed in the context of ecological design and planning, particularly in the work of Joan Nassauer and Anne
Spirn, and in the theoretical criticism of Elizabeth Meyer.[14] This area of writing
and practice is important because it knits together a common divide, which has
historically been promoted by authors who seek to separate the romantic from
the rationalist traditions. Meyer and others who have used the concept of performance to link functional and aesthetic goals present an interesting challenge to
that dichotomy, which suggests a different interpretation of aesthetic goals and
experience in designs that are based in part on scientific theories or evidence.

As the sociologist Pierre Bourdieu noted, aesthetic experience varies based
on our social and cultural context, indicating that they are culturally mediated
experiences rather than universal.[15] And yet within those varied cultural contexts,
and sometimes across them, there are still common themes and experiences.
Narratives can develop from raw experiences that are shared among individuals,
and narratives can also mediate our interpretations of the embodied experiences
that produce aesthetic judgments. Some narratives become so compellingly
familiar within a particular cultural context that they are transformed into complex tropes that act as vehicles for coded knowledge, values, and beliefs. The
stories of Frankenstein's monster and the Salem witch trials provide examples;
there are countless others, and a historical examination of folklore, mythology,
popular literature, and political discourse can reveal that particular narratives can
become more or less resonant in a given era. These narratives influence everything from interpersonal relationships to legal cases to national politics; it is no

FIG. 6 — Wall graffiti in Oakland, California.
Photo by A Sin.

surprise that complexly coded narratives also frequently influence the ways in which we comprehend, alter, interpret, and live in landscapes.[16] (**FIG. 6**)

Designers have often used entire narratives or repeated linguistic tropes to provide a compelling vehicle for interpreting a site, or for framing the interpretation they would like a client or public audience to make of their design proposal. In spite of the power of this approach, it is rare to hear the explicit argument that aesthetic experiences can be linked to narratives in ways that identify strategic priorities for designers of landscapes.[17] It is more common for specific landscape components to be seen as fitting a narrative to a greater or lesser degree, as in arguments about whether the presence of non-native plant and animal species or components of traditional architecture suit particular political positions; but the specific, multisensory aesthetic experiences themselves are rarely linked to a larger narrative by designers.[18]

Aesthetic experiences produced by specific materials and finishes provide useful examples, such as the opportunity to see one's own reflection in a reflective, polished surface. The Vietnam Veterans Memorial (1982) in Washington, DC, by Maya Lin, uses physical reflection as a way to catalyze personal and philosophical reflection. Other designs use aesthetic experiences produced by figurative references in form, such as sculptures that represent animals or specific historical figures. In his design for the Franklin Delano Roosevelt Memorial (1997), again in Washington, DC, the landscape architect Lawrence Halprin included a life-size bronze sculpture of Roosevelt in a wheelchair. Visitors often sit on the lap of the sculpted figure to have their photo taken, which is evident in the polished bronze of the lap versus the rest of the figure. Memorable aesthetic experiences can also be produced by dynamics that are encouraged and made accessible by design, such as interacting playfully with floodwaters. Hamburg's Hafencity district creates this opportunity in public areas that are allowed to flood, while also providing elevated walkways to maintain functional circulation.

From a science-based perspective, it makes sense to see aesthetic experience as potentially instrumental, and ask whether aesthetic experiences can have effects on human cognition and behavior. What if designers used specific aesthetic experiences to support behaviors that might be more adaptive in a changing climate, such as decentralized action and human resourcefulness? Can contemporary design develop a framework for introducing particular sensory experiences that promote equal access to narratives of courage, or resourcefulness, or expanded compassion for people and animals that are outside our familiar experience?

Observed data and predictive models both indicate that the biophysical environment we live in is likely to change more rapidly in the future than it has in the past. Designers can use the small-scale sensory experiences they know how to create to help human beings recognize their potential for successful, autonomous adaptation within and across social networks. We can create designed spaces that support the perception that humans are courageous; that humans have a sense of humor that can sustain us; that we are resourceful; and that we can expand our compassion beyond our own "people" to include others who have fewer resources, and decide to share the resources we control through territory and history.

In short, the design and planning of landscapes can be based on science and still be sensuous and filled with memory. Landscapes can be constructed with a humanistic purpose to adapt to the future global environment that science tells us is likely. By giving up our assumed dichotomies, designers can resolve the long-standing conflict between rationality and romantic sentiment—not by eliminating these contrasting perspectives, but by integrating them with a set of open-ended narratives, expressed in form and materiality. The combined use of empirical and predictive science, memory, and strategy provides us with our design intelligence, in a context of compassion and humanism.

Notes

1

Attributed to the Greek writer Aeschylus.

2

Attributed to the science-fiction writer Isaac Asimov.

3

Clive Oppenheimer, "Climatic, Environmental and Human Consequences of the Largest Known Historic Eruption: Tambora Volcano (Indonesia) 1815," *Progress in Physical Geography* 27 (2003): 230–59.

4

Mary Shelley, *Frankenstein; or, The Modern Prometheus* (London: Lackington, Hughes, Harding, Mavor & Jones, 1818).

5

Jean-François Lyotard, *The Postmodern Condition: A Report on Knowledge*, trans. Geoffrey Bennington and Brian Massumi (Minneapolis: University of Minnesota Press, 1984).

6

Kristina Hill, "Shifting Sites," in *Site Matters: Design Concepts, Histories, and Strategies*, ed. Carol J. Burns and Andrea Kahn (New York: Routledge, 2004), 131–56.

7

These are broad topics, beyond the scope of this essay; but I include this specific mention of theories of probability and possibility because these theories highlight the fundamental concept of knowledge representation. In that sense, they are as critical an epistemological underpinning of the sciences as the scientific method itself, and link the sciences to set theory in mathematics as well as to linguistic and philosophical theories of ambiguity and the awareness that all knowledge is conditional.

8

T. F. H. Allen and Thomas B. Starr, *Hierarchy: Perspectives for Ecological Complexity* (Chicago: The University of Chicago Press, 1982). This theory has been developed further by these authors and by others, notably Valerie Ahl and T. F. H. Allen, *Hierarchy Theory: A Vision, Vocabulary and*

Epistemology (New York: Columbia University Press, 1996).

9

I owe this term *next practices* to my former colleague Jorg Sieweke at the University of Virginia.

10

For examples, see Guy F. Midgley's recent overview, "Biodiversity and Ecosystem Function," *Science* 335, no. 6065, (January 2012): 174–75, and Justin P. Wright, Shahid Naeem, Andy Hector, et al., "Conventional Functional Classification Schemes Underestimate the Relationship with Ecosystem Functioning," *Ecology Letters* 9, no. 2 (2006): 111–20.

11

For an example linked to my previous point, see Stuart L. Pimm, "Biodiversity: Climate Change or Habitat Loss—Which Will Kill More Species?," *Current Biology* 18, no. 3 (2008): 117–19.

12

For examples of species that are adapting to climate changes, see an interview with conservation biologist Stuart Pimm, "Loss of Species Due to Climate Change," *Environmental Review* 11, no. 8 (2004): 1–8.

13

See, for example, a recent proposal by the San Francisco Estuary Institute (SFEI) and San Francisco's urban research group, SPUR, to use operational landscape units as a fundamental unit in coastal adaptation.

14

Joan Iverson Nassauer, "Messy Ecosystems, Orderly Frames," *Landscape Journal* 14 (1995): 161–70; Anne Whiston Spirn, *The Language of Landscape* (New Haven, CT: Yale University Press, 2000); Elizabeth L. Meyer, "Sustaining Beauty. The Performance of Appearance: A Manifesto in Three Parts," *Journal of Landscape Architecture* 3, no. 1 (2008): 6–23.

15

See Pierre Bourdieu, *Distinction: A Social Critique of the Judgement of Taste*, trans. Richard Nice (Cambridge, MA: Harvard University Press, 1984); The anthropologist Setha Low has found similar patterns more recently in the way New Yorkers react to the use of different materials in parks. She found that young men from some ethnic minority groups avoid parks that use what she calls "elite materials" because they expect to be followed and harassed in those parks.

16

There are so many examples of this that it is difficult to choose just a few. For a beautifully documented example of how cultural folklore narratives affected a legal case of apparent murder in Ireland, see Angela Bourke's *The Burning of Bridget Cleary: A True Story* (London: Pimlico Press, London, 1999). On narratives and nationalism, see *Discourses of Collective Identity in Central and Southeast Europe*, vol. 2. *National Romanticism: The Formation of National Movements*, ed. Balázs Trencsényi and Michal Kopeček (Budapest: Central European University Press, 2007).

17

Joan Nassauer's theory of "cues to care" is an important exception. She observed in visual preference experiments that rural people from farming communities in the American Midwest were more likely to find patches of unmown grass and thickets of woody plants aesthetically acceptable if they were surrounded by clear signs of care and intention, such as painted wooden fences and even familiar signage. Nassauer proposed a general theory of cues to care as a way of making landscapes with unusual ecological functions more likely to be accepted, if designers can incorporate patterns, features, materials and finishes that suggest intentionality to counter the perception that naturalistic vegetation patterns are unmanaged.

18

For an example of how others are constructing these local narratives, see Hendrik Ernstson and Sverker Sörlin, "Weaving Protective Stories: Connective Practices to Articulate Holistic Values in the Stockholm National Urban Park," *Environment and Planning A* 41, no. 6 (2009): 1460–79.

PART 3 ——

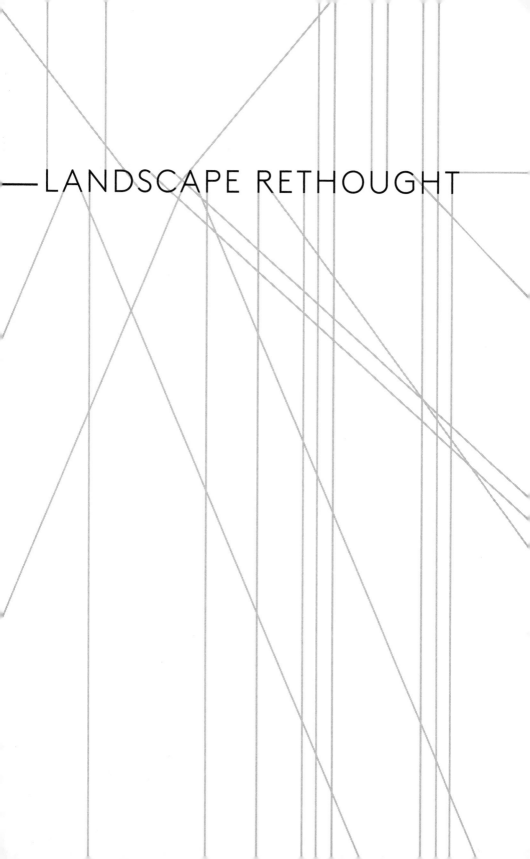

—LANDSCAPE RETHOUGHT

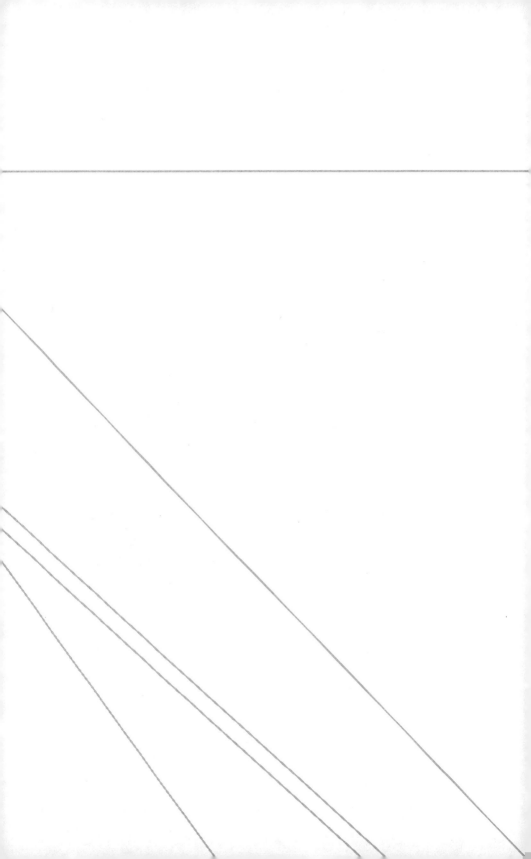

NOT ANYWHERE, NOT ONLY HERE
—*David Leatherbarrow*

The question this brief study addresses concerns the power and significance of terrain in contemporary landscape architecture and architecture, particularly in an age characterized by a high degree of individualization and of globalization. (**FIG. 1**) Briefly stated, my answer is this: the power of terrain today results from its capacity to simultaneously *resist* and *allow* the ambitions of design, particularly its representational ambitions. The significance of designed terrain is not a part of the question that I want to oppose or neglect, only postpone. My concern is with the *constructed* aspect of landscapes and buildings—the fact that they are *made*. Before sites can signify, they must be built. The labor and intentions involved in the latter are what terrain variously resists and allows. My next point is also plain: every built project is built *somewhere*, in some location that is not only territorial but also *dynamic*. With this last term, I mean that they must be subject to a play of forces, both environmental and social, that encompass and reshape what gets built—unnoticeably perhaps, but, over time, decisively. The key, of course, is to grasp the nature of the interplay between construction labor and environmental influence. One of the most challenging developments of the last few years is the reconsideration of the relationships between representation and performance. For many today the first is thought to be largely determined by the second. Built works look as they do because of the ways they behave, although representational aims are never avoided entirely. Today the interplay of *powers* that define both the project and place are thought to largely determine the work's significance.

Now my second premise: *terrain is what the project is not*. To make sense of this simple statement one must try to overcome two longstanding commonplaces: that the significance of a location depends on its familiarity, and that the projects that make them so are somehow native to the place in which they are constructed. I say *try to* overcome these notions because they are too long-standing to be overcome easily. But if landscape architecture and architecture are to be seen as arts—the results of *constructive* intentions—the related ideas of meaning as recognition and construction as cultivation need to be surpassed. When I describe terrain as what the project is not, I am pointing to the latter's essential artificiality.

Let me elaborate this point a little. Designs that intend congeniality with preexisting terrain tend to focus on the aspects of a place that are directly

FIG. 1— Wang Shu, China Academy of Art, Hangzhou, 2014.
All photos by David Leatherbarrow.

perceptible. To some degree, this focus is inevitable. Just as no one can sensibly maintain that terrain is without form or physicality, no one will say that it is imperceptible. Yet, steady dedication to what presents itself immediately often neglects the forces at play in the constitution, development, and deterioration of what we see—forces I have characterized as environmental and social. Neglect for constitutive forces corresponds to concentration on the signifying, not the powerful or formative aspects of terrain.

Project making's basic task, however, is to bring something new to a site— something *not already there*. When that is not carried out, there is no project. And what is imported obtains its place through the labor of construction. A hint about the *constructed* nature of significant terrain can be gleaned from old linguistic usage; specifically, the tensions between three understandings of the word landscape: its scenic sense, its territorial meaning, and the idea of landscape as a constructed domain for social, community, or civic life. The suffix *–scape*, thanks to its early association with painted landscapes, has come to imply the many and varied interpretations of terrain's visual aspects; also the longstanding notion of the landscape as the subject matter of one genre of pictures. Yet, the German equivalent, *–schaft* (as in *Landschaft*), like its English cognate *–ship*, points not to something that is primarily visual, but something made. As verbs, these terms mean to build or create, as in *schaffen*. The old sense of the nouns, on the other hand, can be seen in the ties between the words *ship* and *shape*. A *township*, for example, was a body politic formed under law as well as the territorial domain *shaped* by those citizens. As for the first half of the term, the history of meanings conveyed by the word *land* (in its several European variants) also couples territory with created structures of coexistence. A given stretch of territory would be called *land* because of its legal system or style of governance as much as by its physical characteristics. Defined by laws and customs, *land* gave rise to cultural identity; thus, the English, Danish, and German lands were characterized principally by ways of living. In the eighteenth century, Johann Gottfried Herder's coupling of the ways of a people (*Volk*) and the characteristics of their place and climate expresses the political and territorial sense of land very well.[1] The many nineteenth century variants of this thesis—including but not limited to the materialistic coupling of place and race that provided a pseudorationale for the wars and terror of the twentieth century—both extended and often distorted this same premise. But an earlier and benign articulation of *land* in this double sense can be seen, oddly enough, when paintings are considered. Sixteenth century landscape painting in Northern Europe often portrayed local customs—marrying, trading, and dining—to identify the characteristics of communities that were standing against the Roman Church and its universalizing ambitions. Pieter Brueghel's contemporaries saw his paintings as "pregnant with whole provinces."[2] In his work we see not only the layout and look of terrain but also the life of the place. This point can be made negatively: Albrecht Altdorfer has been described as the first modern landscape painter because his scenes often omit indications of local custom and life, also religious themes, concentrating instead on water, soil, vegetation, and sky—land as such. Traditional subject matter was distinguished from its setting and then replaced by it. What had been the background or supplement became the foreground, although not in a documentary but a fictive sense. Before this time, however, the polar opposite to land was not sea, as with *terrain* in the Latin languages, but forest, because it had not been appropriated into the patterns of society, had not been made fit for life, its dynamism, and cultural norms.

All of the meanings of *land*, *scape*, and *landscape* I have parsed out are available to contemporary usage. The range allows today's writers and designers to alternately emphasize the visual, physical, environmental, or social aspects of landscape. Because so much stress was placed on the visual and signifying sense of landscape in recent decades, contemporary work has reemphasized the landscape's *performative* sense—that is, its environmental and social *operations*.

I would like to join step with this style of thinking, and pursue not the material aspects of projects—discussed so commonly these days—but instead their configurational dimensions; specifically, the mosaic heterogeneity of works that tolerate discontinuous or displaced settings within their expanse, areas that could be called *uncommon grounds*. I have in mind locations in which one is removed from a given area's familiar horizon and relocated to some distant place or time, without, of course, actually going there. Displacement such as this occurs, thanks to the constructive or fictive character of a work, made and made-up. Concrete though it is, the experience is essentially indefinite. Terrain, I will try to show in the example that follows, has the power *to allow* and *to resist* the dislocations we experience today.

PLACE, PAINTING, AND PERFORMANCE

Construction of Wang Shu's designs for the China Academy of Art in Hangzhou started in 2001 and still continues today. While sited at the foot of a small mountain along a river in Hangzhou, it was designed to be seen, sensed, and to perform as both an enlarged version of a traditional garden and a concrete realization of a seventeenth century "mountain-river" painting. (FIG. 2) A commonplace of these paintings is the absence of the axes, metric proportionalities, and enclosures of centralized perspective. Without these constructive means the several distances within the space of the image extend themselves beyond the horizon and the frame. The spread that results allows figures to stand independently and avoid any overlapping that would fix them before or behind one another. A third consequence of this manner of composition is that the painting's middle ground is pervaded by an atmosphere of indefiniteness. One's focus is allowed and expected to move through places that emerge into the fore- and then recede into background, as a result of that very movement. While most architectural elements (when found in these landscapes) are laid out parallel to the picture plane, many also advance toward and beyond the frame at an oblique angle. Diagonal movements lead the eye out of the picture or "over the horizon," as Wang Shu once said of a drawing he made of a project that recalled a mountainous landscape.[3] Depth is there, of course—not constructed according to means Italian Renaissance writers called "legitimate," but through three distancing techniques: high, deep, and level distances; which is to say, up the mountain, into its recesses, and across the waters or terrain at its base.[4] Wang Shu's explanation is as follows: "Chinese landscape paintings never depict the visual image statically, but rather convey a perception of the experience of travelling amidst real landscapes of natural beauty, accompanied by memories and imagination…a garden or a painting is just a temporary pause [in that unending movement]."[5] Through the use of diagonal lines, obliques, or zigzags he approximates these movements in his architecture. "I looked at many traditional landscape paintings related to this region," he wrote, "one [in particular] depicted the lifestyle of rural scholars. A path twisted its way deep into a hollow space formed by the trees, which also

FIG. 2 — Wang Shu, China Academy of Art, Hangzhou, 2007.

FIG. 3 — Wang Shu, Library of Wenzheng College, Suzhou University, 2000.

implied the depth of thoughts. [A peasant's] line of vision was solely from left to right, uninterested in the splendid world outside."[6]

After admitting that the external stairs and ramps that line the facades of some of the campus's buildings are very strange, he said he called them "the mountain."[7] *Mountain* here is less an element of terrain than the type of configuration that encourages unexpected encounters. The hill that forms the center of the campus, however, is insistently present, "heavier than anything he would design," he said, also "speechless."[8] Through his landscape and architecture the hilly terrain obtained its voice, although it sometimes silenced that source.

In explanation of his library at Suzhou University (2000), he wrote:

[M]y purpose was to make people aware that they live between mountains and water, which is the garden style of Suzhou. Backed by a mountain full of bamboo... and facing a lake that used to be a brickfield... the site descends four meters. According to the principles of gardening, buildings between mountain and water should not be prominent. So nearly half of the library is underground... The rectangular main body is floating over the water, facing south, the dominant direction of the winds in summer... The pavilion-like building in the water—the poetry

and philosophy reading room of the library—is from the Chinese literati point of view, in a position where man and nature are balanced."[9] (FIG. 3)
From a narrowly physical point of view the prospect might seem unsuccessfully discordant: white walls against a verdant background, level decks on sloping soil, and hard edges against soft contours. But this view neglects the *operations* Wang Shu tried to accommodate and represent: of breezes through permeable walls, of perspectives that open along the routes between rooms, courts, and pavilions, and of the imagination as readers page their texts.

Discordant performances of this kind were established at the Hangzhou campus at the scale of buildings, rooms, and materials. High differentiation is the result, also the invitation to movement and the accommodation of change. Although architecture initiates these changes, it also relies on forces it cannot control for their continued development, sometimes to the detriment of the project itself. Nevertheless, continual change was proposed from the very start. Wang Shu reported that seven million pieces of broken brick and roof tile were brought to the building site from areas nearby where traditional buildings had been demolished to make room for new construction—part of China's rapid and destructive urbanization. Still bearing traces of their past life and location, the shards were put to use in the new buildings. (FIG. 4)

Describing the initial design, he observed that all the facades are broken down into side views. Insofar as nothing built was allowed to present itself frontally, the mountain preserved its prominence. Why, when the hill is not all that special? "Well," Wang Shu said, "it is still more important than the buildings."[10] I have already observed that he found it impassively silent and ponderous. But that was only one of its faces. A closer view, obtained when climbing its slopes or descending into its hollows, discovers its internal dynamism, its capacity for change, of its own aspects and those of works in its vicinity. The *same* hill presents itself as continually *different*, for its solidities harbor unexpected distances. As such, it allows the imitations the architect has fashioned, but only partly. (FIG.5)

Both phases of the project developed land at the base of the hill, along the course of the area's two streams. Some existing farmlands were preserved, as well as small gardens and fishponds. Pastoral though it may seem, it was to this site that seven million shards of building rubbish were relocated for reuse. Phase one was completed nine years ago. But what one sees today is not what the builders finished. Already, evidences of unintended alterations are apparent: the re- or misuse of spaces, unintended weathering, and two kinds of overgrowth—trees that are now too tall in the courtyards and vines on facades that obscure

FIG. 4 — Wang Shu, Five Scattered Houses, Ningbo, 2006.

FIG. 5 — Wang Shu, Xiangshan Hill, China Academy of Art, Hangzhou, 2014.

FIG. 6 — Wang Shu, China Academy of Art, Hangzhou, 2004.

FIG. 7 — Wang Shu, China Academy of Art, Hangzhou, 2007.

FIG. 8 — Wang Shu, China Academy of Art, Hangzhou, 2004.

apertures. (FIGS. 6-7) Unforeseen, but in hindsight understandable, these changes show the site's capacity to remake itself. What Wang Shu designed and built is not gone, only exceeded by evidences of a metabolism beyond his control. Do the courtyards perform the way they were intended, offering partial views to nearby settings and aspects of the mountain? Yes, but not only that, for they also reveal the growing size and changing lifestyle of today's students. Do the surfaces still attest to the existence of now demolished village houses? Only partly, because they also show the influence of an exceedingly damp and verdant climate. What had been inserted has been absorbed by the terrain, as if the sympathies with the site construction enjoyed were secretly accompanied by a corresponding measure of apathy. Above all else, Wang Shu was impressed by the mountain's brooding silence. (FIG. 8)

When projects take up a conversation with preexisting conditions they generally succeed in making some of their points apparent; but in the course of the dialogue they also suffer some unexpected assertions, different forms of mismaintenance, over- or undergrowth, reuse that tends toward misuse, and so on. The labors of design and construction are not for that reason unsuccessful, for they survive in part, requalifying the location and freeing it into kinds of significance that could not have been realized anywhere, but are not defined by meanings assumed to exist only there. Freedom of that sort—design's greatest task—finds its foothold in conditions that are both specific to the project and seen otherwise, thanks to the qualities of the work itself. (FIG. 9)

FIG. 9 — Wang Shu, China Academy of Art, Hangzhou, 2014.

Notes

1

Although the entire book is abridged, the chapter entitled "National Genius and the Environment" is published in full in Johann Gottfried von Herder, *Reflections on the Philosophy of the History of Mankind* (Chicago: University of Chicago Press, 1968), 3–78. The full text of the entire book can be found in Johann Gottfried von Herder, "*Ideen zur Philosophie der Geschichte der Menschheit*," in *Herders Werke*, ed. Ernst Naumann, vol. 3, bks. 7 and 8 (Berlin: Deutsches Verlagshaus Bong, 1908): 41–109.

2

This term is cited in Kenneth R. Olwig, "Recovering the Substantive Nature of Landscape," *Annals of the Association of American Geographers* 86, no. 4 (1996): 634. I have also benefited from the discussion of terms in this study.

3

Wang Shu, "A Tea Garden and A Reading Room," in *Imagining the House* (Zürich: Lars Müller, 2012), n.p., section 6.1.

4

A brief, introductory description of these "distances" can be found in George Rowley, *Principles of Chinese Painting* (Princeton: Princeton University Press, 1959), especially 64.

5

Wang Shu, "A House as Sleep," in *Imagining the House*, n.p., section 1.0.

6

Wang Shu, "A Picturesque House," in *Imagining the House*, n.p., section 4.0.

7

Wang Shu, "Build a World to Resemble Nature," in *Topography and Mental Space, Architectural Studies* 2 (Beijing: China Architecture and Building Press, 2012), 202.

8

Ibid., 198.

9

Wang Shu, "Library of Wenzheng College at Suzhou University," World-Architects.com, http://www.world-architects.com/en/projects/detail_thickbox/1754.

10

Wang Shu, "Build a World to Resemble Nature," 200.

MAPPING IN THE AGE OF ELECTRONIC
SHADOWS—*Alessandra Ponte*

And yet the great applicability of the musical simile in the field of biology lies in
this very expansion of the concept of tone from a mere heard tone to the meaning
tone of objects which appear in a subject's environment as carriers of meaning.
　—Jakob von Uexküll, *A Theory of Meaning*

P.R.: So architects are not necessarily the masters of space that they once
were, or believed themselves to be.
M.F.: That's right. They are not the technicians or engineers of the three great
variables—territory, communication, and speed. These escape the domain of
architects.
　—Michel Foucault, interview by Paul Rabinow

The shifting nature of the geopolitical events of the last two decades has triggered a debate around the notions of territory and/or territoriality.[1] An analysis
of processes of territorialization and deterritorialization (inspired, initially at
least, by practices identified by Gilles Deleuze and Félix Guattari in *A Thousand
Plateaus*) has been followed by further investigations of the concepts of border
and frontier.[2] In the light of the most straightforward and widely accepted definition of *territory* as "bounded space," the constitution of the idea of space itself
has also come under scrutiny, along with questions relating to sovereignty and
power. A rediscovery of the work of Michel Foucault—prompted partly by the
publication and translation of his lectures at the Collège de France, and partly
by Deleuze's reading or, more recently, Giorgio Agamben's interpretations of
Foucauldian theses on knowledge, power, and biopolitics—has supplied the
theoretical tools with which to approach and unravel the logic of emerging
regimes of spatial politics.[3]

　In addition, over the same period, cartography—a primary tool of territorial representation and governance—has been radically altered by rapid advances
in communication technologies, bringing new forms of data gathering and cal-
culation as well as new platforms and interface systems, and constantly multi-
plying mobile devices for accessing and producing geographic information. A
succinct inventory of these new territories could include satellite imagery, global
positioning and geographical information systems, Google Maps (together

with Street View), Google Earth, Twitter Map and Twitter Trendsmap, and the still-problematic 3-D map app for the iPhone, together with user-generated online maps and different forms of open-source cartographies.[4] One salient character of these new applications and technologies is the almost total suppression of the materiality of the cartographic representation. Information is gathered and presented through screens and displays, while paper seems to subsist only as an occasional support. The near disappearance of material representations of geographical data, with their stable, time-freezing figuration of the world, runs parallel to the upsurge in interest in tracing a more flickering, fluctuating, mobile and event-related reality. Not coincidentally, the opening up of these new realms of cartographic possibilities has contributed (among other things) to current arguments about processes of globalization that, having declared the demise of the territory, bypass territorial investigations and representations in order to focus on networks analysis and mapping.[5]

The interaction with geographical information through screens and displays has also prompted a return to a presumably "original" *navigational* use and interpretation of maps, as opposed to the erroneous and misleading *mimetic* understanding of the cartographic effort. An investigation of the relations between maps, territory, and risks has led Bruno Latour and others to pose the following questions: "Is a map...not a representation of the world but an inscription that does (or sometimes does not) work in the world? Do maps and mapping precede the territory they 'represent,' or can they be understood as producing it?"[6] Latour and his team inscribed these interrogations against the background of conceptual uncertainty regarding the meaning and role of cartographic practices that has characterized studies in the field in recent decades. In their introduction to a recent anthology on mapping theories, Martin Dodge, Rob Kitchin, and Chris Perkins observe that while the plurality of interpretations may appear to undermine the credibility of cartography as a "science," it can also be read as a symptom of an intellectual effervescence that has revived a discipline that had been advancing mainly through improvements in technology and methodology.[7]

In parallel to the upheavals taking place in the geosciences and cartography, design disciplines and artistic practices have exhibited a growing fascination with theories informing geography and a readiness to borrow mapping tools. A brief, far-from-exhaustive inventory of the more recent attempts to renew and "expand" the field of architecture through the appropriation of cartographic techniques and geographical theories could include an expansive range of undertakings: Among these is the psychogeography proposed during the late 1950s

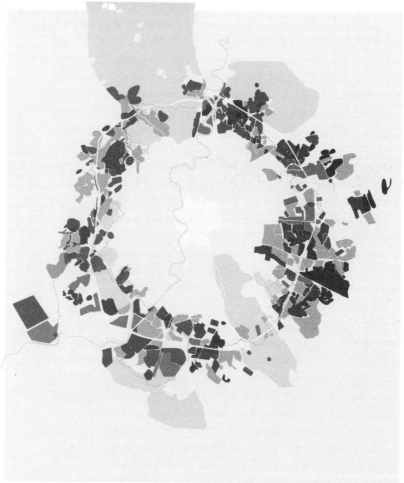

FIG. 1 (TOP) — Stalker "Walking around
the GRA (Rome highway belt)," Spring
2009. *Project PrimaveraRomana. GRA.
Geografie dell'Oltrecittà, Walking for an U
Turn,* 2009.
Photo by Giulia Fiocca.

FIG. 2 (BOTTOM) — Stalker "Rome. Commons
& Eclaves," *Project PrimaveraRomana. GRA.
Geografie dell'Oltrecittà, Walking for an U
Turn,* 2009.
*Edit by Giulia Fiocca, Bennie Meek, Margherita Pisano,
Lorenzo Romito, and Giacomo Zanelli.*

and 1960s by the French situationists, revived in Anglo-Saxon academic milieus during the late 1980s and periodically revisited ever since by various experimental groups of architects and artists like Stalker/Osservatorio Nomade (founded in Rome in 1995).[8] (FIGS. 1-2) We have the cinematic charting of cities initiated by Bernard Tschumi in *Manhattan Transcripts* (1976–81), which was transformed by Nigel Coates and the North Atlantic Treaty Organization into a "narrative" architecture built around installations, performances, and video productions, was adopted as a pedagogical method at the Architectural Association School of Architecture, continues to have a powerful presence today, albeit in transmuted forms (after being revived by Peter Cook at the Bartlett, University College London).[9] Also, the enthusiastic appropriation of the diagram can be understood as a type of map, as a design tool by the "digital" architecture of the 1990s.[10] There is Rem Koolhaas's pedagogical experiment at the Harvard Graduate School of Design, which ran from 1996 to 2000 under the name of the Harvard *Project on the City* (wrongly interpreted by most as a new version of Denise Scott Brown and Robert Venturi's *Learning from Las Vegas*), which provoked an avalanche of so-called research studios.[11] In addition, there are the *datascapes* embodied in the visionary projects of MVRDV, launched by Winy Maas's *Metacity/Datatown* (1999) and the mapping of Israeli architect Eyal Weizman, beginning with his 2002 publication of the first comprehensive charting of Jewish settlements in the Occupied Territories (and the map of Gaza, 2005).[12] This list could also include the plethora of urban studies influenced by Nigel Thrift's nonrepresentational propositions and by the charting of transient webs of relations prescribed by Bruno Latour's Actor-Network-Theory (ANT).[13]

In the field of landscape architecture, James Corner's *Taking Measures Across the American Landscape* (1996, in collaboration with Alex S. MacLean), together with the 1999 essay-manifesto "The Agency of Mapping," signaled the radical renewal of a mapping approach in landscape design that had been inaugurated by the environmental concerns of Ian McHarg in the early 1960s.[14] Corner's exploration, cross-pollinated with architectural theories (his collaboration with Stan Allen, for example), merged with other research projects investigating the "artificial" barriers separating landscape architecture from architecture and urban design, and is now inscribed in the emergence in the late 1990s of landscape urbanism, with Charles Waldheim as its main theorist. In operating on extensive portions of cities and regions, landscape urbanists such as James Corner, Anuradha Mathur, Alan Berger, and Chris Reed privilege maps and the charting of ecological and energetic systems. Mapping remains a central

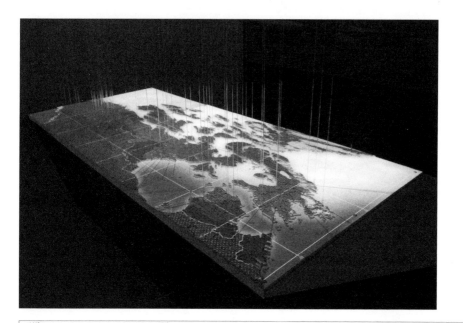

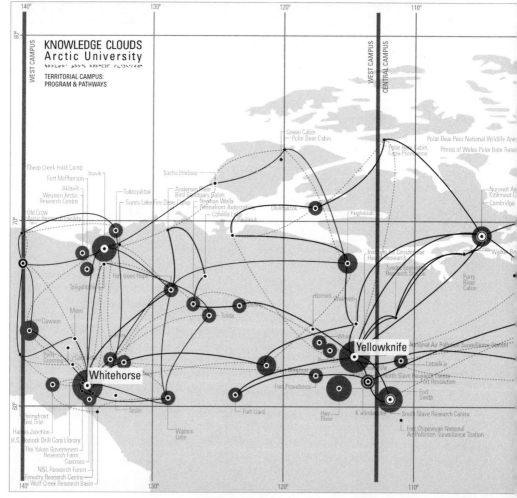

KNOWLEDGE CLOUDS
Arctic University

TERRITORIAL CAMPUS:
PROGRAM & PATHWAYS

WEST CAMPUS

WEST CAMPUS

CENTRAL CAMPUS

Green Cabin
Polar Bear Cabin

Polar Bear Pass National Wildlife Are:
Prince of Wales Polar Bear Rese

Polar Bear Cabin,
Cape Providence

Sheep Creek Field Camp
Fort McPherson
Aklavik
Western Arctic
Research Centre
Old Crow
Arctic Research Facility

Inuvik

Tuktoyaktuk

Sachs Harbour

Anderson River
Bird Sanctuary Cabin
Sunny Lake Fire Base Camp — Norman Wells
Permafrost Autostation
Colville L. — Paulatuk

Nunavut A
Kitikmeot C.
Cambridge

Ulukhaktok

Kugluktuk

Institute for Circumpolar
Health Research

Walker B

Tsiigehtchic

Fort Good Hope

Tundra Ecos
Research Station

Parry
River
Cabin

Mayo

Dawson

Behchoko Wekweeti

Tulita

National Air Pollution Surveillance Station

Yellowknife

Pelly
Crossing

Whitehorse

Teslin

Fort Liard

Fort Providence

Hay
River

K'atlodeeche

Lutselk'e
North Slave Research Centre
Fort Resolution

Fort
Smith

South Slave Research Centre

Permafrost
Test Site

Haines Junction
H.S. Bostock Drill Core Library
The Yukon Government
Research Farm
Carcross
N&L Research Forest
Forestry Research Centre
Wolf Creek Research Basin

Watson
Lake

Fort Chipewyan National
Air Pollution Surveillance Station

FIG. 3 (OPPOSITE) — Lateral Office, "Knowledge Clouds," 2013. Animated mapping projections onto a physical model show existing and proposed education networks across remote Northern Canada. *Photo courtesy of Lateral Office.*

FIG. 4 (BELOW) — Lateral Office, "Knowledge Clouds," 2013. Proposed regional campus of northern education networks.

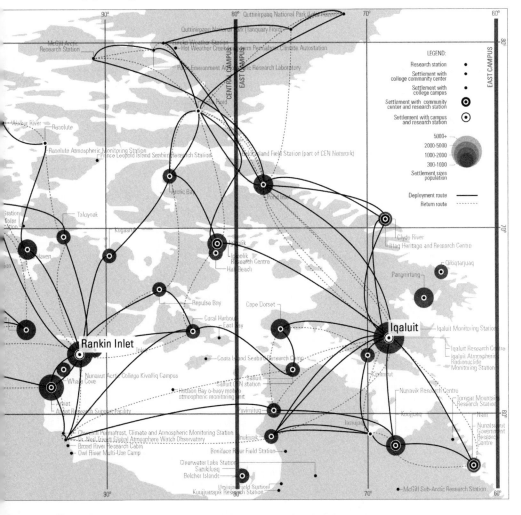

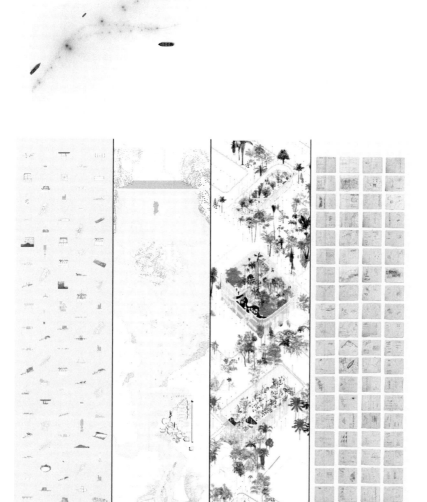

FIG. 5 (TOP) — Luis Callejas / Paisajes Emergentes, Venice Lagoon park. Detail of artificial reefs and vaporetto routes, 2013. *Courtesy of Luis Callejas / LCLA Office.*

FIG. 6 (BOTTOM) — Luis Callejas / LCLA office, "Islands & Atolls: A Taxonomy," 2015. *Courtesy of Luis Callejas / LCLA Office.*

concern of landscape urbanism's recently updated version, ecological urbanism, and an essential preoccupation in the practices of landscape architects and of architects.[15] Both are now advocating the territory or "territorial infrastructure" as a mode and scale of intervention.[16] (FIGS. 3-6)

The geographic and mapping fever of the last decades, rather than indicating (as has been suggested) a "geographic turn" or even a "geological turn," may instead be a symptom of deep anxiety about the waning agency of architects, urban designers, planners, and landscape architects.[17] The search for a merging or hybridization of these disciplines, the attempts to integrate environmental and social sciences into design practice, and the loudly vocalized ambition of architects and landscape architects to reclaim the right to design infrastructure at a territorial scale—all raise at least two orders of problems. The first relates to the obvious need to address the ongoing process of redefinition of the inter-related notions of space, territory, border, and network, a process in which a few architectural theorists are already engaged. The second demands equally urgent investigations of the frontiers and agency of each design discipline. Questions may be formulated as follows: Is there a territory of architecture (or landscape architecture, or urban design)? And if so, what are its borders? Are the disciplines undergoing a process of deterritorialization? Is it advisable to suppress the frontiers between art, architecture, landscape architecture, urban design, engineering, physical sciences, environmental sciences, and social sciences? Is it plausible to think that all these sciences and disciplines are engaged in design practices, and that this is the bond that unites them? If this is the case, how would this coming together of the arts and the sciences under the banner of design differ, for example, from the 1960s' frustrated efforts to build a discipline of "environmental design"? Should the scope and meaning of the notion of design be expanded?

A few years ago, in a lecture titled "A Cautious Prometheus? A Few Steps Toward a Philosophy of Design (with Special Attention to Peter Sloterdijk)," Bruno Latour argued rather persuasively that "design has been extended from the details of daily objects to cities, landscapes, nations, cultures, bodies, genes and . . . nature itself, which is in great need of being redesigned."[18] According to him, the definition of design has expanded both in terms of "comprehension"—because design swallows up more and more components of things—and "extension," since it applies to ever-larger assemblages of production. Here Latour is alluding to his well-known distinction between "objects" and "things," between "matters of fact" and "matters of concern."[19] For him, "things" are artifacts, i.e., "complex assemblages of contradictory issues," in contrast to modernist "objects," on which the focus is materiality and the issue of design is reduced to the application of a fashionable veneer, separate from the "facts" of material and function. In Latour's perspective, therefore, modernist objects are attached to matters of fact, while things pose very different sorts of queries. They are tied to matters of concern, and about a thing we can ask: Does it work? Is it well designed? Should it be redesigned?

According to Latour, "things" may be better understood in the perspective of Sloterdijk's rethinking of the Heideggerian notion of *Dasein*. To follow Sloterdijk's "*Dasein* is design," designers would have to abandon the shores of modernism and sail toward new modes of designing, or redesigning, climates, life-support systems, air-conditioning apparatuses, soundscapes, immunological devices, shielding membranes, and protective envelopes. If *Dasein* means to be thrown into the world, then designers need to identify this world populated by things, human and nonhuman. To define life is to define the *Umwelt*, the envelope surrounding life. The Umwelt is the environment as described by the German biologist Jakob von Uexküll, a notion borrowed by Sloterdijk to talk about the "spheres," or fabricated milieus, inhabited today by humans and nonhumans on life-support systems. If Martin Heidegger's *Dasein* was the philosophy of the German farmer condemned to spend most of the year waiting for his wheat to grow, Sloterdijk's formula "*Dasein* is design" hurls the concept into the space age. This is why the issue today is to decide whether atmospheres are well designed, and why architects, landscape architects, planners, and engineers ought to design and redesign membranes, and move from envelope to envelope, and from fold to fold. Spheres, folds, membranes, and envelopes demand a new understanding and representation of space. Because Latour's "things" are not Euclidian objects traveling in an abstract, Cartesian *res extensa*, new tools are needed to draw together, materialize, simulate, and approximate what things are in all their materiality and conflicting nature. In other words, it may be said that Latour, in the wake of Sloterdijk, is inviting designers to develop new ways of apprehending and charting (human and nonhuman) life and its (designed) milieu.

In so doing, Latour problematizes the concept of environment, which peculiarly seems to have only a tangential impact on contemporary debates and design proposals addressing maps and territories. Or, to be more precise, while the "question of the environment" is often mentioned as a crucial concern in most landscape urbanism schemes and territorial infrastructure projects, designers do not appear particularly concerned to explain precisely what this "question" entails or what "environment" might mean. Yet Latour, following Sloterdijk, strategically selects a very specific understanding of the notion—one developed during the 1930s in von Uexküll's biological model, which differentiated a living being's external surroundings from the subjective, phenomenal world (the Umwelt) it inhabited. Von Uexküll was carefully read by most of the German intelligentsia, including Heidegger and renowned architects such as Ludwig Mies van der Rohe. Picking up the baton, Sloterdijk's trilogy on *Spheres* revisits the biologist's theories, proposing an onto-anthropology or metaphysical (and morphological) investigation of the history of the world-image (environment).[20] His *Domestication of Being: Clarifying the Clearing* applauds von Uexküll's "inspired" definition of *Umwelt*; here, constantly "thinking with Heidegger against Heidegger," he also attempts to transform the now obsolete Heideggerian concept of "land," which opened like a "clearing" (*Lichtung*) in primeval, dark German forests, bringing light (*Licht*) into the darkness through processes of literal illumination, and enlightenment.[21] Sloterdijk thus updates the whole array of notions related to what "surrounds us" today, i.e., an environment made of electric light, airwaves, ultrasound, and electronic shadows.

Interestingly, von Uexküll's famous *A Foray into the Worlds of Animals and Humans* (1934) includes a chapter titled "Heim und Heimat" (translated into English as "Home and Territory"), in which he affirms that "[t]erritory is purely a problem of the environment because it represents an exclusively subjective product, the presence of which even the most detailed knowledge of the surroundings offers no explanation at all." Tellingly, he also suggests a common theme of aggression in human and animal territorial behavior:

> With many animals, one would likely experience that they defend their hunting ground against other animals of their own species and thereby make it into their territory. Any piece of land at all would seem to be a political map for all species if one were to inscribe these territorial areas into it, and this demarcation would be established through attack and defence. It would also turn out that, in many cases, no more free land at all is available, and one territory bumps up against another.[22]

The aggressive rhetoric of the Third Reich's *Lebensraum* (living space) comes to mind. Despite such disturbing undertones, von Uexküll's provided radical reformulations of scientific (and ontological) understandings of the relation between life and its milieu together with a novel conceptualization of the meaning of territorial formations. (**FIG. 7**) Against the life sciences' presumption of a possible "objective" apprehension of reality, von Uexküll poses multiple

Abb. 36. Heim und Heimat des Stichlings.

FIG. 7— "Heim und Heimat des Stichlings" ("Home and Territory of the Stickleback") from Jakob von Uexküll, *Streifzüge durch die Umwelten von Tieren und Menschen*, 1934.

Abb. 54. Fuchs und Eiche.

FIG. 8— "Fuchs und Eiche" (Fox and oak) from Jakob von Uexküll, *Streifzüge durch die Umwelten von Tieren und Menschen*, 1934.

FIG. 9— "Borkenkäfer und Eiche" (Bark beetle and oak) from Jakob von Uexküll, *Streifzüge durch die Umwelten von Tieren und Menschen*, 1934.
(Figs. 7–9 from: Jakob von Uexküll, Streifzüge durch die Umwelten von Tieren und Menschen: ein Bilderbuch unsichtbarer Welten *[Berlin: Springer, 1934]).*

Abb. 57. Borkenkäfer und Eiche.

subjective realities and an equally subjective production of territories. Toward the end of *A Foray Into the Worlds of Animals and Humans*, he writes: "each and every subject lives in a world in which there are only subjective realities and that environments themselves represent only subjective realities. Whoever denies the existence of subjective realities has not recognized the foundations of his or her own environment."[23] Von Uexküll then briefly attempts to explore the interrelations between individual environmental bubbles or, in his own words, to answer the question: "How does the subject exempt itself as an object in the different environments in which it plays an important role?"[24] Von Uexküll introduces the example of an oak tree. The tree itself is understood as a subject responding to selected environmental marks or signs. But it also plays different roles as an object in a multitude of other individual environments: a forester considers how much wood can be obtained from its trunk; a little girl is scared by the dreadful face she sees inscribed on the bark; a fox inhabits the roots while an owl takes shelter in the branches; an ant uses the bark as a hunting ground whereas a bark beetle lays its eggs in it. (FIGS.8-9) Following the musical analogy proposed by von Uexküll, to each subject the oak presents a different "tone": a use tone (for the forester), a magic tone (for the girls), a protection tone (for the fox and the owl), or a food tone (for the ant). Von Uexküll concludes avowing the impossibility of summarizing the multiple tonal characters of the oak tree as an object, while maintaining that such multiplicity represent only partially a subject "solidly put together in itself, which carries and shelters all environments."[25] The musical comparison returns in a later, significant text of von Uexküll's, "A Theory of Meaning" (*Bedeutungslehre*, 1940)—this time as a fully developed theory of "Nature" as composer.

In music, states von Uexküll, at least two tones are required in order to form a harmony. He elaborates: "In the composition of a duet, the two voices that are supposed to melt into a harmony should be composed for each other, note for note, point for point. The theory of counterpoint in music rests on this." In nature, the observer should similarly search for two factors that together form a unity, and therefore begin investigating how a subject situated in its environment establishes harmonious relationships to objects that present themselves as carriers of meanings:

> The subject's organism forms the utilizer of meaning or at least the receiver of meaning. If these two factors join together in the same meaning, then they have been composed together by Nature. Which rules come to the surface thereby— this forms the content of the composition theory in Nature.

In order to decide how two subjects build a harmonious relationship, one of them should be elected as utilizer of meaning and the other as carrier of meaning. It is then possible to explore how their mutual properties perform as point and counterpoint. To clarify the melodic counterpoint of "perception side" and "effect side," and to finally establish the specific meaning rule of a composition, von Uexküll provides numerous examples (including the famous case of the tick), of what he calls "circuits of meaning," or functional cycles that connect subjects and carrier of meanings.[26]

Sloterdijk was not the first to point out the significance of inquiring into the environment while signaling the worth of von Uexküll's theses. Leo Spitzer, in "*Milieu* and *Ambiance*: An Essay in Historical Semantics," a vastly evocative survey of 1942, proposing an archaeology of the layered universe of meanings in which the concepts of milieu and ambiance are historically immersed, mentioned von Uexküll briefly to dismiss his oeuvre as scientific popularization, and focus instead on Heidegger's understanding of the Umwelt (despite the fact that Heidegger was an attentive reader of von Uexküll).[27] Ten years later, however, the philosopher of science Georges Canguilhem retraced in a pioneering essay the history of the concept of milieu, observing that the notion was becoming a universal and required way to capture both the experience and the existence of living beings, and that it was possible to recognize the idea of milieu (or environment) as a category of contemporary thought. In this groundbreaking text Canguilhem analyzed at length von Uexküll's propositions underlying the radical refocusing of the scientific attention on the "irreducible activity of life" and the question of meaning. In fact, Canguilhem's conclusion seems to paraphrase von Uexküll's own while addressing the multiple meanings of the world *milieu* in French, which can be translated as "environment" but at the same time signifies "middle," "center," "in-between," and "medium":

> And thus the milieu proper to men is not situated within the universal milieu as contents in a container. A centre does not revolve into its environment. A living being is not reducible to a crossroads of influences. From this stems the insufficiency of any biology that, in complete submission to the spirit of the psychochemical sciences, would seek to eliminate all consideration of sense from its domain. From the biological and psychological point of view, a sense is an appreciation of values in relation to a need. And for the one who experiences and lives in it, a need is an irreducible, and thereby absolute, system of reference.[28]

Canguilhem's brilliant inquiry inspired a generation of thinkers, notably Michel Foucault and Gilbert Simondon, who together with Gilles Deleuze and Félix

Guattari expanded the investigation of the notion's multiple declinations, and tested their operativity. Notably, Foucault quoted Canguilhem's essay on the living and its milieu in the introductory lecture of his course Security, Territory, Population, delivered at the Collège de France in 1977–78, to elucidate a pivotal shift in the "art of government." According to Foucault, during the second half of the eighteenth century, previous concerns over the government of territories (their acquisition, defense, description, inventory, administration), had given way to the formation of novel (modern) apparatuses of power devised to administer the population and its milieus. At this particular moment in history, milieus became terrains of intervention that targeted a population apprehended as a multiplicity of individuals deeply and biologically bonded to the materiality within which they existed. To explore these new formations, Foucault shifted the focus of his studies toward questions of power and "governmentality," which he defined as "the ensemble formed by the institutions, procedures, analyses and reflections, the calculations and tactics that allow the exercise of this very specific albeit complex form of power, which has as its target the population, as its principal form of knowledge political economy, and as its essential technical means apparatuses of security."[29]

Canguilhem was Foucault's thesis advisor; he was also present at the defense of the doctoral thesis of Gilbert Simondon when a crucial repositioning of the relation between individual and milieu was proposed. Unusually situated in the panorama of French philosophy in the twentieth century, Simondon has been rediscovered mainly as author of *Du mode d'existence des objets techniques* (*On the Mode of Existence of Technical Objects*). Published in 1958, the book presented the materials elaborated by Simondon for his complementary doctoral dissertation, and contributed to his repute as original thinker in the field of technology. However, the main thesis, which appeared in 1964 under the title of *L'individu et sa genèse physico-biologique* (*The Individual and its Physical-Biological Genesis*), should be read in parallel to the first publication in order to grasp Simondon's project in its entirety, i.e., to invent for philosophy a specific mode of addressing all "objects" without espousing science's objectifying relation to knowledge. Refusing dualities or oppositions such as subject/object, form/matter, interiority/exteriority, identity/difference, or vitalism/mechanism, Simondon reformulated ontological and genetic questions beginning with the milieu. Paraphrasing the words of Jean-Hughes Barthélémy, subtle interpreter of Simondon's oeuvre, to enter Simondon's thought means to respect the rule of thinking about the milieu and more precisely about the relation between the individual and its "associated milieu."

If we limit ourselves to thinking about the individual life in relation to its milieu, the suggestion appears rather obvious, but ceases to be so if we follow Simondon in considering from the same perspective the physical individual, and the technical individual. Besides, in Simondon's logic we should think the relation between the two terms (*individual* and *milieu*) without assuming the existence of one or the other anterior to the coming into existence of the relation itself. For Simondon the problem is to account for the genesis of the individual (life or machine) beginning with a primeval phase when individuals and associated milieus are the resultant of each other. Paradigms supplied by contemporary physics allowed Simondon to think of a "pre-physical and pre-vital" (therefore "pre-individual") phase from which the individual, physical or vital, is generated. Such was the condition also for thinking the phylogenetic "individuation" of technical objects in their associated milieus until they become, in the industrial age, machines, or "technical individuals."[30] Simondon's thinking of the genesis of the living and of the technical as analogical processes of individuation opened the way to an affirmative reassessment of technicity and to the perception of the technical object as beautiful in its meaningful encounter with the world. In a 1982 letter addressed to Jacques Derrida, in discussing the foundation of the Collège International de Philosophie, Simondon proposed a "techno-aesthetics." In the note, among other technical objects and buildings, he celebrated the beauty and "intense semantic power" of a set of emission antennas. The antennas, he wrote, like a metal forest playing between earth and sky, testify to the existence of an energetic nonmaterial world: "The technicized landscape also takes on the meaning of a work of art."[31]

Canguilhem, in the second edition of his *Knowledge of Life*, in which the essay on the living and its milieu was included, corrected part of his arguments and applauded Simondon's insights on the individual and his physical-biological genesis—a courtesy that Simondon would not reciprocate, maintaining an ominous silence on the work of the great epistemologist.[32] The person who understood the radical potential of Simondon's oeuvre was Gilles Deleuze, who besides authoring an enthusiastic review of *L'individu et sa genèse physico-biologique*, creatively borrowed concepts from Simondon in *Difference and Repetition*, *The Logic of Sense*, and *A Thousand Plateaus*, written with Félix Guattari.[33] In *A Thousand Plateaus*, Deleuze and Guattari, in a section where they discuss at length the interactions between milieus and territories, write:

> Every milieu is vibratory, in other words, a block of space-time, constituted by the
> periodic repetition of the component. Thus the living thing has an exterior milieu

of materials, an interior milieu of composing elements and composed substances, an intermediary milieu of membranes and limits, and an annexed milieu of energy sources and actions-perceptions. Every milieu is code, the code being defined by periodic repetitions; but each code is in a perpetual state of transcoding or transduction. Transcoding or transduction is the manner in which one milieu serves as basis for another, or conversely is established atop another milieu, dissipates in it or is constituted in it.[34]

This arresting passage evidently reverberates crucial concepts introduced by Simondon including the notion of transduction, which for Simondon referred to the process of individuation of the real itself and was defined as "a physical, biological, mental, social operation through which an activity propagates gradually within a domain, by founding this propagation on a structuration of the domain that is realized from one place to the next."[35] Yet Deleuze and Guattari, in the same chapter, aptly titled "Of the Refrain," in an astonishing *detournement*, while appropriating von Uexküll's theory of nature as composer, attribute the concept to him. They state: "Jakob von Uexküll has elaborated an admirable theory of transcoding. He sees the components as melodies in counterpoint, each of which serves as a motif for another: Nature as music. Whenever there is transcoding, we can be sure that there is not a simple addition, but the constitution of a new plane, as of a surplus value. A melodic or rhythmic plane, surplus value of passage or bridging."[36] The transposition from Simondon to von Uexküll permits to account for the territory as a subjective and aesthetic production. The territory, for Deleuze and Guattari (borrowing from von Uexküll) is an "act that affects milieus and rhythms, that 'territorialize' them." The territory is marked by indexes that "may be components taken from any of the milieus: materials, organic products, skin or membrane states, energy sources, action-perception condensates." A territory materializes when milieu components cease to be directional and functional to become dimensional and expressive. Functions, maintain Deleuze and Guattari, do not explain the territory but presuppose it. The territorializing element resides "in the becoming expressive of rhythm and melody, in other words, in the emergence of proper qualities (colour, odour, sound, silhouette...)." And they ask: "Can this becoming, this emergence, be called art?"[37]

Simondon and von Uexküll, not one or the other, but all the possible relations presupposed by the *and* in-between the theorists—are a perfect example of Deleuze and Guattari's rhizomatic thinking that proceeds from the middle, the *milieu*, and is posited against the totalizing, arborescent model of thought. *A Thousand Plateaus* was Deleuze and Guattari's epic attempt at building a geophilosophy, at charting (literally) new territories for life. Their endeavor, together with the investigations of Spitzer, Canguilhem, Foucault, Simondon, and Sloterdijk, epitomizes a divergent approach that, beyond underlining the complexity of the enquiry and the urgency of the undertaking, may possibly indicate original ways to overcome the 1960s impasse in the building of a discipline of "environmental design." They may likewise clarify how and why researches into the notion(s) of environment should always be related to current investigations, not only of the territory and its representation, but also of processes of territorialization and deterritorialization, of the bonding of technical objects and living individuals, of the possibility of opening the way to the empowerment of subjects and to new production and understanding of aesthetic expressions.

Notes

Epigraphs:
Jakob von Uexküll, *Bedeutungslehre* (1940), translated by Joseph D. O'Neil as "A Theory of Meaning" in *A Foray Into the Worlds of Animals and Humans, with A Theory of Meaning*, Posthumanities 12 (Minneapolis: University of Minnesota Press, 2010), 188.

Michel Foucault, "Space, Knowledge and Power," interview by Paul Rabinow,*Skyline: The Architecture and Design Review* (March 1982): 16–20, 17.

1
Among the most recent literature on the topic, see David Delaney, *Territory: A Short Introduction* (Oxford: Blackwell Publishing, 2005); Saskia Sassen, *Territory, Authority, Rights: From Medieval to Global Assemblages* (Princeton: Princeton University Press, 2006); Stuart Elden, *Terror and Territory: The Spatial Extent of Sovereignty* (Minneapolis: University of Minnesota Press, 2009); Stuart Elden, "Land, Terrain, Territory," *Progress in Human Geography* 34, no. 6 (2010): 799–817; Stuart Elden, "The Space of the World," in *Scales of the Earth*, New Geographies 4, (2011): 26–31; Jeppe Strandsbjerg, *Territory, Globalization*

and *International Relations: The Cartographic Reality of Space* (Basingstoke: Palgrave-MacMillan, 2010). See also Jean Gottmann, *The Significance of Territory* (Charlottesville: University Press of Virginia, 1973); Paul Alliès, *L'invention du territoire* (Grenoble: Presses Universitaires de Grenoble, 1980); Claude Raffestein, *Pour une géographie du pouvoir* (Paris: Librairies Techniques, 1980); Edward Soja, *Postmodern Geographies: The Reassertion of Space in Critical Social Theory* (London: Verso, 1989); and Edward Soja, *Thirdspace: Journeys to Los Angeles and Other Real-and-Imagined Places* (Oxford: Blackwell, 1996).

2
See, for example, Herman Parret, Bart Verschaffel, and Mark Verminck, *Ligne, frontière, horizon* (Liège, Bel.: Mardaga, 1993); Piero Zanini, *Significati del confine: I limiti naturali, storici, mentali* (Milano: Bruno Mondadori, 1997); Henk van Houtum, "The Geopolitics of Borders and Boundaries," *Geopolitics* 10 (2005): 672–79; Henk van Houtum, "Waiting before the Law: Kafka on the Border," *Social & Legal Studies* 19, no. 3 (2010): 285–97; Corey Johnson et al., "Intervention on Rethinking 'the Border' in Border Studies," *Political Geography* 30 (2011): 61–69; and Karine Côté-Boucher, "The Diffuse Border: Intelligence-Sharing, Control and

Confinement Along Canada's Smart Border,"
Surveillance & Society 5, no. 2 (2008): 142–65.

3

Beginning with Giorgio Agamben, *Homo Sacer:
Il potere soverano e la vita nuda* (Turin: Giulio
Einaudi, 1995), trans. Daniel Heller-Roazen,
Homo Sacer: Sovereign Power and Bare Life
(Stanford: Stanford University Press, 1998); the
highly successful (and debated) publications of
Antonio Negri and Michael Hardt, beginning with
Empire (Cambridge, MA: Harvard University
Press, 2000), should also be mentioned. Hardt and
Negri proclaim that their work is highly indebted
to Foucault and Deleuze, a disputed claim, see,
for example, Mathew Coleman and John Agnew
"The Problem with *Empire*," in *Space, Knowledge
and Power: Foucault and Geography*, ed. Jeremy W.
Crampton and Stuart Elden (Farnham: Ashgate,
2007), 317–39.

4

The literature on these recent developments is
vast, see, for example, Jeremy W. Crampton,
*Mapping: A Critical Introduction to Cartography
and GIS* (Chichester: Wiley-Blackwell, 2010);
Jeremy Crampton, "Cartography: Cartographic
Calculations of Territory," *Progress in Human
Geography* 35, no. 1 (2011): 92–103; Sarah Elwood,
"Geographic Information Science: Emerging
Research on the Societal Implications of the Geo-
Spatial Web," *Progress in Human Geography* 34,
no. 3 (2012): 349–57; Sarah Elwood, "Geographic
Information Science: Visualization, Visual
Methods and the Geoweb," *Progress in Human
Geography* 35, no. 3 (2011): 401–8; Paul C. Adams,
"A Taxonomy for Communication Geography,"
Progress in Human Geography 35, no. 1 (2011):
37–57. On Google Earth, see Vittoria Di Palma,
"Zoom: Google Earth and Global Intimacy," in
*Intimate Metropolis: Urban Subjects in the Modern
City*, ed. Vittoria Di Palma, Diana Periton, and
Marina Lathouri (Abingdon: Routledge, 2009),
239–70; Jason Farman, "Mapping the Digital
Empire: Google Earth and the Process of
Postmodern Cartography," *New Media & Society*
12, no. 6 (2010): 869–88. On recent uses of crowd-
maps as support for political activism see Jonathan

Massey, Brett Snyder, "Occupying Wall Street:
Places and Spaces of Political Action," *Places
Journal*, September 9, 2012, accessed on October
20, 2015, https://placesjournal.org/article/
occupying-wall-street-places-and-spaces-of-polit-
ical-action/.

5

See Joe Painter, "Territoire et réseau: une fausse
dichotomie?" in *Territoires, territorialité, territo-
rialisation: controverses et perspectives*, ed. Martin
Vanier (Rennes: Presses Universitaires de Rennes,
2009), 57–66. A splendid book on the challenges
posed by network charting, published by a Parsons
graduate, is Manuel Lima's *Visual Complexity:
Mapping Patterns of Information* (New York:
Princeton Architectural Press, 2011).

6

Bruno Latour with Valérie November, Eduardo
Camacho-Hübner, "Entering a Risky Territory:
Space in the Age of Digital Navigation,"
Environment and Planning D: Society and Space 28
(2010): 581–99, 582.

7

Martin Dodge, Rob Kitchin, and Chris Perkins,
eds., *The Map Reader: Theories of Mapping
Practice and Cartographic Representation*
(Chichester: John Wiley and Sons, 2011). See
also Martin Dodge, Rob Kitchin, and Chris
Perkins, eds., *Rethinking Maps: New Frontiers
in Cartographic Theory* (London: Routledge,
2009); Sarah Whatmore, *Hybrid Geographies:
Natures Cultures Spaces* (London: Sage, 2002);
Nigel Thrift, *Non-Representational Theory:
Space, Politics, Affect* (Abingdon: Routledge,
2008); J. B. Harley, *The New Nature of Maps:
Essays in the History of Cartography*, ed. Paul
Laxton (Baltimore: Johns Hopkins University
Press, 2001); Christian Jacob, *L'empire des cartes:
Approche théorique de la cartographie à travers l'his-
toire* (Paris: Éditions Albin Michel, 1992).

8

On Stalker and other examples of architects or artists
inspired by Situationist's practices or other forms of
mapping by walking, see Thierry Davila, *Marcher,
Créer: Déplacements, flâneries, dérives dans l'art de la
fin du XXe siècle* (Paris: Éditions du Regard, 2002);

Karen O'Rourke, *Walking and Mapping: Artists as Cartographers*, (Cambridge, MA: MIT Press, 2013).

9

A mutated version goes now under the name of "architecture fiction," see Geoff Manaugh, "Architectural Weaponry: An Interview with Mark Wigley," *BLDGBLOG*, April 12, 2007, accessed on October 20, 2015, http://bldgblog. blogspot.com/2007/04/architectural-weaponry-interview-with.html; David Gissen, "Architecture Fiction: A Short Review of a Young Concept," *HTC Experiments*, February 22, 2009, accessed on October 20, 2015, http://htcexperiments.org/2009/02/22/architecture-fiction-%E2%80%94-a-short-review-of-a-young-concept/; Pedro Gadanho, "All the Beyonds," *Shrapnel Contemporary*, May 7, 2009, https://shrapnelcontemporary.wordpress.com/2009/05/07/all-the-beyonds/; Kazys Varnelis, "In Pursuit of Architecture Fiction," *Town Planning and Architecture* 35, no. 1 (2011): 18–20.

10

See Mark Garcia, ed., *The Diagrams of Architecture*, AD Reader (Chichester: Wiley, 2010); and also anticipating recent discussion on infrastructure at a territorial scale Stan Allen, *Point + Lines: Diagrams and Projects for the City* (New York: Princeton Architectural Press, 1999).

11

For an amusing, and appropriate, commentary on the limits of research studios, that often produce just maps and data visualizations ready to be used for exhibition and publication: Mark Foster Gage, "In Defense of Design," *Log* 16, (Spring/Summer 2009): 39–45; a recent product of this type of investigation is, for example, Jeffrey Inaba and C-Lab, eds., *World of Giving* (Baden: Columbia University GSAPP, New Museum, Lars Müller Publishers, 2010).

12

Eyal Weizman is the director of the Center for Research at Golsdmiths, University of London, and cofounder of the architectural collective DAAR (Decolonizing Architecture Art Residency). Among his publications, see Eyal Weizman, Rafi Segal, and David Tartakover, eds., *A Civilian Occupation: The Politics of Israeli Architecture* (Tel Aviv: Babel, 2003); Eyal Weizman, *Hollow Land: Israel's Architecture of Occupation* (London: Verso, 2007); Eyal Weizman and Isabelle Taudière, eds., *À travers les murs: l'architecture de la nouvelle guerre urbaine* (Paris: la Fabrique 2008); Eyal Weizman, *The Least of all Possible Evils: Humanitarian Violence from Arendt to Gaza* (London: Verso, 2011); Eyal Weizman and Thomas Keenan, eds., *Mengele's Skull: The Advent of a Forensic Aesthetics* (London: Verso, 2012).

13

See Bruno Latour, "On Actor-Network Theory: A Few Clarifications Plus More Than a Few Complications," first published 1990, English version on Latour's website: http://www.bruno-latour.fr/sites/default/files/P-67%20ACTOR-NETWORK.pdf; Ash Amin and Nigel Thrift, *Cities: Reimagining the Urban* (Cambridge: Polity Press, 2002); and Nigel Thrift, *Non-Representational Theory* (London: Routledge, 2007); see Ignacio Farías and Thomas Bender, eds., *Urban Assemblages: How Actor-Network Theory Changes Urban Studies* (London: Routledge, 2010). The "spatial products" explored in Keller Easterling's playwritings and the research of Laura Kurgan into digital location strategies and the ethics and politics of mapping should also be mentioned.

14

Denis Cosgrove, ed., *Mappings*, (London: Reaktion Books, 1999). The late Cosgrove's work has been attentively followed by architects, landscape architects, cartographers, and geographers. See also his last two books: *Geography and Vision: Seeing, Imagining and Representing the World* (London: I. B. Tauris, 2008); and *Apollo's Eye: A Cartographic Genealogy of the Earth in the Western Imagination (*Baltimore: Johns Hopkins University Press, 2001); McHarg, founder of the department of landscape at Penn, teacher and then colleague of Corner, was the first to propose the reading of layers of data, charted at a regional scale, as preliminary step to intervention, and is now acknowledged as one the "fathers" of GIS.

See Ian L. McHarg, *Design with Nature* (1969, 25th anniversary ed., New York: Wiley, 1992); Lynn Margulis, James Corner, and Brian Hawthorne, eds., *Ian McHarg: Dwelling in Nature: Conversation With Students* (New York: Princeton Architectural Press, 2007).

15
The former including Pierre Bélanger and Kelly Shannon; the latter, includes Liam Young of Tomorrow's Thoughts Today, Nicholas de Monchaux, Lola Sheppard and Mason White of Lateral Office, Jason Kelly Johnson and Nataly Gattegno of Future Cities Lab, John Palmesino and Ann-Sofi Rönnskog of Territorial Agency, Luis Callejas, and Clare Lyster. Christophe Girot's experiments with video and digital modeling, which attempt to produce topological readings of vast landscapes, should also be mentioned.

16
For a first attempt to trace the history of the emergence of this approach in landscape architecture, see Elizabeth Mossop, "Landscape of Infrastructure," in *The Landscape Urbanism Reader*, ed. Charles Waldheim (New York: Princeton Architectural Press, 2006), 163–77. More recent literature includes *Territory: Architecture Beyond Environment, Architectural Design* 80, no. 3, guest ed. David Gissen, (May/June 2010); Nadia Amoroso, *The Exposed City: Mapping the Urban Invisibles* (London: Routledge, 2010); Kelly Shannon and Marcel Smets, *The Landscape of Contemporary Infrastructure* (Rotterdam: NAi Publishers, 2010); Katrina Stoll and Scott Lloyd, eds., *Infrastructure as Architecture: Designing Composite Networks* (Berlin: Jovis, 2010); Mason White, Lola Sheppard, Neeraj Bhatia, Maya Przybylski, *Coupling* (New York, Princeton Architectural Press, 2011); and Ying-Yu Hung et al., *Landscape Infrastructure: Case Studies by SWA* (Basel: Birkhäuser, 2011).

17
As proposed, for example, by David Gissen in "Architecture's Geographic Turns," *Log* 12 (2008): 59–67; or suggested by the title of a recent colloquium at the University of Michigan, "The Geological Turn: Architecture's New Alliance" (January 10, 2012–February 11, 2012). Geological concerns inform thinkers and designers attempting to address the Anthropocene, see Etienne Turpin, ed., *Architecture in the Anthropocene: Encounters Among Design, Deep Time, Science and Philosophy* (London: Open Humanities Press, 2013).

18
Bruno Latour, "A Cautious Prometheus? A Few Steps Toward a Philosophy of Design (With Special Attention to Peter Sloterdijk)," in *Newtworks of Design: Proceedings of the 2008 Annual International Conference of the Design History Society: Falmouth, 3–6 September 2008*, ed. Fiona Hackney, Jonathan Glynne, and Viv Minton (e-books, Universal Publishers, 2009): 2–10.

19
See Bruno Latour, "Why Has Critique Run out of Steam? From Matters of Fact to Matters of Concern," *Critical Inquiry* 30, (Winter 2004): 225–48.

20
Peter Sloterdijk, *Sphären I: Blasen* (Frankfurt am Main: Suhrkamp, 1998); *Sphären II: Globen* (Frankfurt am Main: Suhrkamp, 1999); *Sphären III: Schäume* (Frankfurt am Main: Suhrkamp, 2004).

21
Peter Sloterdijk, *La Domestication de l'Être. Pour un éclaircissement de la clairière* (Paris: Éditions Mille et une nuits, 2000).

22
Jakob von Uexküll, *Streifzüge durch die Umwelten von Tieren und Menschen* (1934); von Uexküll, *Foray Into the Worlds*, 105.

23
Ibid., 126–7.

24
Ibid., 127.

25
Ibid. 132.

26
Von Uexküll, *Bedeutungslehre*, 172.

27
Leo Spitzer, "*Milieu* and *Ambience*: An Essay in Historical Semantics," *Philosophy and*

Phenomenological Research 3 (1942–43), 1–42, 169–218.

28

Georges Canguilhem, "The Living and Its Milieu" (Le Vivant et son Milieu), initially presented in the form of lecture at the Collège philosophique in Paris (1946–47) and then published in *La connaissance de la vie* in 1952, trans. Stefanos Geroulanos and Daniela Ginsburg, *Knowledge of Life* (New York: Fordham University Press, 2008), 120. The relevance of the works of Canguilhem and von Uexküll on the notions of environment have been recently commented in Michael Hensel, *Performance-Oriented Architecture: Rethinking Architectural Design and the Built Environment*, AD Primers (Chichester: Wiley, 2013).

29

Michel Foucault, "Governmentality," in *The Foucault Effect: Studies in Governmentality*, ed. Graham Burchell, Colin Gordon, and Peter Miller (Chicago: University of Chicago Press, 1991), 87–104, 102.

30

See Jean-Hughes Barthélémy, *Simondon* (Paris: Société d'édition Les Belles Lettres, 2014).

31

Gilbert Simondon, "On Techno-Aesthetics," trans. Arne De Boever, *Parrhesia* 14 (2012): 1–8, 6. See also Yves Michaud, "The Aesthetics of Gilbert Simondon: Anticipation of the Contemporary Aesthetic Experience," in *Gilbert Simondon: Being and Technology*, ed. Arne De Boever et al. (Edinburgh: Edinburgh University Press, 2012), 121–32.

32

See Dominique Lecourt, "The Question of the Individual in Georges Canguilhem and Gilbert Simondon," in *Gilbert Simondon: Being and Technology*, ed. Arne De Boever et al., 11–184.

33

See Sean Bowden, "Gilles Deleuze, a Reader of Gilbert Simondon," in *Gilbert Simondon: Being and Technology*, ed. Arne De Boever et al., 135–53.

34

Gilles Deleuze and Félix Guattari, *Mille Plateaux*, trans. Brian Massumi, *A Thousand Plateaus* (London: Continuum, 2003), 313.

35

Quoted in Jean-Hughes Barthélémy, "Glossary: Fifty Key Terms in the Works of Gilbert Simondon," in *Gilbert Simondon: Being and Technology*, ed. Arne De Boever et al., 202–31, 230.

36

Deleuze and Guattari, *Mille Plateaux*, 314.

37

Ibid., 314–16.

DIETER KIENAST AND THE TOPO-LOGICAL AND PHENOMENOLOGICAL DIMENSION OF LANDSCAPE ARCHITECTURE —*Anette Freytag*

The Swiss landscape architect Dieter Kienast's (1945–1998) works and development as a designer are an example of a lifelong study of how to represent scientific achievements in the research on plant communities or on the habits of users of urban open spaces through a new formal language of landscape design. Through what he "found" and created, Kienast gave an important impetus to a reorientation of the profession of landscape architecture.

At present, the process and the results of Kienast's research are again of great value to enrich the current practice of urban planning and landscape architecture. "Biodiversity"—how to keep it and how to create it in growing cities—is one of the key issues in current debates on sustainabilty. Equally important questions are how to use rainwater and how to keep urban open spaces open to the public and accessible for users of diverse backgrounds. All of these questions also address the problem of form, as bringing "green" to the city is definitely not sufficient on its own, even if some missionaries of the quest for biodiversity might think otherwise. Kienast's experiments in combining ecological necessities and improvements with a new aesthetics for designing with nature in the city remain a source of inspiration for current designers.

This essay presents some aspects of Kienast's work, focusing on his search for a new aesthetic for designing with nature in the city without copying rural motifs or trying to create an "ecological" imagery. His background in the natural sciences shaped his nonsentimental approach toward nature. However, Kienast was a sensuous man, and called himself a romantic.[1] The main goal of the essay is to show how his works embody the topological and phenomenological dimensions of landscape architecture.

Kienast's projects evolved in the realm of postmodernism. His search for forms that make spatial and material qualities more conscious needs to be put in the context of the art, the architecture, and the literature of the day in order to be completely understood. Influenced by the work of artists like Sol LeWitt, Mario Merz, Robert Smithson, and Carl André, architects like Herzog & de Meuron and Jean Nouvel, and writers like Peter Handke, the nature- and social science–oriented education he had received at the University of Kassel went through several processes of reinterpretation. Proponents of the Kassel School soon considered Kienast to be little more than a "postmodern designer of shapes," a label that more accurately applies to those of his imitators who adopted his vocabulary without considering whether it could be integrated into the landscape or not.[2] His works are bound to space and consciousness; they embody the topological and phenomenological dimensions of postmodernism.

Kienast's aesthetic search always focused on the emancipation of the subject. In his later works, he consummated a modification of the emancipatory design paradigm of the Kassel School—from practical to contemplative use, from daily life to aesthetic experience—while the subject-related focus remained constant. Kienast's position in a cultural historical context is therefore ambivalent. Regardless of the extent to which he clearly uses sometimes strikingly postmodern techniques, he remains committed to modernism in his absolute and occasionally utopian vision of the potential effectiveness of open spaces that he acquired in Kassel. Hence, he is difficult to stereotype. Although he excluded formal gimmicks, he did acknowledge the era: "What is meant is not the populist façon of postmodernism that in architecture is improperly reduced to stumps of columns, pediments, and bay windows; what is meant is the postmodernism of Lyotard and Welsch, of Handke and Kundera, of Nouvel and Herzog & de Meuron."[3]

Kienast's constant search for form has one parallel in the literature of the Austrian writer Peter Handke. Handke's story *Langsame Heimkehr* (*Slow Homecoming*) begins in Alaska. Sorger, its protagonist, explores the shapeless vegetation and was "imbued with the search for forms, the desire to differentiate and describe them, and not only out of doors ('in the field'), where this often tormenting but sometimes gratifying, and at its best triumphant, activity was his profession."[4] Sorger is a geologist. The field research he carries out begins to affect his inner state of affairs, and as a result of the bleak nature surrounding him, memories and emotions threaten to erode.

Langsame Heimkehr was published in 1979, the same year that Kienast moved back to Switzerland after spending nine years at the University of Kassel in Germany, where he had studied and earned his PhD. The Kassel School set out to establish a new theory of open space planning supported by science. This theory was based on knowledge gained in both the social and the vegetation sciences: Lucius Burckhardt (1925–2003) was one of the protagonists to found his planning theory and critique in the discursive system of sociology; Karl

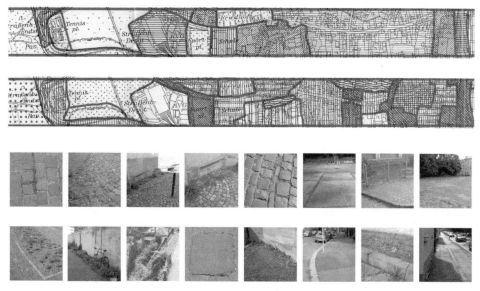

FIG. 1— Dieter Kienast, The city of Kassel's spontaneous vegetation in relation to architectural and urban-structural neighborhood types, 1978. Doctoral thesis, upper map representing the land use, lower map representing the plant communities Kienast found there (both details of a study of 1.8 kilometers), scale 1:5000. Montage with photos taken by Anette Freytag.
Courtesy of ETH Zürich, Archiv gta (NSL), Nachlass Kienast.

Heinrich Hülbusch (1936–) combined it with phytosociology. Kienast was also a natural scientist. With a doctorate in phytosociology, he mapped spontaneous vegetation within the Kassel urban area and investigated traces of human use. (FIG. 1) The illustration shows a small section of a corridor several kilometers long in which Kienast identified the vegetation he encountered. The different fields in the upper map represent various types of land use, for instance agricultural fields, old village centers, and densely populated areas. The areas drawn in on the lower map show the various types of plant communities that Kienast found. These maps provide information about the social structure of different neighborhoods—certain plants, for example, only grow in paved areas, and this is where people have more money. For example, the area around a church is covered in pavers, and plants can grow in the joints in between, whereas the sidewalks and streets in working-class neighborhoods are paved with asphalt, and there are hardly any plants growing there.

The plants that have settled in a particular area also give us information about its use. A parking lot that is seldom used is quickly colonized by plants, whereas other plants will only continue to grow when someone regularly walks on them. In the context of this pursuit of a new type of planning based on science, it becomes clear that this method is an attempt to go back to the roots of the profession: the study of plants and their environment and the coexistence of nature and human beings. Kienast is now able to read and interpret various environments based on the existence of particular plants. This approach to natural science is, in my opinion, the prerequisite for Kienast's later work and helps us to understand the relationship he had with nature in the city.

FIG. 2 — Dieter Kienast, dry meadow biotope for the Grün 80 exhibition in Basel-Brüglingen, 1976–1980. Photo by Georg Aerni, 2012.
Courtesy of the photographer.

This mapping activity also has to be looked at in the context of the time. In the work *Line of Wreckage* from 1968, Robert Smithson precisely mapped different forms of debris.[5] At that time, many similar projects occurred. Be it at the *documenta 5* in Kassel (1972) or the *Kunst bleibt Kunst* (Art Remains Art) exhibition in Cologne (1974)—milieu studies, maps, and searches for clues were the issues of the day.[6] However, Kienast did not carry out his research in an artistic context, but rather as part of a planning process. In 1980 he designed a "phyto-sociological garden" for Grün 80, the second Swiss exhibition for garden and landscape design and architecture near Basel, which is now known as the "dry meadow biotope." (FIG. 2) This was a didactic showpiece at the botanical garden in Brüglingen, which was included in the Grün 80 exhibition. Kienast wanted to vividly show how dynamic plants are, and to illustrate how they compete with one another for soil, water, and light. He wrote that he wished to establish different stages of succession in order to create an object lesson about how Switzerland would look without any human intervention.[7] He was thus interested in chipping away at Switzerland's culturally defined "image of nature" and in showing that alpine meadows are an expression of human methods of production. He also wanted to demonstrate that natural dynamics are much harsher when there is no human intervention. At the same time, the dry meadow biotope, which was part of the "Beautiful Gardens" section of the garden show, was the only part of the show that challenged the aesthetic of lush floral arrangements, and the only part that addressed ecological issues and questions.

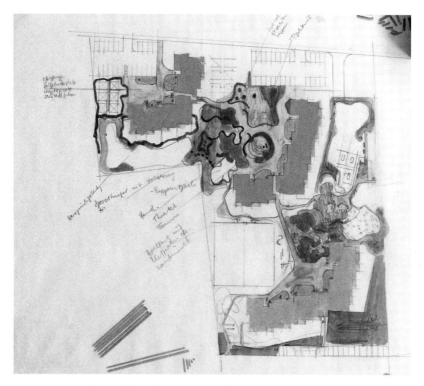

FIG. 3 — Dieter Kienast/Office of Peter Paul Stöckli, sketch for the open space design, 1972.
Felt-tip pen on glassine paper. Kienast's sketches for the residential development in Niederhasli
were heavily influenced by what he had learned in Kassel about emancipatory open space
planning that was focused on the needs of residents. Open space was to be designed so that it
helped people confront the difficulties of their daily lives more easily.
Courtesy of SKK Landschaftsarchitekten, Wettingen.

The Kassel School's interest in the social sciences was reflected in the landscape architectural design of the grounds at various housing developments.
Kienast's first open space design of a residential development, built in the town
of Niederhasli near Zürich (1972–75), was heavily influenced by what he had
learned in Kassel about "emancipatory open space planning" that is focused
on the needs of residents. (**FIG. 3**) Open space was to be designed in such a way
that it helps people more easily face the difficulties encountered in everyday
life. Over the next two decades, Kienast continuously redefined the relationship
people have with their environments—"imbued with the search for forms," like
Handke's hero.

The two pyramids that Kienast included in Stöckli+Kienast's design of
Wettingen's municipal park (1979–83) were a first milestone and showed an
approach to landscape architecture that was rather unusual in the 1970s. (**FIGS. 4–5**)
Naturally formed sledding mounds were originally planned for this location,
and Kienast also integrated functions such as an amphitheater and a fire pit. The
unique spatial planning of the park had a diagonal path leading across it and

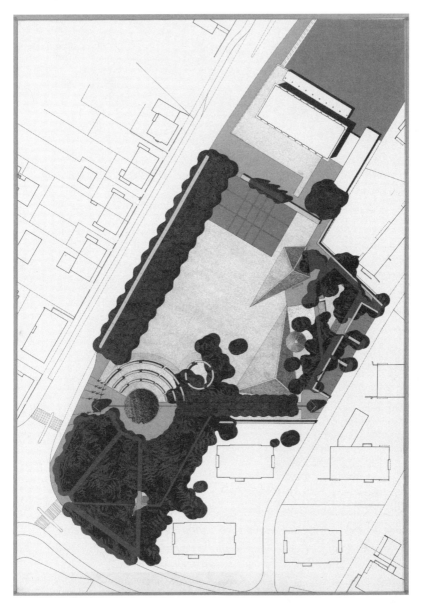

FIG. 4— Dieter Kienast—Office Stöckli + Kienast/
Stöckli, Kienast & Koeppel, Brühlwiese city park in
Wettingen, 1979–1984. Plan view (ex-post from 1994).
Pencil and collage (color transparencies) on copy of
plan, scale 1:200, 33 x 48 in. (83.5 x 121 cm).
Courtesy of ETH Zürich, Archiv gta (NSL), Nachlass Kienast.

FIG. 5—Dieter Kienast—Office Stöckli, Kienast &
Koeppel, Brühlwiese city park in Wettingen—pyramids
and current hedges (former amphitheater), 1979–1984.
Photo by Georg Aerni, 2012.
Courtesy of the photographer.

three rows of tightly planted trees—a rather grand gesture for a provincial Swiss park—as well as the retention of the original meadow as a large open space and the planting of a small grove of trees as a "natural element" that was intended as a counterweight to the new city hall on the other side of the park.[8]

In 1982, Kienast distanced himself from the idea that the mounds had to have a "natural" form, and as a result he built pyramids for sledding. He retained the shapes of the amphitheater and the fire pit, but not their functions, instead integrating hedges planted in stages. In doing so, he wanted his projects, in the truest sense of the word, to "playfully" break through the common patterns of perception that users had, and to expand upon them. At the same time, Kienast strove for a design of contrasts: he covered the geometrically formed earthen pyramids with natural grassland vegetation that slightly counteracted the shapes underneath.

The park in Wettingen was intentionally designed to be an important additional urban element in the new center of this provincial town. Kienast's idea was that the finished product would clearly be seen as an urban park, and not as an idyllic alternative to the city. The materials he used in the park included steel, concrete, paving stones, and asphalt, and he chose shapes that fit the materials with pointed tree guards. In addition to this, he paid careful attention to the topography and created clearly recognizable zones. Upon its completion, the park, which has now aged gracefully, aroused the emotions of other landscape architects in Switzerland, who were much more influenced by the natural garden movement. The cover of Urs Schwarz's book *Der Naturgarten* (The Natural Garden), which was to become a bible for Swiss landscape architects, represents the different aesthetic approach taken by Schwarz as compared to Kienast. (FIG. 6) The latter's more environmentally motivated colleagues considered the fragmentation of Brühlpark and its collage of classical historic garden elements to be scandalous.[9]

Kienast clearly drew inspiration from the history of landscape architecture and was, for example, fascinated by baroque gardens and the collage-like juxtaposition of formally and informally designed areas. He himself considered the park in Wettingen to be an early statement of how social, aesthetic, and ecological concerns in landscape architecture could be linked and the sensual perception of users enhanced. This was made possible through the creation of tension between formed topography and freely growing vegetation, and between light and dark areas or natural and artificial features. He also turned to the tradition of modern Swiss landscape architecture with its protagonists Ernst Cramer (1898–1980) and Fred Eicher. By retaining the park's central meadow and using several large

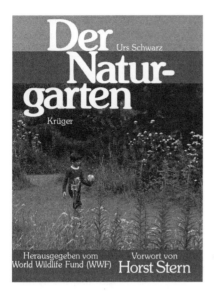

FIG. 6 — Urs Schwarz, book cover of *Der Naturgarten* (The Natural Garden), 1980. (*Urs Schwarz*, Der Naturgarten *[Frankfurt: Krüger, 1980].*)

elements like the pyramids and rows of trees, Kienast adopted Eicher's desire for generosity and reduction in landscape architecture. From Cramer he assumed the courage to use geometric patterns in his designs, something Cramer had done in 1959 with his design for a garden show in Zürich.[10] Within the context of a garden show stressing lush floral decorations, his "Poet's Garden" was scandalous indeed. Kienast's plan graphics are so clearly related to Cramer's project that it is obvious that the former wanted to claim precisely this position of scandal and renewal in the 1980s, only this time his opponent was the natural garden.

Kienast's search for forms that would make spatial and material qualities conscious links him to other artists of the day. In addition to representatives of Conceptual Art and Land Art, he also found inspiration in Peter Handke's *Die Lehre der Sainte-Victoire* (The Lessons of Mont Sainte-Victoire), published in 1980. In an exhibition of his work after becoming a professor in Karlsruhe, Kienast printed Handke's description of a forest onto one of the exhibition walls. A sequel to *Langsame Heimkehr*, *Die Lehre der Sainte-Victoire* deals with the struggle to express the visible world in words. Handke does not want to describe them, but instead—like his role model Paul Cézanne—desires to create "constructions and harmonies parallel to nature": "the order and connection of ideas is the same as the order and connection of things...At the end of a story it must be possible to make mere words stand for things."[11]

Like Handke, Kienast was likewise seeking to create such "constructions and harmonies parallel to nature." His language consisted of his built projects and also drawings. A plan of his own garden, drafted after its redesign in 1991, shows his finesse in representing the external world. (**FIG. 7**) Kienast worked on these kinds of drawings for days, but only once a particular project was complete. Three different aspects are striking about this drawing activity: first, the

FIG. 7— Dieter Kienast, Private garden of the Kienast family in Zurich, 1991. Ink, pencil, colored crayon on chipboard, plan view, scale 1:100, 33 in. x 35.5 in. (84 x 90 cm).
Courtesy of ETH Zurich, Archiv gta (NSL), Nachlass Kienast.

drawings seem to be a type of meditation about what has been created; second, one may detect Kienast's wish to record the garden as he created it, before it is altered by nature and other people; and third, the drawings show Kienast's desire to see his work considered as art.

When studying the original plans, the thought occurs that Kienast may also have been trying to illustrate the material qualities of the elements he used in the garden.[12] To do so, he used pencils of varying thickness and hardness, as well as techniques like frottage. Individual areas of the plan, such as those parts that represent gravel areas, are hatched over a rough surface so that the texture is visually similar to the actual material. The roof of the greenhouse that was part of his parents' nursery, on the other hand, has a completely different appearance than the gravel or the soil in the planting beds, or the hedges that surround the beds.

Kienast was drawing in such a way that you can almost hear the crunching of the leaves, as is the case with the topiary. Water bodies are drawn with black ink, but Kienast lets the color of the paper on which he draws come through as if the sun were perhaps reflecting off the surface of the water. In a way, these plans and their different layers are a kind of microtopography and, to invoke Handke again, are "constructions and harmonies parallel to nature."[13]

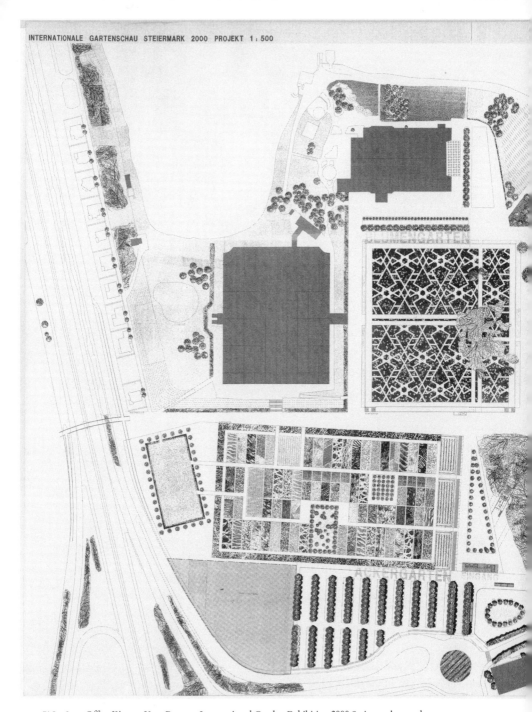

FIG. 8 — Office Kienast Vogt Partner, International Garden Exhibition 2000 Steiermark, template for the final competition plan, 1997. Collage of black-and-white photocopies, ink, and pencil on glassine paper, collated on a laser print, plan view, scale 1:500, 50 x 79.5 in. (127 x 202 cm).
Courtesy of ETH Zürich, Archiv gta (NSL), Nachlass Kienast.

Kienast retained the textures drawn by hand in his plans, which were drafted using a collage technique, even creating his own pattern books.[14] The photographs that he always used—here for water, there for gravel—are very close to his drawings made by hand. He added new textures to this collection. The collage technique eventually replaced the handmade drawings, because as the success of the office grew, and due to the large number of competitions the office entered, it became impossible to draw all the plans by hand. A plan made for the competition for the International Garden Show 2000 in Graz, where Kienast designed a Mountain Garden—a kind of folded landscape in which he once again integrated one of Peter Handke's texts in an unfolded "landscape reader"—shows all kinds of different textures. (FIG. 8) The Mountain Garden with its meter-high pyramids was repeatedly criticized as a self-referential landscape created by a narcissistic landscape architect who was interested not in the users but in the illustration of his own grandeur.[15] In a continuation of the idea created at the park in Wettingen, however, the Mountain Garden aims to sharpen and change the perception of its visitors and to activate their playful and creative potential. In a particularly concise way, Kienast was also illustrating the core theme of landscape architecture: the changing of topography in order to create new spaces.

In the Mountain Garden, Kienast's search for form, which had begun in the 1980s, was now taken to an extreme—and if he had not died prematurely in 1998 at the age of fifty-three, he probably would have taken a new direction after this project. Apart from inventions for garden shows, Kienast was clearly interested in making specific locations more legible through landscape architectural interventions: "We have to accept that there are more and more houses, and that we have to design the little area we have in an urban way and break with the existing rural models."[16] In the context of urban and suburban space, Kienast wanted to achieve a "coherence of meaning, form, and material."[17]

Handke's and Kienast's respective quests for literal things marked an era in which ideologies had lost their guiding function. As the significance of utopias faded, the environment changed considerably during the 1960s and 1970s: cities grew, and urban sprawl spread out over the landscape. According to Kienast, this new reality could no longer be understood with tried and tested sign systems: "The old dichotomy between cities and the countryside has dissolved; the boundaries are blurred. We assume that neither the city nor the countryside can be dismantled. The legibility and experiencing of the world is, however, based on the principle of inequality. The future task of the simultaneity of the city and countryside is therefore the prevention of any further blurring of internal

FIG. 9 — Hansruedi Wildermuth, book cover of *Natur als Aufgabe* (Nature as Quest), 1978. *(Hansruedi Wildermuth*, Natur als Aufgabe: Leitfaden für die Naturschutzpraxis in der Gemeinde *[Basel: Schweizer Bund für Naturschutz, 1978].)*

boundaries and fractures. They must be made perceptible to the senses again."[18] Kienast rejected simulated idylls—just as Handke rejected natural descriptions. In Switzerland he came into conflict with landscape architects and environmental planners who wanted to give each design a natural form and who opposed all kinds of urbanism, as you can see on a book cover from 1978. (**FIG. 9**) In order to make a given site legible, Kienast developed a vocabulary for the landscape in the 1980s and 1990s that traced, accentuated, and at times contradicted the given topography and the clear creation of zones for different functions, as is plainly visible in the plan for the École Cantonale de Langue Française. (**FIGS. 10–11**) The individual kindergarten and school buildings and the various athletic fields are all both separated and connected by a circulation system that widens to a funnel-shaped playground. Differences in elevation and hedges reinforce this functional separation. The playground is paved in asphalt, which has a number of concrete strips with linear drainage inlets for the infiltration of rainwater running across it. The edge is formed by a single row of lime trees, benches, and a strip of concrete slabs (see **FIG. 10**). Kienast intentionally used wide joints, as well as gravel areas and tree grids, so that vegetation could spontaneously grow. At the end of each linear infiltration inlet, he planted ivy that grows up the long wall connecting the school buildings and acts as a visual base for the residential tower blocks located behind it. In the first of the "Ten Theses on Landscape Architecture" that he formulated in 1992, Kienast notes: "Our work is the search for the nature of the city, the colors of which are not only green, but also grey. Nature in the city means a tree, a hedge, a lawn, but also permeable surfaces, broad spaces, canals, high walls, axes that are maintained to provide fresh air and views, the center, and the periphery."[19]

In the project for the school grounds, the various manifestations of "urban nature" play an important role in the effectiveness of the overall facility.[20] The different areas of the grounds are clearly demarcated through the use of design,

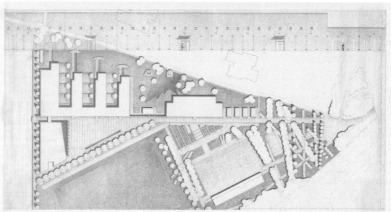

FIG. 10 (TOP) — Office Stöckli+Kienast/
Stöckli, Kienast & Koeppel, École Cantonale
de Langue Française, Berne (French School of
Bern), 1984–1987. Photo by Georg Aerni, 2012.
Courtesy of the photographer.

FIG. 11 (BOTTOM) — Dieter Kienast—Office
Stöckli, Kienast & Koeppel, Freiraumgestaltung
École Cantonale de Langue Française in Bern
(Open space planning for the French School of
Bern), November 2, 1987. Ink, pencil, colored
pencil, laserprint on chipboard, plan view,
scale 1:200, 68.5 x 35 in. (174 x 89 cm).
*Courtesy of ETH Zürich, Archiv gta (NSL), Nachlass
Kienast.*

materials, and plants. While the design of the play area reacts to the tower blocks, and the edges of the open and clear sports fields enable the viewing of matches, on the other side of the wall connecting the buildings there is a kind of "hinterland" where children, hidden by the buildings, can play in privacy. The meadow here is seldom mown, and the entire area reflects the remnants of a rural landscape that still exists in this part of Bern, adjacent to the tower blocks that were built in the 1960s.

Kienast used his knowledge as a gardener and a plant sociologist in developing the planting plan for the project. In doing so, he created what he considered to be adequate images for each individual area. On the other hand, the details show that he put the ecological experiences gained in Kassel to use in creating an improved microclimate, as is evident, for example, in the plants that continuously and deliberately threaten to take over the pathways. The consistency of function and design—as he taught in Kassel, aiming to improve the well-being of the users—is present everywhere, for instance in the small play areas directly adjacent to the classrooms on the ground floor, where children can relax and have fun. These spaces have the minimum of equipment that Kienast felt was necessary to create a feeling of well-being: a well-defined space, here using hedges, a tree that provides shade with a bench underneath it. In this simplicity, he understood landscape architecture.

Kienast developed, through his investigation of phytosociological methods and his research on spontaneous vegetation in urban settings, a new aesthetic for designing with nature in the city. He was able to go from a study and interpretation of spontaneous urban vegetation to making his work legible through an emblematic and symbolic use of plants. Similarly, the use of "urban" and "ordinary" materials, such as concrete, cement, and steel, played an important role in his development of a new aesthetic for landscape architectural design in the city. In the courtyard of the reinsurance company Swiss Re, Kienast presented the conditions necessary for designing with nature in urban areas. (FIG.12) This courtyard is situated on top of a parking garage, and he drew attention to the artificial subbase by inclining the surface toward the building. Perhaps due to an unconscious memory of plants growing in the joints between pavers, he planted blue flag irises in the drainage strips running across the courtyard, as a sign of the moisture that infiltrates there. When designing with nature in the city, Kienast wanted to pursue neither the ideas of ecologically motivated landscape architects, nor the lush floral decorations of urban gardeners and other pastoral images, but instead to develop his own language. Despite a reduction in the

FIG. 12—Dieter Kienast/Günther Vogt—
Office Kienast Vogt Partner, Courtyard at the
Reassurance Company Swiss Re in Zurich,
1994–1995. Photo by Georg Aerni, 2012.
Courtesy of the photographer.

use of plants, Kienast found the sensual experience of the existing plants very important. The katsura trees change color in the autumn, and the leaves falling to the ground smell like gingerbread.[21]

Upon returning to Switzerland from Kassel, Kienast used his concepts based on form to confront and oppose the wildlife gardening movement influenced by Swiss garden and landscape architecture. The question of the suitability for daily use of his increasingly form-driven open spaces, which culminated in the 1990s and are always mentioned by his critics, is put into a new perspective when one reflects on his roots in Kassel. As stated earlier, Kienast modified the design paradigm of the Kassel School in his later works from practical to contemplative use, from daily life to aesthetic experience while keeping the subject-related focus constant. Kienast attempted to capture both processes of perception and material qualities through his methods of visualization, thereby coming to the heart of the matter itself: the users of his completed projects should be afforded a similar aesthetic experience. Sensory experience and the envisioning of plants and materials are at the heart of his endeavors. Thus, Kienast's works indeed embody the topological and phenomenological dimensions of postmodernism and of landscape architecture in general.

Notes

1

Dieter Kienast, "Cultivating Discontinuity," in *Between Landscape Architecture and Land Art*, ed. Udo Weilacher (Basel: Birkhäuser 1996), 150.

2

Reto Mehli, "Die mit den Förmchen spielen. Über die 'Bühnenbildnerei' in der Gartenarchitektur," in *Notizbuch der Kasseler Schule* 40 (1996), 77. This essay was based on a lecture related to his oral diploma examination at the University of Kassel, September 23, 1993.

3

Dieter Kienast, "Von der Notwendigkeit künstlerischer Innovation und ihrem Verhältnis zum Massengeschmack in der Landschaftsarchitektur," in *Die Poetik des Gartens: Über Chaos und*

Ordnung in der Landschaftsarchitektur, ed. Prof. für Landschaftsarchitektur ETH Zürich (Basel: Birkhäuser, 2002), 109 (translation from German by David Skogley).

4

Peter Handke, *Langsame Heimkehr* (Frankfurt am Main: Suhrkamp, 1979), 9 (translation from German by David Skogley).

5

For an image, see Robert Smithson, *Robert Smithson: The Collected Writings*, ed. Jack Flam (Berkeley: University of California Press, 1996), 205.

6

See Anette Freytag, *Dieter Kienast: Stadt und Landschaft lesbar machen* (Zurich: gta, 2016), 58–63.

7

Dieter Kienast, "Botanischer Garten Südteil. Naturnahe Biotope" (unpublished manuscript, January 4, 1980), Archives SKK Landschaftsarchitekten, Wettingen.

8

For full imagery, see Freytag, *Dieter Kienast*, 164–219.

9

See the videofilm by Marc Schwarz and Annemarie Bucher, *D. K. Eine Spurensuche* (Zürich: Schwarzpictures, 2008).

10

For an image of the plan, see Freytag, *Dieter Kienast*, 216; and Udo Weilacher, *Visionary Gardens: Modern Landscapes by Ernst Cramer* (Basel: Birkhäuser, 2001), 109.

11

Peter Handke, *Die Lehre der Sainte-Victoire* (Frankfurt am Main: Suhrkamp, 1980), 80 (translation from German by David Skogley); Peter Handke, *Die Geschichte des Bleistifts* (Salzburg: Residenz Verlag, 1982), 320 (translation from German by David Skogley).

12

For details from images and more information, see Anette Freytag, "Back to Form: Landscape Architecture and Representation in Europe since the Sixties," in *Composite Landscapes: Photomontage and Landscape Architecture*, ed. Charles Waldheim and Andrea Hansen (Ostfildern: Hatje Cantz, 2014), 98–103.

13

Handke, *Die Lehre der Sainte-Victoire*, 80.

14

Freytag, "Back to Form," 100.

15

For example by Ilse Helbich, "Von unbetretbaren Gärten" in *Neue Parkideen in Europa. Zwischen Arkadien und Restfläche*, ed. Anette Freytag and Wolfgang Kos for Broadcast Diagonal, Radio für Zeitgenossen, Austrian Broadcasting Corporation (ORF), Station "Österreich 1" (Ö 1), first broadcast October 10, 1998.

16

Dieter Kienast, "Funktion, Form und Aussage: Interview mit Robert Schäfer," in *Die Poetik des Gartens*, 186 (translation from German by David Skogley).

17

Ibid., 183.

18

Dieter Kienast, "Zehn Thesen zur Landschaftsarchitektur," in *Die Poetik des Gartens*, 207 (translation from German by David Skogley).

19

Ibid.

20

For images and more information, see Freytag, *Dieter Kienast*, 87–114.

21

See Freytag, *Dieter Kienast*, 136–48.

MEMORY, DIRECT EXPERIENCE, AND EXPECTATION: THE CONTEMPORARY AND THE CHINESE LANDSCAPE

— *Stanislaus Fung*

> But even now it is manifest and clear that there are neither times future nor times past. Thus it is not properly said that there are three times, past, present, and future. Perhaps it might be rightly said that there are three times: a time present of things past; a time present of things present; and a time present of things future. For these three do coexist somehow in the soul, for otherwise I could not see them. The time present of things past is memory; the time present of things present is direct experience; the time present of things future is expectation.
>
> —St. Augustine, *Confessions*, Book XI, Chapter 20

In the fifteen years since I last wrote about the prospects of cross-cultural dialogues in landscape architecture, Chinese landscape architecture has decisively entered the awareness of contemporary landscape architects in many parts of the world.[1] From Turenscape "designed ecologies" winning American admirers and prizes, to the increasing number of mainland Chinese students in Western schools of landscape architecture, to China's massive environmental problems, we see a picture of internationalization with some glimmers of success, as well as big challenges for educators and designers alike.

Two trends have intensified this progress of internationalization: the rapid expansion of tertiary education and the proliferation of teaching programs in landscape architecture in China have opened up the horizons of Chinese designers and students. Joint design studios for Chinese and foreign students have also revealed notable difficulties in promoting genuine collaboration. Chinese publishers and journal editors, riding on a boom in publications, have promoted a novel sense of what is "current" and "new" in the world of landscape architecture. However, not only is the readership small, the relatively poor quality of translations has also ensnared Chinese readers in a seemingly endless quagmire of semantics. Behind these trends is the growth that the Chinese economy has achieved in the last decade, such that it is now economically conceivable for Chinese entities to buy out *both* the *Journal of Landscape Architecture* and *Topos* from their European publishers. Overall, the vocabulary of Chinese landscape architecture has been broadened to include a host of concerns and techniques in landscape management and ecological studies. It is tempting to see in this a happy narrative of Western institutions helping Chinese landscape architects achieve a new (shared) sense of cultural values after ditching their feudal past.

For mainland Chinese designers emerging from decades of relative isolation from the world, it is easy to understand why a new vocabulary and know-how would be met with uncritical reception: First, the language of critical thinking had not been widely accepted in Chinese public discourse for more than half a century. Instead, an authoritarian mentality and a concern for personal welfare often informed an etiquette of reticence. Second, for young Chinese students and teachers who have been intensely aware of the differences in design cultures between mainland China and the West, the latest ideas and techniques from Britain or America compensated for perceived deficiencies in local education and carried a sense of being contemporary in a world of peers. This is not to say that dissent found no space for expression. On the contrary, the momentous advent of the Internet in China over the last fifteen years has enabled self-publication of individual views; sometimes, critical views appeared in conditions of semi-anonymity using online monikers. For several years in the first half of the 2000s, the bulletin boards of ABBS were filled daily with frank and sometimes critical comments.[2] In those years, the efforts of this website, with half a million registered users, outpaced conventional print media in allowing mainland Chinese readers access to new thinking and discussions. These developments in China had a higher impact in the field of architecture compared to that of landscape architecture, but even in the field of architecture, broadening horizons and critical comments were answered by the inertia of educational practices on the one hand and by the use of international links as a marker of institutional legitimacy on the other. By the second half of the 2000s, increasingly better-funded Chinese academic institutions recaptured a sense of initiative in advancing the field of landscape architecture through international links, academic exchanges, translations, and publications. Many Chinese may take these developments as the workings of progress in which the past is superseded and the present comes to be, and an even more exciting future beckons.

In what follows, I shall argue, with St. Augustine, that the linear conception of past, present, and future is problematic and that the coexistence and resonance of three registers of "time present"—memory, direct experience, and expectation—are the crux of a renewed understanding of the contemporary and the Chinese landscape.[3] On this view, the contemporariness of "Chinese landscape architecture" is not just something underwritten by a concern for the ecological, or by renewed public relevance through provision of life-saving street drainage, or by the implementation of advanced imaging techniques for municipal risk management. Rather, I hope to evoke a conjunction of the contemporary and the Chinese landscape that is already before us and yet slightly beyond the range of conventional understanding.

The focus of my discussion is a significant tourist site that receives millions of visitors each year: the Zhuo Zheng Yuan in Suzhou, popularly known as the Humble Administrator's Garden.[4] A garden called Zhuo Zheng Yuan was first established on this site in 1509, but the relationship between the name and the site varied over the centuries. This name was set aside from 1661 to 1872, and in 1872, when the name was reinstated, it referred to the middle of the three parts of the garden that stands today. This central part will be the focus of my discussion here. After the renovation in 1951–52, the name referred to the central and western parts and, from 1960 onwards, this was extended to include the eastern part as well. The tripartite division of the site derives from the Qianlong period (eighteenth century) and this has been the basic schema of the site for about half of its five-hundred-year history. The present-day eastern part of the garden occupies an area that had been grassland and cultivated vegetable plots for about 150 years until it was renovated in 1959–60; this is why this part of the garden appears more parklike to tourists as they enter the garden nowadays. In recent years, the garden has remained open to new changes. In response to large numbers of visitors, the Suzhou Bureau of Gardens proposed adding four covered walking galleries. I wish to consider this site as an open work or process in which additions and alterations are not necessarily taken as injurious to the integrity of a work.

Before I begin, I would like to offer three remarks in order to ward off possible misunderstandings: Firstly, the historical texts about this site that have survived do not convey a clear sense of the original intentions of the sixteenth-century persons who were involved in the design of this garden. In what follows, my discussion is directed purely at the level of effects. Consistency in effects does not demonstrate intentionality in a conclusive way, but I would argue that it rewards our attention. Secondly, the medium of analysis is mostly photographs, mainly taken during 2014–15. The analysis of a garden is not the same as an analysis of photographs of it, and I do not wish the photographs to be taken as conclusive evidence. Rather, photographs are indexical images; they point to situations and aspects of the garden and assist us in attending to nuances in effect. Lastly, the analysis is abbreviated for the purposes of this discussion but an effort has been made to demonstrate the crucial variety of situations.

INSTABILITY OF SPATIAL DEPTH

It is a well-known platitude that Chinese gardens refer to the poetic world of Chinese paintings.[5] At the most superficial level, we can imagine similar elements in gardens and in paintings: pavilions, covered walkways and other built elements, plants, rockeries, and misty scenes. People mildly misled by what they imagine to be stylistic analysis would focus on positive elements, and Chinese designers might consider the reuse of these elements in a general discussion of "inheriting the tradition." Designers may consider "reuse" positively or negatively, and some may take a modernizing form of abstraction or a historically accurate re-creation to be a viable design approach, or not. In any case, a designer's position on what contemporary landscape design is can be sounded out along these lines. We may recognize in these attitudes echoes of age-value and newness-value that Alois Riegl considered to be modern values. Newness-value, for example, demands that new works recalled historical works as little as possible.[6] In what follows, I shall argue that the crux of how Chinese landscape sensibilities may enter contemporary experience is not to be found by thinking about the selection and treatment of compositional elements but by attending to the instability of spatial depth that is well known in Chinese painting.

In a pavilion called Xiu Qi Ting, popularly known as the Embroidered-Silk Pavilion, located close to the eastern entry to the central part of the Zhuo Zheng Yuan, a wall opening offers a framed view of the eastern part of the garden, the part that had been vegetable fields for 150 years. (FIG. 1) A small building in the central part and the walking gallery that divides the central and the eastern parts of the garden are in the foreground. The occlusion of the ground surface in this view creates the impression of indeterminate depth and spatial compression.[7] When one moves to the parts of the garden framed in this view, one realizes that spatial compression is a momentary effect of the height and size of the frame and the sectional relationship of the frame to the eastern surrounds. Sunlight comes into the framed view from the right and in the afternoon, the white walls may become backlit; this may have an impact on the reading of depth and spatial compression. In mist, parts of the background of the framed view are occluded and the desaturation of color can be factored into the reading of spatial depth. (FIG. 2)

Looking south from this pavilion, the view is not framed explicitly by a wall opening, but the occlusion of the ground surface sets up a similar effect. (FIG. 3) Here we see the sun mostly to the south of the buildings. Whether the buildings appear backlit in sunny weather or stand in diffuse light on cloudy days, spatial

FIGS. 1–4 (FROM TOP) — Views from Xiu Qi Ting (Embroidered-Silk Pavilion) looking east, looking east in morning mist, looking south, and looking south in morning mist. *Courtesy of Liu Xu.*

compression can be sustained in this view. The southernmost building in this view would disappear on a misty day. (**FIG.4**) This leads us to the observation that two orders of subtraction are involved in the visual field. On the one hand, the coordination of topography and architectural elements opens up the possibility of views in which the occlusion of the ground plane leads to a sense of indeterminate depth and spatial compression. This can be intensified or weakened by weather conditions: sunny or cloudy, in the morning or afternoon, winter or summer sun angle, etc. On the other hand, mist plays a soft hand in subtracting elements from the visual field. It introduces a different and varying sense of depth, and it can intensify and attenuate a sense of delicacy in a setting.

FIG. 5 — Looking west from the eastern entry to the central part of the Zhuo Zheng Yuan, an elevated zigzag bridge overlaps with a distant embankment to the west.
Courtesy of Hou Xinjue.

Returning to the area near the eastern entry to the central part of the garden, looking west, we see that a zigzag bridge in the middle ground is unusually elevated above the surface of the pond. (FIG. 5) Normally, one would expect this kind of bridge to be much closer to the surface of the water. Yet at this height, the bridge is aligned with the embankment behind it. The distance between the bridge and the embankment is about forty meters, yet they appear much closer together compared with the distance between the bridge and the vantage point of this view, which is about seventy meters. In other words, the alignment of bridge and embankment from this vantage point renders the water surface between them much less obvious. The effect is a momentary spatial compression that brings together the middle ground and background of this view. When the visitor walks over to the bridge or embankment, the effect of spatial compression would be canceled. Noting that this is the longest visual corridor in the whole garden, we realize that the alignment of bridge and embankment evokes the traditional dictum, "In the small see the large, and in the large see the small."[8] The movements of the body activate an experience of the relativity of size, and, at the same time, trigger and cancel experiences of indeterminate spatial depth.

Very near the eastern entry to the central part of the garden, slightly to the north, there is a small pavilion called Wu Zhu You Ju (Secluded Lodge of Wutong Trees and Bamboo). It is a building with circular doorways on all four sides. Standing outside on the northern side of the pavilion and looking south, one sees a framed view of a small intimate setting. (FIG. 6) A stone table obscures the view

FIG. 6 (TOP) — Looking south from Wu Zhu You Ju (Secluded Lodge of Wutong Trees and Bamboo), the water surface outside the Lodge and around a small bridge has been occluded.
Courtesy of Hou Xinjue.

FIG. 7 (BOTTOM) — Looking south from Wu Zhu You Ju (Secluded Lodge of Wutong Trees and Bamboo), with a change in vantage point, spatial depth appears different.
Courtesy of Hou Xinjue.

FIG. 8 — Looking northwest from Wu Zhu You Ju (Secluded Lodge of Wutong Trees and Bamboo), in morning mist.
Courtesy of Sun Xiong.

of the pond outside. A small stone bridge appears very close to the embankment and the effect of spatial compression is evident. Moving a short distance toward the south and standing closer to the southern circular opening, one sees clearly the foreground and the effect of spatial compression is no longer. (FIG. 7) In heavy mist, the stage is given to the trees. In autumn, a soft intensity is revealed. (FIG. 8)

Finally, we encounter a large mirror set on a whitewashed wall. (FIG. 9) The size of this mirror is architectural, large enough for the elements in the reflection to show a similar level of illumination and scale as the elements in the surroundings. The overall effect recalls other actual doorways in the garden and draws our attention to a game of illusions. The interplay of the real and the illusory reminds us how difficult it is to tell them apart. With this realization the experience of the whole garden is cast more deeply into the horizons of an illusory world of garden-as-painting.

Thus, we can see that the garden experience we have just studied calls upon several relatively autonomous elements: topography, architectural elements, climatic and seasonal conditions, and the movement of human bodies. Sectional alignments—between vantage point, bridge, and embankment, or between frame, architectural elements, and topography—can play a crucial role in generating the effect of indeterminate spatial depth. These alignments are inexact, for we are in a world of the seeming, not in the Archimedean world in which geometry is made real. In the words of Alexandre Koyré, it is a "world of the more-or-less of our daily life" and not yet "a universe of measurement and precision."[9] The instability of spatial depth triggers, and relies on, memories at several timescales: memories of the impressions of the garden at other times and from other

FIG. 9 — Looking southwest from Xiao Fei Hong (Little Rainbow) toward a large mirror in the De Zhen Ting (Pavilion for Obtaining the Real).
Courtesy of Tang Xiaoying.

vantage points (both from the same visit and from previous visits), memories of paintings, and memories of the stories evoked by the settings and by the names of various buildings and places in the gardens.[10] Memories of repeated visits and memories of literary compositions and paintings can also engender expectations or anticipations that may be answered or elided in surprising ways. One visits a garden in a similar manner to the way in which a music lover enjoys the performance of the same piece of music on different occasions. Familiarity with the piece of music and a developed idiomatic sense of a sound world sustain the listener's nuanced attention to subtle variations and differences between different traversals of the same work.

The interplay of the far and the near in the instability of spatial depth, the work of the mist in generating the full and the empty: these are aspects of *yin* and *yang*, which originally meant "the sunny" and "the shaded." Wu Kuang-ming explains *yin* and *yang* as "reciprocals, that is, counterparts and counterpoints."[11] He writes, "Counterpoints are contraries and contrasts such as yes and no...dark and light...construction and destruction...Counterparts are mutuals such as this and that, form and content, body and mind....When these reciprocals are constitutively involved with one another, the situation is 'beautiful.'"[12] Thus, the *yin*-and-*yang* understanding of our garden is not achieved by classification: mountain or rockery is *yang*, whereas water is *yin*. Rather, the *yin* is becoming *yang*, and everything is caught up in polar motion.[13] Thus, we follow the effects of de-distancing (the far brought near) and consider how movement cancels these effects.

Form and content are mutually constitutive in this garden. Content (what it says): garden as painting, world as illusion, or the Buddhist *saṃsāra*, among other things. Form (how it says it): sectional alignments; insisting on a nuanced response to topography; composing, i.e., standing together, with the weather and the seasons; correlation of the image with the imaginal. Framed views inside a pavilion, unframed views under the sky, a virtual scene in a mirror—they echo each other and enhance the message that the garden is not just appearing similar to paintings in some aspects. The garden is an exercise in walking and dwelling that triggers metalepsis. Diegetic framing elements that correspond to points of view are incorporated into "the mimetic level of those contents that have been framed."[14] We are close to the genre of the fantastic in literature: the double (mirrors, places that recall other places), the story within the story (literary allusions, garden enclosure within another enclosure), travel in time (evoked by place names and literary allusions), and contamination of the everyday with the dream or with fiction.[15]

The effects in the Zhuo Zheng Yuan that I have tried to evoke in the previous discussion have not attracted much attention among Chinese landscape architects and other visitors. This should not be surprising and is not a matter of personal failing. We can consider it on two levels. From the point of view of professional formation, Chinese landscape architects have been trained in the skillful but indiscriminate use of Western orthogonal drawings and photography. The assumptions of objective vision have been drilled into them since the beginning of their professional training. Instructors routinely teach their students linear perspective by taking them into gardens and asking them to make freehand sketches. The assumptions of objective perspectival space were inculcated into students from the beginning of professional training. From the tourism viewpoint, visitors typically focus on individual scenic elements—a pavilion here, a rockery there; these are often used as backgrounds against which to take photographs of themselves and their family and friends. But, to borrow the words of Martin Seel, a pavilion with a wall opening, or a zigzag bridge over a pond are not appearances; "appearances *reveal themselves*" on them.[16] "The aesthetic appearing of an object," Seel points out, "is a *play of its appearances*."[17] A nuanced photography, with multiple shots instead of single shots, is often desirable to call attention to a play of appearances. If we have been blind to this play of appearances and imaginations, it might be because we have fetishized objective vision, forgetting the notion of subjective vision that was elaborated in nineteenth-century Europe, according to which "the human body, in all its contingency and specificity… becomes the active producer of optical experience."[18]

Tourists are understandably focused on what they see before them within the duration of a brief visit, but Seel sets the bar a bit higher for everyone:

"exclusive concentration on mere appearing is nothing special; what is required here is an interpretative perception that allows a *different* appearing to emerge. Correspondingly, the thesis of an aesthetic 'recourse to the present' does not entail the assumption that reflection on the past and the future does not play a role in aesthetic intuition."[19] In fact, place names and poetic couplets display on buildings in the Zhuo Zheng Yuan have already been sending hailing signals to all who enter it. Literary allusions have been actively engaging visitors to shuttle to other times and places imaginatively. We are reminded of the way experience involves both perception and memory.

Jacques Rancière's concept of *partage du sensible* may clarify the predicament of this seeing-and-not-seeing and "exclusive concentration on mere appearing." Variously translated as "the threshold of the sensible," or "the distribution of the sensible," *partage du sensible* carries two senses. On the one hand, it refers to a sharing of the sensible as if it was an experience or a piece of knowledge that is shared. It is about "an act of giving, of making something that is not common, common to all."[20] We can think of the shared habits of perception occasioned by the introduction of Western imaging techniques to the study of Chinese landscape, shared assumptions of landscape representation or of touristic enjoyment, as well as the difficulties of sharing the aperspectival sensibilities of the Chinese landscape. On the other hand, *partage du sensible* refers to a division or separation, or the establishment of a threshold within the "common to all." Rancière invokes a related concept of *dissensus*, "a dissent from inequality and . . . an inability to be sensed, noticed or accounted for."[21] The aim of dissent, in our case, would be to highlight the inability to notice and account for instability of spatial depth in conventional readings of Chinese gardens, and then to mount a broader challenge to the assumptions of Cartesian space in our disciplinary production of knowledge in landscape architecture.

CONCLUDING REMARKS

In an essay entitled "What Is the Contemporary?" Giorgio Agamben offers two memorable images of thought. First, he offers an image of the starry night in relation to a definition of the contemporary. "The contemporary is he who firmly holds his gaze on his own time so as to perceive not its light, but rather its darkness."[22] Agamben rejects the simplistic view that contemporaries are simply people who live through the same period of time. He urges us to think of the contemporary as someone engaged in a singular activity, avoiding focusing on the bright lights but perceiving a special darkness that attends the bright lights.

It is like remote galaxies moving away from us at such speed that their light is unable to reach us and so we perceive only darkness in the heavens where they are. He writes, "To perceive, in the darkness, of the present, this light that strives to reach us but cannot—this is what it means to be contemporary."[23]

Second, Agamben defines the contemporary in relation to the archaic: "Only he who perceives the indices and signatures of the archaic in the most modern and recent can be contemporary."[24] Here archaic does not mean prehistoric time in a chronological sense of time. Rather the archaic carries the force of the origin and the original in our present. The search for the archaic and the original is not a regression to a specific historical past but is a return to "that part within the present that we are absolutely incapable of living.... The attention to this 'unlived' is the life of the contemporary."[25]

The contemporary is not an attribute acquired naturally by virtue of one's birth and survival. It is an achievement attained by virtue of a cultivated form of attention to what is present and yet beyond our everyday capacity for experience.

In the foregoing discussion of the Zhuo Zheng Yuan, I attempted to figure the garden as part of our present that is liminal to the scopic regimes of landscape architecture and called for a cultivated form of attention to a play of appearances. This form of attention takes its bearings from a (re)turn to the (Chinese) aesthetic, and focuses on situations in which, to borrow Wu Kuangming's words again, "reciprocals are constitutively involved with one another." But we shall take a hint from Martin Seel, for whom aesthetic appearance is a play of appearances. (Sometimes, in order to enliven this sense of play, one takes inspiration from more than one tradition of thinking.) In these senses, what I propose here is a form of dissent against the use of Western imaging techniques as a cognitive mainstream in China and elsewhere, but this stance is avowedly open-ended, unfinished, and available for "further involvement, devolvement and development."[26]

The work described in this paper was partially supported by a grant from the Research Grants Council of the Hong Kong Special Administrative Region, China (Project No. CUHK 14618615). I also thank the Social Science Panel of the Chinese University of Hong Kong for a Direct Grant (Project No. 4052071) that supported my research during 2014–15. I am happy to thank members of my research team for their assistance: Jeffrey Cheng, Du Songyi, Hou Xianjue, Leung Yee Hang, Liu Xu, Lu Xiao, Mao Jianyuan, Mu Xiaodong, Htet Thiha Saw, Sun Xiong, Tang Xiaoying, Ernest Hon

Yin To, Wu Hongde, Xu Chenpeng, Yan Yu, and Zhu Hanlin. For helpful sugges-tions and comments on various drafts of this essay, I am indebted to Chen Wei, Patrick Hwang, Meng Zhaozhen, Mu Xiaodong, Kai Ming Wong, and Zhang Peng.

Chinese proper names and terms are transliterated in standard pinyin. *Chinese and Japanese proper names are given in the traditional order: surnames first. Where the name of a modern Chinese author is known in a different form of transliteration, I have followed the author's preferred form.*

Notes

1

Stanislaus Fung, "Mutuality and the Cultures of Landscape Architecture," in *Recovering Landscape: Essays in Contemporary Landscape Architecture*, ed. James Corner (New York: Princeton Architectural Press, 1999), 141–51.

2

ABBS website has a bulletin board for landscape architecture, accessed April 10, 2015, http://www.abbs.com.cn/bbs/post/page?bid=16&sty=3&age=0.

3

In the context of Chinese cultural studies, "con-temporary China" refers to the period of reform since 1979. See, for instance, Edward L. Davis, ed., *Encyclopedia of Contemporary Chinese Culture* (London: Routledge, 2005).

4

The principal sources on the Zhuo Zheng Yuan are: Kate Kerby, *An Old Chinese Garden: A Three-fold Masterpiece of Poetry, Calligraphy and Painting* (Shanghai: Chung Hwa Book Co., 1923); Liu Runen, "L'allégorie de 'l'incapacité': La culture du jardin du Jiangnan dans la Chine impériale tardive, l'exemple du Zhuozhengyuan: Jardin de l'activité politique d'un incapable." (PhD diss., Université Paris 1 Panthéon-Sorbonne, 2011); Andong Lu, "Deciphering the Reclusive Landscape: A Study of Wen Zheng-Ming's 1533 Album of the Garden of the Unsuccessful Politician," *Studies in the History of Gardens and Designed Landscapes* 31, no. 1

(2011): 40–59; Suzhou shi yuanlin he luhua wei-yuanhui, *Zhuo Zheng Yuan zhi* (Shanghai: Wenhui chubanshe, 2012).

5

Tong Jun was among the first to affirm a relation-ship between painting and garden design. In an essay of 1936, he states: "Chinese garden design takes its direction from the art of painting. It has no rational logic and no rules. For example, meandering paths, covered galleries and bridges; apart from a painterly beauty [in them], there are no explanations for them." In 1970, Tong Jun reaf-firmed his basic understanding: "Garden design and painting share the same principles, establishing correlative positions, contrasting the sparsely distributed and the densely clustered, with the high and the low staggered with each other, winding and turning to perfect effect. A garden is merely a painting in three dimensions." Tong Jun, *Tong Jun wenji*, 4 vols. (Beijing: Zhongguo jianzhu gongye chubanshe, 2000–2006), 1: 239. See also, Li Xi, "Ruping de shanshui: Zhongguo meixue shiye xia de 'fengjing ruhua,'" *Zhongguo yuanlin* 4 (2014): 108–13; Liang Jie, "'Hua' yu 'shen'— *Yuan ye* yu *Fusheng liuji* zhong 'hua' de hanyi dui zaoyuan yingxiang bijiao tanjiu," in *2012 Guiji fengjing yuanlinshi lianhehui (IFLA) Yataiqu huiyi ji Zhongguo fengjing yuanlin xuehui 2012 nian huiyi wenji*, 2 vols., 1: 68–71.

6

Alois Riegl, "The Modern Cult of Monuments: Its Character and Its Origin," *Oppositions* 25 (Fall 1982): 20–51.

7

David Leatherbarrow, *Uncommon Ground: Architecture, Technology, and Topography* (Cambridge, MA: MIT Press, 2000), 17.

8

Shen Fu, *Fu sheng liu ji* (1808), trans. Lin Yutang, *Six Records of a Floating Life*, (Shanghai: Xi feng she, 1949), 92–95; Shen Fu et al., *Fu sheng liu ji: wai san zhong*, ed. Jin Xingyao and Jin Wennan (Shanghai: Shanghai guji chubanshe, 2000), 59.

9

Alexandre Koyré, *Metaphysics and Measurement: Essays in Scientific Revolution* (Cambridge, MA: Harvard University Press, 1968), 91.

10

Gao Juhan [James Cahill], Huang Xiao, and Liu Shanshan, *Buxiu de linquan: Zhongguo gudai yuanlin huihua* (Beijing: Sanlian shudian, 2012); Alison Hardie, "Chinese Garden Design in the Later Ming Dynasty and Its Relation to Aesthetic Theory," 3 vols. (PhD diss., University of Sussex, 2001); Cao Lindi, *Suzhou yuanlin biane yinglian jianshang*, 3rd ed. (Beijing: Huaxia chubanshe, 2009; John Makeham, "The Confucian Role of Names in Traditional Chinese Gardens," *Studies in the History of Gardens and Designed Landscapes* 18, no. 3 (Autumn 1998): 187–210.

11

Wu Kuang-ming, "Chinese Aesthetics," in *Understanding the Chinese Mind: The Philosophical Roots*, ed. Robert E. Allinson (Hong Kong: Oxford University Press, 1989), 238.

12

Ibid.

13

Ibid.

14

Donald Kunze, "Metalepsis of the Site of Exception," in *Architecture Against the Post-Political*, ed. Nadir Lahiji (Abingdon: Routledge, 2014), 128.

15

Kunze, "Metalepsis," 129. See also Wai-yee Li, "Gardens and Illusions from Late Ming to Early Qing," *Harvard Journal of Asiatic Studies* 72, no. 2 (December 2012): 295–336. Richard E. Strassberg, "Mirrors and Windows: Fictional Imagination in Later Chinese Garden Culture," in *Gardens and Imagination: Cultural History and Agency*, ed. Michael Conan (Washington, DC: Dumbarton Oaks, 2008), 191–205.

16

Martin Seel, *Aesthetics of Appearing*, trans. John Farrell (Stanford: Stanford University Press, 2005), 38.

17

Ibid., 37.

18

Jonathan Crary, *Techniques of the Observer: On Vision and Modernity in the Nineteenth Century* (Cambridge, MA: MIT Press, 1990), 69.

19

Ibid., 35.

20

Davide Panagia, " '*Partage du sensible*': The Distribution of the Sensible," in *Jacques Rancière: Key Concepts*, ed. Jean-Philippe Deranty (Durham: Acumen, 2010), 96; Jacques Rancière, *Figures of History*, trans. Julie Rose (Cambridge: Polity Press, 2014), 31–44.

21

Panagia, " '*Partage du sensible*,'" 96.

22

Giorgio Agamben, "What Is the Contemporary?" in *What is an Apparatus? And Other Essays*, trans. David Kishik and Stefan Pedatella (Stanford: Stanford University Press, 2009), 44.

23

Ibid., 46.

24

Ibid., 50.

25

Ibid., 51.

26

Wu, "Chinese Aesthetics," 240.

LANDSCAPE AS A CONSTRUCT, ENGINEERING AS A MEMORY— *Adriaan Geuze*

Translated by Michael O'Loughlin

Recent developments in landscape architecture have been strongly influenced by the fierce debates about the planet's limitations when it comes to housing and feeding an exploding world population, the exhausting of primary sources like water and fossil fuels, and the visible facts of climate change. The "systems approach" seems to be winning. The landscape architect has to become an engineer again, making cautious interventions on the basis of knowledge of the systems and cycles of nature. Opposed to this is the idea that the landscape is always the expression of collective memory. In fact, landscape architecture must operate on the basis of a tradition in which meaning, memory, and our mythic desires are fostered. In this essay I want to argue in favor of bringing together the two concepts of landscape as a product of engineering and landscape as memory, using as example a historic man-made landscape that was created in the sixteenth and seventeenth centuries: the Netherlands.

THE INVENTION OF LANDSCAPE

The invention of perspective and the horizon ushered in the new worldview of the Renaissance. The idea of *landschap* (landscape) as a separate object became a major theme in the sixteenth century Netherlands. Visiting Joachim Patinir in 1521, Albrecht Dürer observed in his diary that Patinir is "the good landscape painter." Joachim Patinir (ca. 1480–1524), who worked in Antwerp, is a pioneer of the genre of landscape painting. He was painting biblical scenes, but they were dominated by the context, the landscape. The landscapes were painted with naturalistic detail. Puny figures were set in a lyrical fantasy of hills, bays, coasts, and hamlets. The motifs of his native realm are striking: there is always a suggestion of the coast, and beautiful skies with low-hanging clouds. Patinir was the pioneer of the newly objectified landscape, the painter between Hieronymus Bosch and Pieter Bruegel. Less than a century later, the Dutch masters would be painting the euphoria of the everyday landscape.

The introduction of the landscape as subject did not appear out of nowhere. The Renaissance was the time of voyages of discovery, people setting off to discover terra incognita, going literally over the horizon. They had to once again consciously orient themselves and learn to navigate. At first, they went along the coast, and reproduced it as a cognitive map.[1] Later, they used the stars, as an interconnected universe. This is exactly what happened in painting: the introduction of perspective and choosing a point of view with regard to the object and the horizon enabled painters to construct a subjective, aesthetic view of the world. In this way, the fifteenth century became the moment of escape from the closed frameworks of the Middle Ages. The appearance of the landscape is a symptom of a profound change in the Western space and therefore of the Christian way of life as a whole. The painted horizon replaced the transcendental God. That is the counterpart of the Copernican drama in which the earth loses its central position, and the notion of the positive infinity of the world prevails. In *Filosofie van het Landschap* (The Philosophy of Landscape) Ton Lemaire talks of the explosion of the medieval enclosed space of the soul, of the discovery of the horizon, which is literally made visible in the new landscape of the Netherlands.[2] Formerly, the horizon only existed at sea; now it dominated the unrelieved flat polders. The horizon retreats into the distance with the help of perspective, and makes space for the unknown.

Simon Schama calls landscapes imaginative constructs, which are projected onto the forest, the water, or the rocks.[3] He characterizes the pre-romantic Dutch masters as the artists who turned the landscape into a dream, a desire, or a refuge. In his analysis, geology, history, mythology, and art are fused together. For Schama, the representation of landscape in Western culture is hardly an exact copy of reality. It is used to reveal other meanings. Just as the still life makes reference to death, lust, and sexuality, so does the landscape painter create allegories of the seasons, morality, the worship of creation: Paradise and Arcadia, battlefield and the banal everyday.

THE EPIC OF THE WATER

Nothing has been more instrumental in the formation of the Dutch mentality than the sea and the menace of water. Just as the Alps define the collective memory of the Swiss, and the permanence of volcanoes, earthquakes, and tsunamis impels the Japanese to ritualize order, the Dutch challenge their fate by building dikes and dams and institutionalizing their water management. The flood became the ground zero of Dutch culture.

There are two facets to the territories of the Netherlands. Half of the landscape developed on rolling high ground with river valleys, characteristic of continental Europe, with scattered settlements that came into being in the feudal era, and now known as the Old Land. The other half is the so-called alluvial

Netherlands, the landscape that developed on the coastal plains in the delta of three European rivers and in the marshes. We know that early historical settlement was concentrated on the high ground, the banks of the rivers and the higher parts of the fertile coastal planes. But from 1000 CE onwards, the great marshes in-between were chosen as a new basis. Why did the monastic orders and farmers choose this nonland of impenetrable forested bogs? Was their urge to reclaim the marshlands an expression of the idea that after Adam and Eve had been expelled from Paradise, mankind had to toil and labor to make his own Paradise, if necessary, in places that were not intended for this?

Monks and farmers cut their way through the dense marshland forests and dug thousands of kilometers of ditches. An open landscape on an organic base came into being. The endless rhythm of ditches and narrow parallel plots had a unique appearance. The drainage ditches were connected to the existing creeks, which were dammed at the estuaries and equipped with sluices so that in the event of a storm, floodwater from the big rivers and the sea no longer had access. This medieval New Land was unique. Whereas feudal Europe was building cathedrals in a competition for the highest spires or airiest structures, here, it was the horizon that was being built. The medieval society on the New Land was confronted with mortality and the vulnerability of existence. Not through the plague or epidemics or wars and feudal exploitation, which were rare in these prosperous and well-organized lowlands—the real threat came from elsewhere. Without being aware of the real cause, life on the New Land was undermined by two geological factors: the rising sea levels and the unsuitability of marshlands for durable habitation. Between 1100 and 1300, there was a substantial rise in sea levels, which in geological terms would lead to a serious transgression of the delta. The thick cushions of marshland that had formed in the postglacial period in the big lagoon, jammed in safely between the dunes and the high ground, could offer no resistance to the sea, which broke through the dunes at various points along the coast. In geological terms, the thick layer of marshes—the soft, spongy organic base—was pushed away by the sea and the lagoon gradually filled up with sediments, sand, and clay. Another defining parameter for the unsuitability of marshland for habitation is subsidence. The unintentional side effect of the efficient drainage of the New Land is the inevitable oxidization of the organic base. This led to a dramatic subsidence of the New Land. Sometimes the ground could sink by up to four meters with regard to the original level. In just two centuries, areas that were once comfortably above sea level had sunk too close to it. This geological rise revealed itself in a series of successive storm surges that appeared when extremely high tides coincided with an Atlantic storm. The coastal plains were flooded and the sea penetrated deep inland through the ditches and rivers. Large chunks of the marshes were swept away. Between 1170 and 1219 there were four such superstorms. They were named after the calendar saints: in 1170, the All Saints' Flood; 1196, St. Nicholas's Flood; 1212, the Great Storm Flood; and 1219, St. Marcellus's Flood.

The effects of this cycle were clear. The northern regions in particular were affected. The Almere creek, which was the estuary of the Vecht, expanded into the Marsdiep. Large areas of Friesland disappeared into the sea. A permanently open connection with the North Sea was created so that the ebb and flood could reach deep into the center of the New Land. It is known that in the northwestern part of the New Land, the Storm Flood of 1212 claimed sixty thousand victims. The sea had separated this part of Friesland, which from then on would be called West Friesland. After the St. Marcellus's Flood a big inland sea was formed, the Zuiderzee and the Waddenzee. An inhabited area of one million hectares of marshlands had disappeared. In the southwest part, a complex of deeply scored gullies was created at the estuary of the Schelde and the Maas: Zealand.

Exposed to this harsh natural violence, medieval society saw in it the hand of God. The Bible provided an unambiguous allegory: God, who threatened mankind with a flood because of their misbehavior and the wrongs they inflicted on each other. Mankind paid no heed to repeated warnings. God told Noah to build an Ark and to gather together all the animals, both male and female; he must save himself and his family and all the animals from the flood, which would wash away all mankind. After 150 days, the waters receded and the ark was stranded on the top of Ararat. Noah built an altar and resumed his life. The destructive work of the Flood was not actually the definitive end to life on earth—it was a new beginning. Mankind would be taught to live in harmony and righteousness.

The cultivation of the flood plain had become a precarious and macabre life with the sea. Living in the coastal marshes, you challenge the sea. The next stop in the history of the development of the Lowlands was the serious beginning of dike building to defend the unprotected land. All the marshland streams were dammed, and dikes built on the rivers. Primitive dikes were built around the new Zuiderzee. In the thirteenth century, the southern part of West Friesland was the first integrated polder area to get an enclosing dike, which was 126 kilometers long. Water management became a serious task for water boards, with voting rights and a mandate to levy their own taxes. But there was never enough money or memory. Neglected dikes and overdue maintenance led to countless disasters,

FIG. 1 — *The Elizabeth's Day Flood*, Master of the St. Elizabeth Panels, Anonymous, ca. 1490–95. Oil on panel, 50 x 43.5 in. (127.5 x 110.5 cm).
Rijksmuseum Amsterdam.

on a greater and lesser scale. In the beginning of the fifteenth and the sixteenth century, however, another series of devastating storm floods made their appearance, whose names would be engraved in the collective memory. It was precisely during a period of fierce social conflict (known as the "Hook and Cod Wars") with much rattling of swords and sieges of the competing towns of Dordrecht and Geertruidenberg that the tragedy of two successive storms took place, the Second (1421) and Third (1423) St. Elizabeth's Floods. (FIG. 1) The economic center of the region above Antwerp, the Grote Waard behind Dordrecht, was devoured, literally swallowed up by the sea. The chronicles speak of the disappearance of seventy-two villages. A fifty-kilometer-long salt inland sea, with the major city of Dordrecht like a lonely and landless island at the edge, was a reminder of the Apocalypse. The Cosmas and Damian Flood (1509) created another inland sea between Leiden and Amsterdam, the Haarlemmermeer. The

St. Jeronimus Flood (1514) caused the inundation of the entire West. In Zealand, Stevenisee disappeared. The St. Felix's Flood (1530) was epic, and echoed the St. Elizabeth's Floods. The heart of Zealand, on the banks of the Schelde, disappeared under the waves. The town of Reimerswaal, with a hinterland of eighteen villages, ended up on the seabed of what then became the Oosterschelde. In the St. Pontian's Flood (1570) and the Second All Saints' Flood (1570), once again large regions with villages in Zealand and Flanders were drowned, including the region of Saeftingen. The Dutch landscape would always be connected to disasters of mythical proportions. In terms of narrative significance, they would equal those of Atlantis, or those of Homer's *Odyssey*.

THE FINE ART OF MAKING THE NEW LAND

The sea and the rivers had penetrated deeply into the marshland landscape, but they also brought it sediment. The delta grew from the erosion of the continental agriculture upstream. The shores of the inland sea created by the St. Elizabeth's Floods and that of Zealand and the northern coast, were the first to profit from this accretion. Using simple techniques like dams perpendicular to the shores and rows of faggots (bundles of sticks), they were able to accelerate the sedimentation process so that the seafloor silted up many centimeters per year until it reached the high-water mark. These raised sandbanks were then surrounded by dikes. Drainage ditches and canals were then dug in an orthogonal relationship, and were linked up to the original creek. A drainage sluice was built in this dammed creek so that at low tide the excess water was discharged into the sea. This impoldering was a serious legal and administrative task with patents, estimates, investors, consortia, bonds and property rights, leases, and bailiffs. The final awarding of the "patent" was a matter for the highest authorities. New polders of extremely fertile young marine clay were extremely valuable. In the region around Dordrecht, with its inherited trauma of the St. Elizabeth's Floods, the specialized craft of landmaking developed, with land surveyors, dike builders, and polder workers.

An important milestone was the impoldering of the Middelzee, a long tidal gulley consisting of mudflats in the North Frisian marsh landscape. For this it was necessary to raise a dike fourteen kilometers long at the top of the estuary. This could only be done in the short period of nine months between winter storms. By 1505 they were ready. After the patent had been obtained fifteen hundred dike workers were recruited from the Dordrecht region. This army was divided into fifteen so-called *homannen*, a tightly knit group of one hundred polder workers with spades and wheelbarrows, each of which had to build one kilometer of dike.

In that same autumn, the new polder Het Bildt was completed. The polder had been given the early modern block layout, which was also used in the south. Three villages were built for the polder workers, called after their place of origin, and most of them settled there permanently. In this way a Dutch colony came into being, and constructed a prosperous agricultural community on the Frisian seafloor. Years later the right to this lucrative silt deposit was claimed by at least twelve different legal entities. The Frisians had harsh feelings about the geopolitics of Holland.

As mentioned earlier, the area where the St. Elizabeth's Floods had washed away the Grote Waard was an important incubator for the crafts of dike building and impoldering. Ultimately it was the Counts of Holland, the Lords of Breda and the Marquess of Bergen op Zoom who granted the patents for the reclamation of the land lost under the waves, which resulted in the large-scale modern polder landscape that is now called West Brabant, the Island of Dordrecht and the Hoekse Waard. From the mid-sixteenth century onwards, this huge area was added to the New Land in record time. The steadily improving techniques for accelerating the silting up process and building dikes was codified and given a scientific basis in the *Treatise on Dykology for the Construction of Dykes* by Andreas Vierlingh (1507–1579).[4] This early engineer, who guided the impoldering of West Brabant, was an eye witness to the St. Felix's Flood with the inundation of Sint Philipsland, and the land around Borssele and Reimerswaal (1530). He blamed the inundation at Reimerswaal on the neglect of the dikes and expressed his exasperation in this manual. Under his charge an immeasurable area of seafloor was reclaimed, a valuable territory behind the strong dikes of the Hollands Diep, De Merwede, and the Kil. All that remained of the inland sea was the most central, deepest part, a brackish tidal marsh called De Biesbosch. The new polders were well-thought-out Cartesian artworks by land surveyors who set to work using drawings made beforehand. These sea clay polders with fossilized gullies were laid out in a block pattern or in Renaissance-style rectangular plots. Their plans, in which the meandering patterns of the original mudflats gulleys contrast with the razor-sharp orthogonal pattern of the ditches and roads, were published as cartographic masterpieces with beautiful names. This New Land was irresistible to farmers. The combination of light clay with lime from the seashells, and a completed regular and controlled water level is the best ground possible. In the autumn when the fields had been ploughed and the low sun was reflected like silver on the smooth black clay, they saw a gently lapping sea—a magical optical illusion in which sea and seabed became one.

The third notable evolution came about in West Friesland. In the Sipe, a passage to the sea that was the result of a Middle Ages collapse of the dunes near Hondsbosch and Callantsoog, a mudflats area developed with a deep gully. Many patents had already been awarded for the closing up of this sea passage. Partly inspired by the successful enclosing dike in the nearby Burghorn creek (1456), het Bildt, and West Friesland, in 1552 serious new plans were drawn up for the Sipe and for the reclamation of het Achtermeer, a lake of about thirty-six hectares below Alkmaar. In 1533, this last plan succeeded. The Sipe plan was an initiative of the cleric and painter Jan van Scorel (1495–1562). As his name suggests, van Scorel was born in a village in the dunes called Schoorl, an island that had been separated from the West Friesland mainland by successive storm floods. In the period from 1549 to 1553 he developed a comprehensive plan for the impoldering of an extremely large stretch of mudflats above West Friesland. In the plan, which he dubbed Nova Roma, the mudflats and the various islands, including his native village of Schoorl, would be joined to the mainland of the West Friesland Ring dike. His years in the Venetian Lagoon must have inspired him to create this visionary plan for his native region. (FIG. 2) He presented the intended design as a painting, which helped him to secure the patent from Karel V in 1552. With some merchant friends he succeeded in organizing the financing of the southern part of this megalomaniac plan, the Zijpe polder. With the money from Antwerp, work started that very same year. By 1554 the canals and roads were completed, but in 1555 the sandy dike shifted and was washed away. The polder was lost. Second and third attempts (in 1570 and 1572), in which ten windpumps were used, were not successful either. The polder could not be consolidated. The All Saints' Flood (1570) and war damage destroyed the recently reclaimed new land. The fourth attempt was at the initiative of both local and Amsterdam investors. This plan finally succeeded. In 1597 the dike around the Zijpe and Hanze polders was closed off and the hired laborers excavated a main watercourse in the north-south axis of the polder, the Grote Sloot. The polder plots were the property of wealthy Amsterdammers with a cadastral and water management layout of twenty "wards," indicated by the letters *A* to *U*. A windpump was built for every twenty wards (1600), which guaranteed that the water could be pumped out.

The old organization of the water boards was the basis of the continuous expansion of the New Land in West Brabant, Zealand, and the South Holland Islands, West Friesland, the Wadden coast, and the Dollard. The new dikes on the coast seldom collapsed. The making of land had arrived at the next stage of

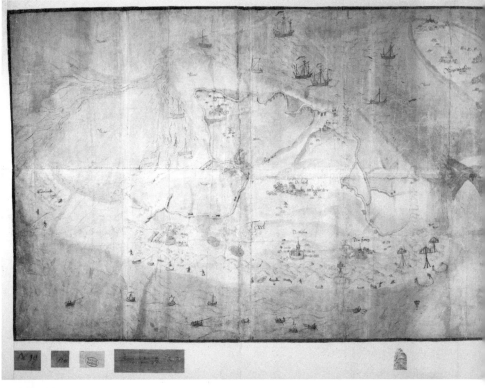

FIG. 2 (TOP)— Jan van Scorel, Illustrated map of Texel and Zijpe, ca. 1552. 94.5 x 30 in. (240 x 78 cm).
Nationaal Archief, The Hague (Maps Hingman, V.T.H., inv.nr. 2486).

FIG. 2a— Detail of the map.

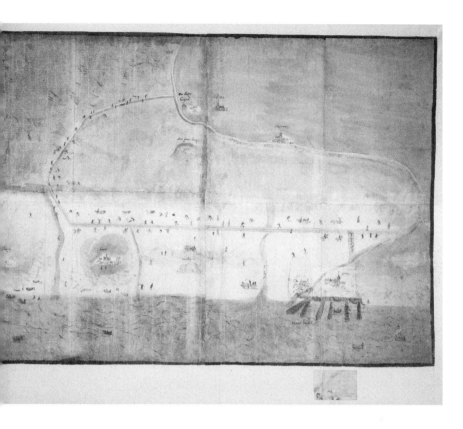

development with a new self-confidence, the technology of wooden construction and the wealth of the early seventeenth century. The next logical step was to attempt, with unprecedented ambition, the unthinkable on the Zijpe polder, which had been drained at sea level: to pump the sea dry!

Due to the looming threat of the salt water, in 1607 the States of Holland and West Friesland had given mayors and merchants permission to drain the many lakes. The water board expert Jan Adriaanszoon was appointed to carry this out. The land surveyor Pieter Cornelis Cort mapped out the area with precision. By placing windpumps in series of three and extracting the water in stages he could ultimately store water up to a depth of three to four meters in a ring canal that had been built around the lake. These rows of windmills were miracles of ingenuity. Zaandam was the center of shipbuilding and sawmills where big series of extremely efficient mills could be constructed. Leeghwater, the windmill contractor who got the concession, started with forty-three mills. In 1610, the drainage was almost ready. However, due to a disastrous breach in the Zuiderzee dike, the polder was full again in a couple of days. Consequently, the Ring dike was raised a meter higher than the surrounding land. In 1612, the polder was dry, and "the drained lake" De Beemster became a reality. (FIG. 3) The patterns of roads and ditches had been constructed as perfect mathematical squares, according to the Renaissance ideal.

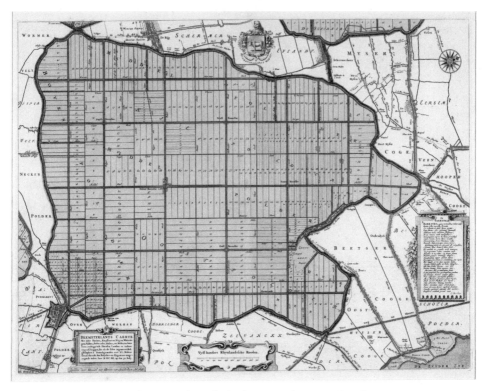

FIG. 3 — Historic map of Beemster, the Netherlands (Beemsterlants Caerte), 1658, engraver Daniël van Breen.
Geheugen van Nederland, Kaartencollectie Provinciale Atlas.

The area of North Holland turned into a region of lakes by centuries of disastrous storms underwent a true metamorphosis. Within twenty years all the lakes above and to the east of Amsterdam were New Land. This drainage of old sea clay brought unprecedented possibilities. Cattle markets and warehouses full of smoked meat made Purmerend famous. Alkmaar established a reputation for cheese and ham. The reclamation of North Holland helped feed the big fleet of the western shores of the Zuiderzee. Enkhuizen, Hoorn, Medemblik, and Amsterdam had the hinterland they dreamed of. Van Scorel's Nova Roma vision finally got a mighty apotheosis. Within twenty years its landscape had changed into a fascinating machine-dominated horizon, where hundred of windmills restlessly rotated clockwise. The new mill technology was able to continue draining the already reclaimed peatlands to far below sea level. Other large peatlands were dug out for turf, which was used as fuel for the cities. This large-scale fuel extraction created new lakes between Rotterdam and Gouda, and on the border of Holland and Utrecht.

The livestock from the polders became famous. The new polders provided hemp, flax, madder, linseed, cabbage, and grains. The marshes and shallow waters provided city dwellers with game, fish, and shellfish. The invented ideal world with its energetic horizon of hundreds of windmills was more than just agricultural land: it was the proudest possession of a people, the identity of a

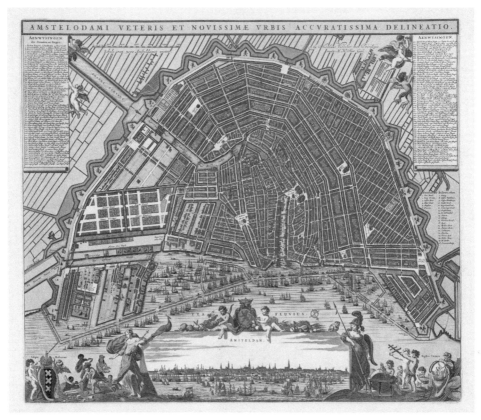

FIG. 4 — Hand-colored Map of Amsterdam, Anonymous, Nicolaes Pietersz Berchem, 1685–1695. Engraving, 19 x 22.5 in. (48.5 x 57.5 cm).
Rijksmuseum Amsterdam.

new nation. Unlike formerly, it was not created by land clearing—this world had literally been created. The making of land had acquired a cultural dimension. It was an art form.

The system of newly dug tow-canals linked all the cities with unprecedented efficiency according to a reliable timetable between Rotterdam, The Hague, Leiden, Harlem, Amsterdam, and Muiden. The rivers and sea inlets linked all the other cities on the water. The Zaan region was the beating industrial heart, with sawmills, oil mills, whale oil works, and shipyards. There were more than 350 mills along the Zaan. The new land gave birth to the first network society in which goods and services were traded. From the noiseless *trekschuit,* a horse-drawn canal boat, or from an open sailing boat, people watched the new land gliding by from a low perspective. The empty land with silhouettes moving on the horizon was enchantingly beautiful, even intoxicating!

In his historical analysis *The Dutch Republic,* Jonathan Israel shows how sweeping was the restructuring of trade as a consequence of the new political situation between 1590 and 1650, which led to an explosive growth of the cities in the coastal areas of Zealand and Holland, although death rates exceeded birth rates.[5] This was all possible due to a high surplus settlement. The immigrants came from the countryside and from abroad, until 1620 mainly from the Southern Netherlands, and afterwards mainly from Germany. The rapid progress of the cities of the coastal zone changed the Republic into a country with two economies, that of the western New Land, expansionary, dynamic and prosperous, and that of the country provinces, largely stagnating and much poorer. There was a gap—wages were half what they were in the west.

The undisputed epicenter of this explosive growth was Amsterdam. (FIG. 4) The city was bursting at the seams and in 1606 was given permission by the States of Holland for a new fortification. In 1613, the city government started phased implementation of the city's expansion, based on Simon Stevin's principles of the ideal city. The primal version of the Dutch town was a ditch with a road with buildings on either side of it, joined by a bridge in Woudsend. Along the shores of the Zuiderzee this typology had developed into a version with a central canal with quays and warehouses (as seen in Bunschoten and Monnickendam). Towns with a trading fleet had a number of parallel canals with side streets. The mathematician, physicist, and engineer Simon Stevin drew his ideal city as a grid of canals and streets, with a market square and scattered churches, all imprisoned in a square fortification, with mills on the bastions. This organizational model was applied to Amsterdam by laying three parallel canals in a semicircle, the birth of the Amsterdam ring of canals. Functionality, aesthetics, and profit came together. Amsterdam became the ideal city without squares, without hierarchy, with churches spread around for every belief. The extensive waterfront was fenced off with stakes and equipped with islands with docks. To construct these rings of canals and quays, vast volumes of sand were excavated from the dunes to the southwest of Haarlem and shipped to Amsterdam on the new tow-canal. This mining operation resulted in wonderful flat land that was then cultivated for tulips and bulbs, adding to the New Land legacy one of the most unusual and colorful landscapes ever made. Cities like Rotterdam, Schiedam, Enkhuizen, Zierikzee, and others also got canals and spectacular new harbors. The Hague and Batavia were built according to Stevin's ideal. The New Land was the most densely populated region in Europe, without there being a single metropolis.

NEW NATION, NEW RELIGION, NEW LANGUAGE

In this flat world, every position was identical. The unavoidable need to cooperate nourished ideas of equality. The flatlands would tolerate neither pope nor tyrant. In the polders there are only two conceivable positions: inside the dike, or outside the dike. The New Land of the polders enforced a straightforward and principled view of the world, in which the choices were to cooperate or be excluded.

The inhabitants of the delta had a tendency toward the principles and values that later crystallized into the Protestant faith, values in which sacrifice, straightforwardness and the inclination toward purity were virtues. After all, the sea had not given up the land so easily. Dogmatism became the mental equivalent of toiling in the heavy clay, and the theological hair-splitting seemed the logical equivalent of land surveying. The so-called *beeldenstorm*, or Iconoclastic Fury, which had first appeared in the Southern Netherlands in 1562, raged like a hurricane over the polders in 1566. In 1568, this would lead to a definitive revolt against the king and the Catholic Church. People started to fight for religious freedom and they chose Calvin's version, the ideologically most puritan form of Protestantism—the ideal philosophy for the man of the polders. The Reformation had many causes. Early on, the humanistic tradition had put down deep roots in the Netherlands. There was also great discontent among the aristocratic landowners with regard to the extensive centralization of power, and the taxes and legal system that the Spanish and Hapsburg ruler Philip II wanted to impose from Brussels. The year 1566 was one of famine, as a result of grain shortages and high prices due to the closure of the Sont (1565) in the war between Sweden and Denmark. In that same year the Flemish linen industry and Antwerp trade were hit hard by the English import duties and by the Great Storm that winter. In 1570 came another fatal blow for large parts of Zealand and Flanders: the All Saints' Flood.

The Revolt started in August 1566 in the Flemish Steenworde. Within three weeks, four hundred monasteries and churches in Flanders had been pillaged. In the Northern Netherlands the revolt against the king turned into war and decision to separate from Spain. The campaign by Europe's most superior land army got bogged down at the sieges of Alkmaar and Leiden (1573 and 1574), where cleverly organized flooding broke the Spanish encirclement. A new chapter was added to the Dutch mythology of flood disasters: repelling the enemy with water. In 1579, the northern provinces signed the Union of Utrecht. This was the de facto declaration of independence of the Republic of the Seven United Provinces. For the first twenty years of the war, the rebels' position was extremely precarious. Around 1590, the tide turned in favor of the Republic. In the watery west, using rapid movement of troops by ship, and reverse impoldering, that is, flooding, the Republic's troops defeated the Spanish enemy. The Republic's ultimate victory was made possible by the Spanish Empire's imperial overstretch, it being in a state of war with France, England, and the Ottomans, the skillful military leadership of Prince Maurits of Orange, and the maritime expansion of the Netherlands. A country with a population of just 2.5 million had developed into a world power. The seventeenth century is regarded as the Republic's Golden Age in the economy, science, and culture. For the Calvinists, it was also the period in which their political influence was at its height. The territory of the northern United Provinces overlapped with that of the New Land constructed in the marshlands and on the seabed itself. With the Republic, a new nation was founded here inspired by a new religion.

The Republic's Protestantism, germinated in a context of storm floods, the Spanish Inquisition, and war, was not mild and flexible. The Reformation was taken hostage by preachers and clergymen, each with his own claim to be the true Protestant belief: a violent polemic that came close to civil war. This destructive impasse, which lasted for years, resulted in the decision to summon a great Calvinist Synod in Dordrecht (1618–19), where the definitive principles of Protestantism would be formulated. Here too, the Bible translation authorized by the States would be established. In order to be free of the Papist Latin Bible, the Bible would be translated directly from Hebrew, Greek, and Aramaic, and made legible for the people in a language that would be a compromise between the various dialects. The result of the heavily politicized Synod was that the Calvinist denomination became the officially dominant faith. The second product was an impressive "States Bible" in a new language, Standard Dutch, which became available in 1635. It was a language with new words including the word in which the epic of the New Land had its roots: from then on, the great, destructive Biblical Flood would be called the *zondvloed*, joining the words for "sin" and "flood" into a single word.

THE REPRESENTATION OF THE NEW LAND, THE SUBLIME OF THE ORDINARY

The earliest representation of the new land was cartography. In Antwerp, in the second half of the sixteenth century, mapmaking had become a highly developed craft that was given a scientific basis by precise trigonometry and the copper engraving of reality. It developed into a flourishing business with richly illustrated printed atlases. In a period when new colonies were found, maps were of great military and commercial importance. In 1558, Jacob van Deventer (1505–1575) was appointed royal geographer, and entrusted with the task of mapping all the towns of the Netherlands. This would be the pinnacle of his career, with

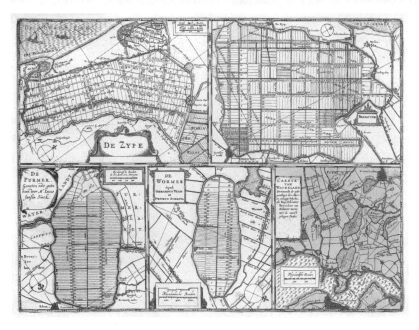

FIG. 5 (TOP) — Map of the Netherlands (Hollandiae antiquorum catthorum sedis nova descriptio, auctore Iacobo a daventria), by Abraham Ortelius, Jacob van Deventer, 1600.
Nationaal Archief, The Hague (Kaartcollectie Zuid-Holland Ernsting).

FIG. 6 (BOTTOM) — Petrus Kaerius, *Five Polder Map*, 1631.
Collection of the Zijper Museum, Schagerbrug.

the first systematic maps of 260 towns and their landscape. (**FIG. 5**) The development of cartography coincides with the late sixteenth century phase of land reclamation. Patents for impoldering and precise determination of the New Land with survey maps commissioned by the Water Boards are common from this period. The most important cartographers left Antwerp when war broke out. In this fashion a second generation settled in Amsterdam where cartographic enterprises came into being, publishing maps and atlases.

The orthogonal universe of the New Land in Zealand and Holland and the new urban expansions with their fortifications was published in beautiful maps. A famous example is the Five Polder Map (*Het Kaerius-Pitt kaartje van de Zijpe*) of 1631 by Petrus Kaerius (1571–ca.1646). (**FIG. 6**) The delight in the reclamation of North Holland fairly leaps off the wall map with its collage of the Zijdepolder, the Beemster, the Wormer, the Purmer, and the Waterland polders. The wall maps of the New Land adorned the interiors. These big wall maps appear in a number of paintings by Jan Vermeer. The maps of the North Holland impoldering show a strictly ordered world that resembles the later America. The maps of the Zealand and South Holland New Land show the land of pioneers who imposed a rectangular structure on the twisting creeks of the marshes.

There has been much speculation about the reason why it was precisely in this new Republic that landscape painting exploded. The decline of the central power of the court and the church as patrons deprived artists of their market. Protestantism, emphasizing the *beeldenstormers'* argument about God's second commandment, forced the artist to restrict themselves to the inoffensiveness of everyday life and the world around them: the landscape, the community, and still lifes. Although not necessarily untrue, these seem like explanations by outsiders, historians who are probably unfamiliar with the scale and importance of the actual evolution of the landscape. After all, the new society had arisen on the New Land. Only Johan Huizinga seems to be aware of this. In *Dutch civilisation in the seventeenth century* (1968; original Dutch published in 1941), he makes the very plausible argument that the free and down-to-earth citizens with an open and eager view of the world could be proud of the hard-won landscape in all its flatness and simplicity.[6] This thesis can easily be illustrated by a few obvious examples in art.

The polder landscape with windmills, the horizon, and the clouds was so overwhelming and stimulating that it became a main theme of poets and painters. They seemed to be hypnotized by the beauty of the flat landscape, the religious dimensions of the light of the skies, the clouds, the waves, the livestock,

FIG. 5 — Meindert Hobbema, *The Avenue at Middelharnis*, 1689. Oil on canvas, 41 x 55.5 in. (103.5 x 141 cm).
National Gallery, London.

the windmills, the silhouettes of the towns and the boats. The euphoria of the flat land would give rise to the Dutch masters who together would immortalize every aspect of the New Land. The young Paulus Potter (1625–1654) was a specialist in painting livestock. As a West Frisian, he witnessed the enormous transformation of his native region and the big impoldering of this province. It is no coincidence that in his paintings, the dogs, the horse, and the cows are projected against the horizon. In his famous painting *The Young Bull* (1647) the new nation seems to be symbolized as a vain young bull in a landscape whose horizon Potter make pass through its legs. Meindert Hobbema (1638–1709), a student of Ruisdael, excels in the theme of the horizon. He painted the polders on the island of Flakkee, newly diked in the late sixteenth century. The *Avenue at Middelharnis* (1689) is a veritable ode to the land surveyors, a glorification of the new orthogonal world. (**FIG. 7**) This painting is proof of the monumental beauty hidden in the simplicity of the polders. A land made by human hand, born of pure pragmatism. Jan van Goyen (1596–1656) seems to be the painter who devoted himself to painting mankind in his new setting. He painted the sailors and fishermen, the ferryman on the water, the farmer, the dredger, the bargemen, the rambler in the polders with windmills and the Dutch cities in the background. No one would depict the polder land like Rembrandt van Rijn (1606–1669). He went on long rambles through the polders around Amsterdam. He was enraptured by everyday life in the polders and sketched the obscure hamlets, barns, and windmills of Diemen, the Gein, and the Amstel. In his paintings you experience the

FIG. 8 — Rembrandt Harmenszoon van Rijn, *The Three Trees*, 1643. Etching with drypoint and engraving, 8.5 x 11 in. (21.3 x 28.3 cm).
Courtesy of the Metropolitan Museum of Art, New York.

muddy path, you feel the mist and smell the muck and dung of the polder land. Of course, the New Land is an aesthetic work of art with perspective and low skies, but Rembrandt is interested above all in the primal characteristics of the land of the polder workers and farmers: water, clay, weeds, bog, reedy edges, odors of fermentation, and willow bushes. Rembrandt provides a framework for looking at the New Land. Beside the windmill of the Blauwhoofd bastion, chimneys and cannon become characters. The other primal power of the New Land is the dynamic sky and the light. The etching *The Three Trees* (1643) has a sky with rain approaching, shafts of light, and racing clouds. (**FIG. 8**) This lends enormous charisma to the three trees (Golgotha or innocence?) above the perfect polder horizon. It is obvious that it is precisely the polder landscape that in its openness in a low sun and approaching weather offers the spectacle of sunlight piercing the clouds. A fragment of the landscape is made radiant while the rest of the landscape fades into dark shadow. It is as if God is choosing to send the light to one particular spot.

Albert Cuyp (1620–1691) was the master of the river forelands, the muddy land outside the dikes with cows served as foreground for his panoramas of Dordrecht, with their cows, ships, and waterfront. He commands the technique of capturing the light of the lowlands with somber colors. Jacob van Ruisdael (1629–1682) and Philips Koninck (1619–1688) painted the everyday but lent it more meaning. They climbed the inner sides of the dunes and the Heuvelrug in order to better experience the breathtaking emptiness of the New Land. Beneath

FIG. 9— Jacob Isaacksz van Ruisdael, *View of Haarlem from the Northwest, with the Bleaching Fields in the Foreground*, ca. 1650–1682. Oil on canvas, 17 x 19 in. (43 x 48 cm). *Rijksmuseum Amsterdam.*

their low-hanging cloudy skies the vanity and mortality of toiling mankind in his self-made creation was inescapable. They sublimated the Atlantic clouds and the bounteous light. In Koninck's *A View over Flat Country* (1655–1660), the wildly twisting river has difficulty in leaving the beautiful polder landscape. In Ruisdael's *View of Haarlem from the Northwest, with the Bleaching Fields in the Foreground* (ca. 1650–1682), of which he painted more than one version, the city of Haarlem seems blessed in the low-lying land beneath the mighty columns of cloud. (FIG.9) Both painters knew the country well. Koninck had a shipping company with regular services between the cities of Amsterdam and Rotterdam. He must have had a good view of the New Land from the rivers and tow-canals. Ruisdael traveled a lot. It is known that he scaled the Westertoren in order to be able to draw the peerless rows of windmills of the city polder to the west of Amsterdam, backlit with a low horizon. Rembrandt would sketch the same horizon of a thousand sails from the west. The *Panoramic View of Amsterdam looking towards the IJ* (1665–1670), for which view he scaled the scaffolding surrounding the tower of the new Town Hall, has the Damrak, the Amsterdam waterfront, the IJ, and to the north the horizon of the Waterland polders. Just like Haarlem, he painted Rhenen and Wijk bij Duurstede on the forelands of the Rhine, where he had the Cuneratoren and the Korenmolen dominate the fluvial lands of the Betuwe. Ruisdael was fascinated by the monumentality of the New Land's infrastructure. Windmills, bridges or the waterwheels are the leitmotif for a dramatized reality. Albert Cuyp, Jan van Goyen, Johannes Vermeer, and Rembrandt van Rijn were impassioned about the everyday, and made use of the magic of the polder light. The clear Dutch light was never so well captured as by Vermeer (1632–1675), who didn't even need to paint the landscape in order to evoke it. The way in which he has his hometown of Delft loom up out of the empty polder is obvious. In The *View of Delft* (1660/61) this city becomes the pearl of Holland's polder lands. The city is radiant in the morning light, mirrored in the newly dug harbor on the Schie. In the foreground, there are women on the quay and a modern barge, which traveled between Leiden, Delft, and Schiedam/Rotterdam along the canal de Schie, dug in 1655. The morning sunlight sparkles over the tiled roofs, Delft's skyline playfully pierces the low-hanging clouds.

ENGINEERING AS A MEMORY

From 1650 onwards, the society that cherished the simple and the ordinary was changing. Wealth brought complacency and the inevitable hedonism to the Republic. The black clothes and regulation plainness changed into colorful velvet, extravagant embroidery, high heels, and wigs. For the second part of the Amsterdam ring of canals, the sober Dutch style was replaced by classicism, with expensive stone ornamentation. The power and wealth rankled the other great European powers. The sudden success of this small nation was not in isolation from the simultaneous impasse within European geopolitical relations. This came to an end in 1672, and the natural great powers turned on the dwarf. Led by the Sun King, Louis XIV, France, England, and Münster decided to attack the Republic.

However, the first part of the seventeenth century continues to reverberate through history as the miraculous moment of landmaking, the quest that led to the synthesis of religion, nation building, the formulation of a shared new language and culture and economic euphoria. This unique convergence could be explained in terms of an existential desire resulting from the accumulated trauma of the threat from the sea, Catholic intolerance, and the subjection demanded by Spain. It could also be argued that the pragmatic polder culture sought redemption in a Calvinism in which simplicity and plainness were fostered. This became the DNA of the *beeldenstormers*. The mythology of the Flood, the engineering of the land on the seabed and the proud enjoyment of everyday life under the low sky ultimately became a closed circle. Ill fortune and the construction of the ideal world are logically connected. Within this the culture of the ordinary is the shining moment, the climax. In the collective memory, the self-made land of artificial nature is the benchmark. In the idiosyncratic Dutch perception of nature, nostalgia and engineering are the same.

Notes

1
History of Cartography, ed. David Woodward, vol. 3, part 1, *Cartography in the European Renaissance* (Chicago: University of Chicago Press, 2007).

2
Ton Lemaire, *Filosofie van het Landscap* (Amsterdam: Ambo, 1970).

3
Simon Schama, *Landscape and Memory* (New York: Knopf, 1995).

4
Andries Vierlingh, *Tractaet van dyckagie*, ed. J. de Hullu and A. G. Verhoeven (The Hague: Martinus Nijhoff, 1920).

5
Jonathan Israel, *The Dutch Republic: Its Rise, Greatness, and Fall, 1477–1806* (Oxford: Clarendon Press, 1995).

6
J. H. Huizinga, *Dutch Civilization in the Seventeenth Century* (New York: Harper & Row, 1969).

ACKNOWLEDGMENTS

We would like to thank all the authors for their inspiring and incisive texts, which not only discuss central issues in the contemporary landscape, but also give deeper insight into the ideas that motivate their practice. Without the thorough engagement of the entire ETH Chair—and most particularly Anette Freytag, Suzanne Krizenecky, Albert Kirchengast, and Dunja Richter, who helped conceive and organize the "Thinking the Contemporary Landscape" conference in Herrenhausen Hanover in June 2013—this publication could not have been born. We would also like to thank all the participants of the conference; their varied presentations and subsequent discussions became the foundation of this book. We would like to thank the Volkswagen Foundation, especially Wilhelm Krull and Anorthe Kremers, for their generous support and the gracious organization and hospitality in Hanover.

CONTRIBUTORS

Susann Ahn — is a landscape architect and research associate to the Chair of Landscape Architecture of Christophe Girot, ETH Zurich.

James Corner — is a landscape architect and urban designer, founder of James Corner Field Operations, and professor of landscape architecture and urbanism at the University of Pennsylvania School of Design. He is author of *The Landscape Imagination: Collected Essays of James Corner 1990–2010* (Princeton Architectural Press, 2014), and coauthor of *Taking Measures Across the American Landscape* with Alex MacLean (Yale University Press, 1996).

Vittoria Di Palma — is associate professor of architecture at the University of Southern California, a coeditor of *Intimate Metropolis: Urban Subjects in the Modern City* (Routledge, 2009), and the author of *Wasteland, A History* (Yale University Press, 2014).

Sonja Dümpelmann — is associate professor of landscape architecture at the Harvard Graduate School of Design. She is the author of *Flights of Imagination: Aviation, Landscape, Design* (University of Virginia Press, 2014).

Anette Freytag — works as scientific advisor of landscape politics for the Swiss Federal Government; she was formerly a senior lecturer and Head of Research at the Chair of Landscape Architecture at ETH Zurich. Her latest book, *Dieter Kienast—Stadt und Landschaft lesbar machen* (gta Verlag, 2015), retraces the evolution of European landscape architecture education and practice between the 1960s and 1990s.

Stanislaus Fung — is associate professor and director of the MPhil-PhD Program of the Chinese University of Hong Kong's School of Architecture. His recent work has appeared in *Oxford Bibliographies in Chinese Studies* (ed. Tim Wright, New York, 2014), and *Dentō Chūgoku no teien to seikatsu kūkan: Kokusai shinpojiumu hōkokusho* (ed. Tanaka Tan and Takai Takane, Kyoto, 2013).

Adriaan Geuze — is one of the founders of West 8 urban design & landscape architecture b.v., a leading urban design practice based in Rotterdam, New York, and Belgium, and frequently lectures and teaches at universities worldwide.

Christophe Girot — is professor and chair of landscape architecture in the Department of Architecture at ETH Zurich, and founder and director of Atelier Girot, Zurich. His most recent publication is *The Course of Landscape Architecture* (Thames & Hudson, 2016).

Kathryn Gustafson — is a landscape architect and a founding partner of Gustafson Guthrie Nichol, Seattle, and Gustafson Porter, London. Her award-winning work includes a widely known series of projects in France, and recently acclaimed projects have ranged throughout Europe, North America, and the Middle East.

Kristina Hill — is a scholar and practitioner of landscape-based urban design, and associate professor of Landscape Architecture & Environmental Planning and Urban Design at the University of California at Berkeley. She wrote and edited *Ecology and Design: Frameworks for Learning* (Island Press, 2002) and is currently advising public agencies in the San Francisco Bay area on typologies for urban adaptation to sea level rise.

Dora Imhof — is an art historian and a postdoc in the Department of Architecture at ETH Zurich. She recently published *Museum of the Future* with Cristina Bechtler (JRP Ringier, 2014), and *Kristallisationsorte der Kunst in der Schweiz. Aarau, Genf und Luzern in den 1970er-Jahren* with Sybille Omlin (Scheidegger & Spiess, 2015).

Regine Keller — is professor of landscape architecture at the Technical University, Munich, and founder and partner of Keller Damm Roser Landscape Architects, Munich.

David Leatherbarrow — is a professor of architecture and chairman of the Graduate Group/PhD Program in Architecture at the University of Pennsylvania. His recent publications are *Surface Architecture* (with Mohsen Mostafavi; MIT Press, 2005), *Topographical Stories: Studies in Landscape and Architecture* (University of Pennsylvania Press, 2004), and *Architecture Oriented Otherwise* (Princeton Architectural Press, 2008).

Alessandra Ponte — is a professor at the École d'architecture, Université de Montréal. She curated the exhibition Total Environment: Montreal 1965–1975 at the Canadian Center for Architecture in 2009 and collaborated on *God & Co: François Dallegret Beyond the Bubble* (Architectural Association Publications, 2011) with Laurent Stalder and Thomas Weaver. She published a collection of essays on North American landscapes titled *The House of Light and Entropy* (Architectural Association Publications, 2014).

Jörg Rekittke — is a landscape architect and an associate professor in the Master of Landscape Architecture Programme at the Department of Architecture, School of Design and Environment, National University of Singapore.

Saskia Sassen — is the Robert S. Lynd Professor of Sociology and cochair of the Committee on Global Thought at Columbia University. Her recent books include *A Sociology of Globalization* (W. W. Norton, 2007), *Territory, Authority, Rights: From Medieval to Global Assemblages* (Princeton University Press, 2006), the fourth fully updated edition of *Cities in a World Economy* (2012), and *Expulsions: Brutality and Complexity in the Global Economy* (2014).

Emily Eliza Scott — is an interdisciplinary scholar and an artist. Currently a post-doc in the Department of Architecture at ETH Zurich, she is the cofounder of two collaborative art-research projects: the Los Angeles Urban Rangers (2004–) and World of Matter (2011–). She is coeditor with Kirsten Swenson of *Critical Landscapes: Art, Space, Politics* (University of California Press, 2015).

Charles Waldheim — is John E. Irving Professor at Harvard University's Graduate School of Design. He edited *The Landscape Urbanism Reader* (New York: Princeton Architectural Press, 2006) and *Landscape as Urbanism: A General Theory* (Princeton University Press, 2016).

Kongjian Yu — is founder and president of Turenscape, one of the first and largest private landscape architecture practices in China, and founder of the College of Architecture and Landscape Architecture at Peking University, China.

Published by
Princeton Architectural Press
A McEvoy Group company
37 East Seventh Street
New York, New York 10003

Visit our website at www.papress.com

Printed and bound in the United States by Thomson-Shore
20 19 18 17 4 3 2 1 First edition

ISBN: 978-1-61689-520-4

Front cover:
Bet Figueras with Carlos Ferrater and Josep Lluis Canosa,
Barcelona Botanical Garden, 1999. Photo by Christophe Girot.

Project Editor: Barbara Darko
Designer: Jan Haux

Special thanks to: Janet Behning, Nicola Brower,
Abby Bussel, Erin Cain, Tom Cho, Benjamin English,
Jenny Florence, Jan Cigliano Hartman, Lia Hunt, Mia Johnson,
Valerie Kamen, Simone Kaplan-Senchak, Stephanie Leke,
Diane Levinson, Jennifer Lippert, Kristy Maier, Sara McKay,
Jaime Nelson Noven, Esme Savage, Rob Shaeffer, Sara
Stemen, Paul Wagner, Joseph Weston, and Janet Wong of
Princeton Architectural Press —Kevin C. Lippert, publisher

Library of Congress Cataloging-in-Publication Data
is available from the publisher upon request.